The Ethiopian–Adal War 1529–1543

The Conquest of Abyssinia

Jeffrey M. Shaw

Helion & Company

Helion & Company Limited
Unit 8 Amherst Business Centre
Budbrooke Road
Warwick
CV34 5WE
England
Tel. 01926 499 619
Email: info@helion.co.uk
Website: www.helion.co.uk
Twitter: @helionbooks
Visit our blog http://blog.helion.co.uk/

Published by Helion & Company 2021
Designed and typeset by Mach 3 Solutions Ltd (www.mach3solutions.co.uk)
Cover artwork by Maxim Borisov © Helion & Company 2021. Cover designed by Paul Hewitt, Battlefield Design (www.battlefield-design.co.uk)

ISBN 978-1-914059-68-1

British Library Cataloguing-in-Publication Data.
A catalogue record for this book is available from the British Library.

For details of other military history titles published by Helion & Company Limited contact the above address or visit our website: http://www.helion.co.uk.

We always welcome receiving book proposals from prospective authors.

Contents

Foreword

The interest and complexity of African military history emerges clearly from Jeff Shaw's excellent account of the Ethiopian–Adal War in the sixteenth century. This overdue account is particularly valuable because the subject has received insufficient attention, and there is a misleading tendency to focus on an Atlanticist account of African history. This first English language book on the topic incorporates an interdisciplinary approach to the cause and the outcome of this war. Shaw's account takes on special value because of the role of outside participants in the shape of the Ottomans and the Portuguese, but the story does not put them first. Instead, we see the interplay of alliances and enmities as well as the role of weapons, leadership, logistics, the role of religion, and an assessment of the strategies employed by the participants, each one seeking to achieve different objectives. Indeed, this war set the stage for the rise of Cold War rivalries in the region, and the consequences of this tragic affair still resonate throughout Ethiopia to this day.

The subject is difficult due to limitations in the sources and the need to reconcile different accounts and throw light on many angles. Keeping the focus on the Ethiopian view of events is particularly a challenge since most of the sources are from the Arabic and Portuguese perspectives. Despite the numerous challenges, Jeff Shaw is to be congratulated for an engaged and informed account that is of value not only to specialists in the region but also to all those interested in African history, the history of the wars of religion, and the sweeping panoply of sixteenth-century military history.

Jeremy Black

Preface

In the summer of 2009, I travelled to Ethiopia on a business trip. Once we finished our work in Addis Ababa, I had the opportunity to visit the Portuguese Bridge – a popular tourist attraction, about two hours north-west of the city, located near the famous Debra Libanos monastery. Situated on the edge of the Great Rift Valley, the bridge and its surroundings are a marvel to behold. No photograph can do justice to the valley's views. The source of the Blue Nile, the Great Rift Valley, is a natural phenomenon that defies description. A few years after my return, I found myself editing a three-volume work entitled *War and Religion: An Encyclopedia of Faith and Conflict*, for which I wrote an entry on the Ethiopian–Adal War. This little-known conflict sparked my interest to investigate further, and now, nearly a decade later, this book has found its way to print.

The Ethiopian–Adal War was fought while the Protestant Reformation consumed Europe. The conquistadors were planting the Spanish flag in Mexico and Peru, and the Ottoman Empire's mighty army was besieging Vienna. The Ethiopian–Adal War has, for too long, been hiding in the shadows behind these monumental historical events. In the few instances when the war is mentioned, whether in history books or scholarly articles, there are certain unexamined assumptions that have come to characterise this conflict that have recently been challenged. For example, the role of firearms in the war and the Ottoman Empire's contribution to the Adal war effort are topics that scholars and historians have recently explored in greater depth. This book relies on much of this new interpretation. I have referenced all the primary source material written by participants in the Ethiopian–Adal War and hundreds of scholarly articles and book chapters in order to frame this war as a significant sixteenth-century event. While some authors have begun to include the war in their research on Ethiopian, African, Portuguese, and Turkish history, this stand-alone book seeks for the first time to bring the Ethiopian–Adal War to a broader audience. This is the first book in English (and may perhaps also be the first book in any language) to focus specifically on the entire 14 years of the Ethiopian–Adal War. I thank Helion and Company for bringing it to print.

Sources for the Ethiopian–Adal War

Primary source material covering this war is limited. There are only four known accounts written by actual eyewitnesses to the war. Three are from Portuguese participants, and one is from the Adal perspective. There are no known Ethiopian or Ottoman written accounts from participants in the war.

The most useful primary source is the *Futuh Al-Habaša,* Arabic for "the conquest of Abyssinia", written by Šihab ad-Din Ahmad bin Abd al-Qader bin Salem bin Uthman (referred to hereafter as Arab Faqih). Arab Faqih accompanied the Sultan of Adal, Imam Gurey (1506–1543), on his campaign to conquer Ethiopia. Arab Faqih recorded the events that occurred from 1529 to 1537, although the war continued until 1543. He wrote the *Futuh Al-Habaša* in 1559, and copies of the book made their way to India within a few decades. Among the first Europeans to obtain a copy of this book was the British governor of Sudan, Sir Charles Gordon (1833–1885). Italian and French translations of the *Futuh Al-Habaša* were published in the nineteenth century. In 2003, Paul Lester Stenhouse translated the *Futuh* and published it in English for the first time. It is a historical record of invaluable worth for those studying the Ethiopian–Adal War and provides extraordinary insight into sixteenth-century African history. Although the *Futuh Al-Habaša* ends in the year 1537, some Ethiopian scholars claim to have seen a second volume covering the end of the war, "though they were unable to say where it is now kept".[1] It is unlikely that such a volume exists, and it is not even known if Arab Faqih lived beyond 1537. Even if he was still alive in 1537, it would have been a good year to end the story of the conquest since Imam Gurey's campaign against Ethiopia seemed to have been brought to a victorious conclusion. For the last six years of the war, 1537–1543, Portuguese sources of varying reliability are the only first-hand accounts available.

1 Hussein Ahmed, 'The Historiography of Islam in Ethiopia', *Journal of Islamic Studies*, Vol. 3, No. 1 (January 1992), p.16, note 39, referencing an interview with Shaykh Muhammad Walĕ bin Ahmad (interviewed in Addis Ababa, 25 June 1982) and Shaykh Muhammad Jamma (interviewed in Dasĕ, 4 May 1982). If true, the second volume of the *Futuh al Habasa* would be a historical find of tremendous importance for our understanding of the final years of the Ethiopian–Adal War, and for Muslim–Christian relations in sixteenth-century Ethiopia and the Horn of Africa.

The three Portuguese accounts include journals written by Miguel de Castanhoso, João Bermudez, and Gaspar Correa, all of whom were present with the Portuguese expeditionary force in Ethiopia from 1541-1543. Scholars and historians have debated which source is more reliable, and the vast majority support Castanhoso's version of events, which were written immediately after the war upon his return to Portugal. The three narratives were first published in English by the Hakluyt Society of London in 1902 with an introduction by R.S. Whiteway. This introduction provides a concise summary of the Portuguese participation in the war, and many of Whiteway's names and dates help clarify some of the Arabic and Ethiopian sources' contradictions, as well as reconcile some of the discrepancies between the three Portuguese accounts.

Among the secondary sources, Francisco Alvarez, a Portuguese missionary, recorded his experience in Ethiopia as a member of a diplomatic mission between the years 1520 and 1526. His observations of the Ethiopian government, customs, and geography are useful in any study of the Ethiopian–Adal War, although Alvarez was not in Ethiopia during the war years. His account was also published in English by the Hakluyt Society in the early twentieth century. The Portuguese captain Dom João de Castro recorded the voyage from India to Suez, which was led by Estêvão da Gama (he referred to him as Stefano da Gama), second son of Vasco da Gama. Castro's account was written between 1545–1548 and was translated into English for the first time in 1664. It is widely available online.

Other Portuguese missionaries and priests travelled to Ethiopia after the war, and many of them recorded their discussions with Ethiopians who shared their memories and recollections of the war. Pedro Paez arrived in Ethiopia in 1618, and his account of the land and its people was also published in English by the Hakluyt Society in the nineteenth century. Paez describes the Ethiopian–Adal War from a second-hand perspective, but like Alvarez, he probably also spoke with many Portuguese and Ethiopian veterans while writing his narrative.

About 80 years after the war ended, Father Jerome Lobo, another Portuguese missionary, visited Ethiopia. He spent the years 1624 to 1634 travelling throughout the country, visiting many of the sites destroyed during Imam Gurey's invasion. It is unlikely that he had read Castanhoso's account of the war, but Lobo may have spoken with Ethiopians who recalled their own versions of the many war stories which even today are freely shared in Ethiopia. Even the youngest veterans of the conflict whom Father Lobo could have met would have been in their upper nineties, their views of the past possibly distorted by the passing of time. However, Lobo provides interesting information about the Ethiopian–Adal War and its impact on Ethiopia, its church, and its people. He wrote, "what I have here related of the death of Don Christopher de Gama I was told by an old man, who was an eye-witness of it: and there is a tradition in the country that in the place where his head fell, a fountain sprung up of wonderful virtue, which cured many diseases otherwise past remedy."[2] Lobo's perspectives on the war and the legends that arose surrounding it are a fascinating addition to the literature.

---

2 Fr. Jerome Lobo, *A Voyage to Abyssinia.* Translated from French by Samuel Johnson (London: Cassell & Co, Ltd, 1887), n.p.

Finally, Father Balthazar Tellez, another Portuguese priest who visited Ethiopia, published a combined account of his countrymen's observations which was published in English in 1710. In addition to the first-hand accounts written by Castanhoso, Bermudez, and Correa, we can add Alvarez, de Castro, Paez, Lobo, and Tellez to the list of Portuguese observers who provided specific accounts of the Ethiopian–Adal War which have been translated into English.

From the Ethiopian perspective, *The Chronicle of King Gelawdewos (1540–1559)* covers the war's final years, although it was written about 15 years after the war ended. This chronicle is a unique literary work composed to glorify King Gelawdewos' reign. Like all the Ethiopian kings' chronicles, it emphasises Gelawdewos' many accomplishments in a somewhat hagiographical manner. The author's identity is unknown. Written in the flowery prose one would find in Ethiopian royal chronicles, the book begins with a short benediction to the Lord Jesus Christ, followed by a tribute to the great King Gelawdewos, which reads:

> We begin here to write the fine story, sweeter in the mouth and palate than the taste of honey and sugar, which brings benefit of blessedness for the ears of those who hear it and which gives joy to those who understand it, like a mixture of canticle and wine – from the story and account of the glorious and most high king, the owner of a great name and the owner of a virtuous commemoration, whose deeds are more praised than the deeds of his forefathers, whose ordinance is proper, whose law is sincere, whose name is notable, whose judgment is right, whose verdict is righteous and whose commandment is blessed.[3]

The Chronicle of King Gelawdewos is considered one of the finest literary works of sixteenth-century Ethiopia. One of its primary shortfalls as a historical work is that it gives little credit to the 400 Portuguese soldiers who helped stem the tide against Imam Gurey between 1541 and 1543, barely mentioning them at all. The author attributes Imam Gurey's defeat solely to Ethiopian forces, neglecting to note that the Portuguese effort contributed to the eventual Ethiopian victory.

Other journals that are useful in studying this era and in situating the Ethiopian–Adal War into its proper historical perspective include those written by the Italian explorer Ludovico de Varthema, one of the first Europeans to make the pilgrimage to Mecca about 20 years before the Ethiopian–Adal War began. His observations of the region and its people help shed light on the events and issues that led to the war's outbreak. The Scotsman James Bruce travelled throughout Ethiopia in the early eighteenth century. His accounts of the dates and locations for some of the battles and other events of the Ethiopian–Adal War clarify some of the discrepancies between the Portuguese, Arabic, and Ethiopian sources.

Ethiopian historical accounts written by contemporary scholars include research done by Merid Aregay, Deresse Ayenachew, Mohammed Hassen,

3 Solomon Gebreyes, trans., *Chronicle of King Galawdewos (1540–1559)* (Lovanii: Peters, 2019), p.3.

and Taddesse Tamrat. These historians and scholars have added much to our understanding of the Ethiopian–Adal War. Also of importance in researching East African history is the work done by George Wynn Brereton (G.W.B.) Huntingford (1901-1978). His lifelong study of eastern Africa and Ethiopia contributed tremendously to this book. The same is true of Richard Pankhurst (1927-2017), another British scholar and the founder of the Institute of Ethiopian Studies. Pankhurst was also a professor at the University of Addis Ababa in Ethiopia and was married to the legendary suffragette and anti-fascist activist Sylvia Pankhurst. Huntingford and Pankhurst remain the leading non-native Ethiopian experts on Ethiopia, and their substantial research on Ethiopian history, culture, religion, language, and geography is unmatched.

All the primary sources mentioned above, journals, and accounts written by participants, explorers, and scholars help contemporary historians piece together the Ethiopian–Adal War. This violent conflict nearly resulted in Christian Ethiopia's destruction in the sixteenth century. Until now, the war has been mostly unknown in the west, overshadowed by other events, many of which arguably have had far less impact than the Ethiopian–Adal War has had on the contemporary international order. I hope historians and general readers alike will find this book to be a useful addition to the literature on Ethiopia, especially at this critical time in her history.

Author's Note

The various authors of the primary source documents often use different names to refer to the same people and places. The bewildering variety of dates used to identify when the battles and other events took place requires some attempt at standardisation. Of particular interest is the variety of calendars used in the sixteenth century, whether in Europe, Arabia, or Africa. Identifying exact dates for many of the events of the Ethiopian–Adal War is complicated, and in some cases, quite impossible. For example, the author of *The Chronicle of King Gelawdewos,* discussing the Battle of Wayna Dega, gave the following date:

> During that third year in the last Hebrew month, in the sixth month among the Coptic months which is the main fasting month among the fasts of the Church, in the year 7035 of the creation of the world, and in the 28th of the month we mentioned [before], on Wednesday, our lord Mar Gelawdewos fought Imam Ahmad, the son of Abrahim, whose soldiers were numerous like locusts and their number exceeds thousands upon thousands and ten thousand [times] thousands.[1]

Sparing the reader from trying to figure out the actual day to which the author is actually referring, I have decided to go with the accepted Gregorian calendar dates for these events. The most common estimate for when the Battle of Wayna Dega was fought is 21 February 1543. Other such dates from the Gregorian calendar will be used when they are known. In most cases, these dates come from research done by Huntingford and Pankhurst, although some of them are taken from R.S. Whiteway's introduction to Castanhoso's journal.

For simplicity and clarity, the name Ethiopia will be used to refer to the kingdom which appeared in East Africa nearly 2,000 years ago. Although originating as the Kingdom of Da'amat, which became the Kingdom of Aksum, and later Abyssinia, a name deriving from the Arabic word *al-Habasa*, "Ethiopia" will be used along with these names to refer to the political entity situated in the highlands of the Horn of Africa. Also complicating matters is the fact that many different names are used to refer

1 Gebreyes, *Chronicle of King Galawdewos*, p.16.

to Ethiopian kings in historical narratives and chronicles. For example, the Ethiopian monarch during most of the Ethiopian–Adal War, King Dawit II (1496–1540), was named Lebne Dengel at birth but was also known by his moniker Wanag Segued (to whom the lions bow) in the Arabic sources. King Gelawdewos (1522–1559), whose name is the Amharic word for "Claudius", was also referred to as Asnaf Segued, "to whom the horizon bows". His throne name was Asnaf Segued I. These Ethiopian kings will be referred to by the names most commonly used in the historical sources, Lebne Dengel and Gelawdewos. On the Adal side, the main protagonist in this story, Imam Ahmed bin Ibrahim (1506–1543), the leader of the *jihad* against Ethiopia, is referred to in various sources as Imam Ahmed, Ahmad ibn Ibrahim al-Ghazi, Ahmed Gran, or Imam Gurey. The Somali nickname "Gurey" means "left-handed", and in all the historical accounts, he is depicted as having been one of the rare individuals to be able to wield a sword with his left hand. For simplicity's sake, his Somali nickname Ahmed Gurey will be used to refer to him before his designation as an imam, after which Imam Gurey will be used.

Many of the battle sites and other locations in which the events described in this book occurred are difficult or impossible to render on a map. Determining their location with any precision is a nearly impossible task for contemporary scholars and historians. In some cases, the historical record lists more than one name for some of these places. The place names used throughout the book are primarily those used by Huntingford and Pankhurst in their study of Ethiopia and the Horn of Africa. Huntingford illuminates the challenges inherent in identifying some of the places mentioned in the *Chronicle of King Gelawdewos*:

> The topography of this early period of the invasion is extremely difficult. Assuming Antukyah is the place suggested near Wärrä Ilu, the statement that between Watmat and Ayfārs was a river called 'Arah suggest that several of the intervening stages have been left out by the chronicler ... It would thus appear that the names 'Arah, Majlah below Ayfārs, Janbah below Sarkah 'Andurah, and Qanburah are all to be sought many miles south of Antukyah ... This is not a satisfactory solution, but I cannot think of a better one.[2]

Fortunately, the war's overall narrative can be written without relying on a description of every place and person mentioned in the sources, whether these sources are the *Futuh Al-Habaša* or *The Chronicle of King Gelawdewos*. I have relied primarily on the work of G.W.B. Huntingford and Richard Pankhurst for their interpretation of sixteenth-century historical geography.

2 G.W.B. Huntingford, *The Historical Geography of Ethiopia, From the First Century A.D. to 1704* (New York: Oxford University Press, 1989), pp.126–27.

Acknowledgements

Many colleagues and friends helped bring this book to print. Dr Grant Rhode, friend, and colleague, and distinguished scholar at Boston University's Pardee School of Global Studies, provided expertise on sixteenth-century maritime history, photos from his travels, and insight and encouragement, which is deeply appreciated. My very good friend and colleague, Dr Michael Pavkovic, suggested useful ideas for formatting and presenting the book. From Salve Regina University, friend and colleague Jones Ofuasia graciously shared pictures from his time in Ethiopia. From England, Dr Jeremy Black also suggested helpful ideas for presenting this book and took the time to write its foreword, for which I am indebted.

I benefitted tremendously from the scholars working on Ethiopian history at the *Centre National de la Recherche Scientifique* in France, especially Dr Amélie Chekroun and Dr Margaux Herman. Amélie and Margaux have done ground-breaking work on Ethiopian history, and their research helped clarify the events leading up to the Ethiopian–Adal War and the role played during the war by the Ottoman Empire. I am especially indebted to Amélie for allowing me to use her hand-drawn maps of the Ethiopian–Adal War, maps which she created in 2013 for her doctoral dissertation. These are the most meticulously researched maps of the war available, and I am grateful for her permission to bring them to a wider audience. Dr Verena Krebs of the Ruhr-Universität Bochum provided valuable insight into Ethiopian history as well. Dr Mukerrem Miftah, professor of religion and policy analysis at the Ethiopian Civil Service University in Addis Ababa, pointed me towards several valuable sources which helped fill in some of the gaps in the narrative of both Ethiopian history in general as well as the Ethiopian–Adal War. For their assistance in pointing me towards relevant scholarship and sharing their own, I would also like to thank many professors and researchers from around the world who helped me identify the best and most recent scholarship on Ethiopia, the Ottoman Empire, and Portugal. Professor Marco Vigano of the University of Addis Ababa provided his time and energised many of his colleagues working in the fields of Ethiopian history and archaeology, including Dr Enrico Piero Bossi of Italy, Dr Manfred Kropp, professor of Semitic and Islamic Studies, Johannes Gutenberg-Universität Mainz, and Meftuh Abubaker, an independent researcher in Islamic History and Archaeology in Ethiopia. Also providing their assistance were professors Giulia Bonaci, a faculty member at the *Institut de Recherche pour le Développement* (IRD – France), and Zahit Atçıl, professor of Ottoman history at the Istanbul Medeniyet University. Jean-Claude Latombe, Professor Emeritus in the School of Engineering at Stanford University, granted permission to use his stunning photographs of the Ethiopian landscape. He trekked through central Ethiopia in 2013 and recorded his journey in pictures, all of which can be found at his website, <https://ai.stanford.edu/~latombe/mountain/index.htm>.

For assistance with inquiries on weapons and firearms, I would like to thank the Milwaukee Public Museum's Jennifer Tetzlaff and Sara Podejko, and Professor Ben Nicholson of the School of the Art Institute of Chicago. Alison Gerber and Robin Rudd of the Chattanooga Times Free Press granted permission for the use of images from their newspaper, for which I am indebted. Dr Kathryn Bard, Professor of Archaeology and Classical Studies at Boston University, graciously shared photographs from the 2004 excavation of Mersa/Wadi Gawasis, Egypt, undertaken in conjunction with the University of Naples' L'Orientale. I would also like to thank Mikael Muehlbauer for sharing his photos of the churches at Lalibela. Mikael is an art historian who specialises in Medieval Ethiopian and Egyptian Architecture and is currently a core lecturer at Columbia University, where he earned his PhD in 2020. Yves-Marie Stranger, author of *The Anthology of Ethiopia through Writer's Eyes*, provided me with links to stories and blog posts on Ethiopian culture and history, which were most helpful in framing the general narrative of the war.

Alex Saikowski of the Maritime Museum in San Diego assisted in obtaining permission to use Robert Camp's photographs of the replica of the Spanish sailing vessel *San Salvador*. Alex also serves as the *San Salvador*'s first mate. Journalist Julia Lee also shared many of her photographs of the *San Salvador*. Thank you, Alex, Robert, and Julia, for your assistance and permission to use your photos.

The reference librarians at the Naval War College, Robin Lima, and Heidi Garcia, procured books and articles to support this project from libraries worldwide. Without their assistance, I could not have written this book.

My wife Robin and daughters Kara and Erin also encouraged me in this endeavour, and as always, I owe any success I have found in life to them. Ultimately, I dedicate this book to my mother, Pat Shaw (1942–2019). May you rest in peace.

Chronology

~350 Ethiopian King Ezana converts to Christianity
~700 Islam spreads across the Arabian Peninsula and North Africa
~900 The Ethiopian Kingdom of Aksum declines, surrounded by Islam and cut off from its land and maritime trade routes to Europe, India and Arabia
1299 Sultan Osman I establishes the Ottoman Empire in modern-day north-western Turkey
1329 Ethiopian king Amda Seyon I leads a military campaign against the lowland Sultanate of Ifat
1389 An Ottoman army defeats the Serbs at the Battle of Kosovo and advances into the Balkans
1415 Ethiopian king Zara Yaqob subjugates the Sultanate of Ifat. In the same year, the Portuguese capture Ceuta in Morocco, establishing a presence on the continent that would last until the twentieth century
1453 The Ottomans capture Constantinople, the capital of the Byzantine Empire, disrupting European overland access to the Orient
1509 Ethiopian Queen Eleni sends an envoy to King Manuel of Portugal, requesting a diplomatic mission
1514 The Ottomans defeat the Persians at the Battle of Chāldirān, employing gunpowder weapons
1515 The Ottoman–Mamluk War begins. By 1517 the Mamluk Sultanate of Egypt is incorporated into the Ottoman Empire
1520 The Portuguese diplomatic mission requested by Queen Eleni in 1509 arrives in Ethiopia
1526 An Ottoman army defeats the Hungarians at the Battle of Mohács
1529 Imam Gurey, the Sultan of Adal, invades Ethiopia and crushes the Ethiopian army at the Battle of Shembra Kure
1529 An Ottoman army besieges Vienna
1531 Imam Gurey's army defeats the Ethiopians at the Battle of Antukyah
1536 The King of France, Francis I, allies with Ottoman Sultan Süleyman the Magnificent
1538 The Portuguese–Ottoman War begins; the Ottomans lay siege to the Portuguese port city of Diu in India
1540 Ethiopian King Gelawdewos succeeds King Lebne Dengel

1541 Cristóvão da Gama and 400 Portuguese soldiers, including Miguel de Castanhoso, land on the Ethiopian coast at Massawa

1542 Portuguese troops, heavily outnumbered, defeat Imam Gurey's forces at the battles of Amba Senait and the Antalo Plain. In August, Cristóvão da Gama is killed at the Battle of Wofla

1543 The Battle of Wayna Dega, the death of Imam Gurey, and the end of the Ethiopian–Adal War

Introduction

The Ethiopian–Adal War nearly resulted in the destruction of the Ethiopian Christian kingdom at the hands of invading Muslim armies from the Sultanate of Adal, a kingdom located to the south-east of Ethiopia in what is today part of eastern Ethiopia, western Somalia, and Djibouti. The war began in 1529 as a continuation of the ethnic and religious conflict common for centuries in the Horn of Africa. Warfare between the highland Christians and the lowland Muslims was common throughout the fourteenth and fifteenth centuries. These wars were fought primarily to ensure that the small sultanates and principalities along Ethiopia's southern and eastern border recognised Ethiopian overlordship and ensured Ethiopia's access to the many lucrative trade routes in the region.

During the war, the Portuguese intervened on Ethiopia's behalf, while the Ottoman Empire provided some support to the Adal army. Economic and religious motives propelled both the Portuguese and the Ottomans into the conflict, although it would be inaccurate to portray the conflict as a religious war. Religious considerations were an essential factor in both the Portuguese and the Ottoman decision to intervene in Ethiopia. In a pattern not unique to this war, religion "was important in transforming local conflicts into either general European ones or, at least, into national conflicts".[1] Defending their Ethiopian Christian brethren was an important factor in the Portuguese decision to intervene to protect Ethiopia from further Muslim intrusion. However, economic reasons were also essential factors in the Portuguese decision to enter the conflict in 1541. For the Ottomans, containing Portuguese expansion in the Indian Ocean and protecting their trade routes through the Red Sea were important factors that led to their support to the Sultanate of Adal. Economic factors were more critical to the Ottomans than religious factors, although the responsibility to protect their fellow Muslims throughout the Islamic world was a factor in the Ottoman decision to lend support to Adal. The Ottoman Empire was in the process of affirming its position as the pre-eminent Islamic political entity, having recently subjugated the Egyptian Mamluks and the Shi'a Safavid Persians. Although the term "Turkish" is often used to describe the Ottoman Empire,

1 Jeremy Black, *Why Wars Happen* (London: Reaktion, 1998), p.59.

the Ottomans did not refer to themselves as Turks, "which meant rustic peasant or country bumpkin".[2] The Ottomans were rulers of an empire, while Turkey is a modern nation-state. The terms Turkey and Ottoman Empire imply distinctly different political entities and should not be conflated, and throughout this book, the term "Ottoman" will be used.

Condensing thousands of years of historical events into a series of short chapters, the first part of this book presents the historical background information necessary to set the stage for the Ethiopian–Adal War. The story begins with the early Ethiopian kingdoms of Da'amat and Aksum, the adoption of Christianity by the Aksumite king Ezana, and a description of Islam's rise and its impact on Ethiopia, which found itself surrounded by Muslim states in the closing years of the Aksumite kingdom. The constant conflict between Ethiopia and the Muslim sultanates was influential in developing the Ethiopian military organisation and doctrine employed against Adal from 1529-1543. In the fifteenth century, the Portuguese empire's rise coincided with Ethiopia's re-emergence as a regional power in the Horn of Africa. The Ottoman Empire also began to influence events in the Red Sea and the Horn of Africa by 1500. The chapters that follow include a brief history of the Portuguese and Ottoman Empires and a historical account of the Sultanate of Adal, which rose to prominence in the early sixteenth century, challenging and nearly vanquishing Christian Ethiopia after the initial invasion in 1529.

The war between Ethiopia and the Sultanate of Adal can be divided into two phases, the first of which lasted from 1529-1541. During this time, the Adal forces, composed mostly of Somali warriors led by Imam Gurey, nearly defeated the Ethiopians. Following their victory at the Battle of Shembra Kure, Imam Gurey's forces maintained the upper hand throughout 12 years of fighting. The second phase of the conflict took place from 1541-1543. During the sixteenth century, the contest between the Ottoman Empire and the Portuguese for control of trade routes, which included the Red Sea, had found an outlet in the Horn of Africa, and both sides entered the conflict, upsetting the balance of power in what was "an entirely internal matter".[3] Ottoman contribution to the Adal war effort did not match the level of support that the Portuguese provided to Ethiopia. The Ethiopians managed to secure the assistance of the great Portuguese explorer Vasco da Gama's fourth son, Cristóvão, and 400 Portuguese troops. These troops were at the forefront as the Ethiopians stemmed the Muslim advance, and by 1543 the combined Ethiopian/Portuguese force drove the invading Muslim army from Ethiopian territory. This decisive Portuguese expedition ensured that Ethiopia remained a Christian nation, and rarely in history have "results so momentous been attained by means so disproportionate".[4] While the conflict appeared to be a religious war between Christians and Muslims, the religious

2 Jeremy Black, *European Warfare, 1494–1660* (London: Routledge, 2002), p. xi.

3 Mesfin Wolde Mariam, 'The Background of the Ethio-Somali Border Dispute', *The Journal of Modern African Studies*, 2 (July 1964), p.196.

4 R.S. Whiteway, *The Portuguese Expedition to Abyssinia in 1541–1543* (Alpha Editions, 2019), p.xviii.

element was secondary to controlling the Red Sea and Indian Ocean trade routes. These routes were crucial to both the Ottomans and the Portuguese as they competed for maritime dominance.

The Ethiopian–Adal War led to a cultural resurgence in Ethiopia. The spirit of this resurgence was captured in the words of a contemporary who said: *"Comme un nuage sombre, les devastations de gragne passent sur l'empire chretien, plus la lumiere revient et l'on s'apercoit alors que la toute perspective d'histoire est change. L'ethiopie medievale a disparu; un nouvel age est en train de naitre."* (Like a dark cloud, the devastations of Imam Gurey pass over the Christian empire, the more the light comes back, and one realises then that the whole perspective of history is changed. Medieval Ethiopia has disappeared; a new age is being born.)[5]

Ethiopian children are still told tales of Imam Gurey and the war that was fought nearly 500 years ago. The Ethiopian emperor Haile Selassie (1892–1975) referred to Imam Gurey in his memoirs, stating that villagers in northern Ethiopia "point out sites of towns, forts, churches, and monasteries damaged or destroyed by [Imam Gurey] as if these catastrophes had occurred only yesterday."[6] Ethiopians have not forgotten this war, and they continue to grapple with its impact in the twenty-first century.

---

5 J. Doresse, *L'Empire du Pretre-Jean,* Vol. II (Plon, 1957), p.323. Translated by Jeffrey M. Shaw.

6 Paul B. Henze, *Layers of Time: A History of Ethiopia* (New York: Palgrave, 2000), p.90.

Chapter 1

History of the Horn of Africa Region

The Horn of Africa is the easternmost tip of the African continent, composed of Somalia, Eritrea, Djibouti, and Ethiopia, and is home to some of the earliest traces of human development. Along with Peking Man and Java Man, the earliest evidence of *Homo Erectus*, dating back to over 1.5 million years, was discovered in the Horn of Africa. Stone spear tips found in the region have been dated to around 280,000 years old. Evidence of human civilisation can be found in the Ethiopian savannah, indicating that some 60,000 years ago humans developed tools and weapons in the Awash valley and the Dire Dawa region of modern Ethiopia.[1] The ancient Egyptians interacted with the people of this land, and surviving Egyptian texts indicate that a mysterious "land of Punt" could be reached by "traveling south along the Red Sea after crossing the Eastern Desert".[2] The land of Punt referred to the area south of Egypt along the Red Sea coast, in what is today Somalia and south-eastern Ethiopia. The ancient Egyptians considered the land of Punt, from which the life-giving Nile River emerged, "to be a source of curiosity and mystery", and when the river flooded Egyptian priests concluded that the Gods had been offended.[3] These same Egyptian texts also indicate the importance of sea routes for trade. The sea features prominently throughout Egyptian as well as Ethiopian history. Access to the Red Sea was crucial to Ethiopia's economy from ancient times to the twenty-first century. Menelik I, the first recognised Ethiopian emperor, reigned in the tenth century BC. Legend claims that Menelik was the son of King Solomon and the Queen of Sheba, and he is thus the first recognised king in the Solomonic line. This line continued to the reign of Haile Selassie (1892-1975), with only a few interruptions. The *Kebra Nagast,* the chronicle of Ethiopia's founding, attests that Menelik I brought

1 Harold G. Marcus, *A History of Ethiopia* (Berkeley, CA: University of California Press, 1994), p.2.

2 Jacke Phillips, 'Punt and Aksum: Egypt and the Horn of Africa', *The Journal of African History*, 38, No. 3 (1997), p.425.

3 Henze, *Layers of Time*, p.15.

the Ark of the Covenant to Ethiopia. Ethiopian Christians believe the ark to be there to this day.

In the fifth century BC, the Greek historian Herodotus described a land south of Egypt, which he referred to as Ethiopia. He wrote:

> these Ethiopians ... are said to be the tallest and handsomest of all men; and they say that they have customs different from those of other nations, and especially the following, with regard to regal power; for they confer the sovereignty upon the man whom they consider to be of the largest stature, and to possess strength proportional to his size.[4]

Through trade and commerce, knowledge of the Greek world permeated Ethiopia and vice versa. The great poet Homer wrote that the Greek gods, including Zeus, frequently visited the Ethiopians. References to Ethiopia also appear in the Bible. Psalm 68 states, "Princes shall come out of Egypt; Ethiopia shall soon stretch out her hands unto God."[5] Over the following centuries the Romans traded with Ethiopia much more so than the Greeks had done. Trade and economics were the foundation of Ethiopian civilisation, and ensuring access to trade routes, whether overland or by sea, was among the Ethiopian kings' top priorities. The Ge'ez language, a language of the south Semitic branch, was developed during this era.

Geographically diverse, The Kingdom of Da'amat boasted high mountains, deep gorges and river valleys, and flat, lowland pastoral regions. There are five major river systems in Ethiopia, each with numerous tributaries. The rivers in the highlands are not navigable, and the major rivers throughout Ethiopia disrupt travel and communication between the provinces.[6] Lake Tana, the source of the Blue Nile, lies in the mountains, some 5,600 feet above sea level. The Great Rift Valley runs north-east to south-west through the centre of modern Ethiopia. Some 50 miles wide, the valley separates the Ethiopian highlands into two distinct mountainous zones. A temperate climate marks the highlands, while the lowlands to the south-east and south-west are hot and are subject to frequent drought. Swarms of locusts occasionally plague both highlands and lowlands, devastating crops and leaving apocalyptic destruction in their wake. Forests line the gorges in the highlands; pines, sycamores, and gum trees are just a few of the various species found in the river valleys. Elephants, crocodiles, rhinoceroses and giraffes are among the many species of wildlife that inhabit the lowland areas.

The fertile highlands were suitable for growing wheat and barley, plentiful once the plough broke the land. Widely cultivated throughout the highlands, teff is a crop indigenous to Ethiopia – the most characteristic of all Ethiopian grains. It is used primarily as an ingredient in the flatbread known as *injera*. It has a high nutrient and mineral content and is a staple of Ethiopian cuisine to this day. Irrigation and efficient government storage and distribution systems

---

4 Herodotus, *The Histories*. Translated by Henry Cary (New York: D. Appleton & Co., 1904), p.160.

5 *The Holy Bible*: King James Version (Dallas, TX: Brown Books Publishing, 2004).

6 Huntingford, *Historical Geography*, p.31.

The Great Rift Valley, about 100 miles north-west of modern-day Addis Ababa. (Author's photo)

ensured that Da'amat, and later the Kingdom of Aksum, had enough food to maintain stability and growth. Despite the best efforts of early kings and later monarchs, Ethiopia's fragmented geography, especially in the highlands, significantly impacted the country's political and cultural unity. Isolated and remote mountainous plateaus "have proven to be almost insurmountable obstacles to political leaders who have sought to unify the country, to the invaders who desired to conquer it, and to those who have sporadically attempted to develop its economic resources".[7] Throughout her long history, the contrast between the north-western highlands and the south-eastern lowlands has contributed to turmoil, tension, and conflict.

The Kingdom of Aksum

As the Ethiopian Kingdom of Da'amat declined in power, the Kingdom of Aksum arose in its place. The city of Aksum, known to both the Greeks and Romans, would rise to prominence shortly after the beginning of the Christian era, in the first century AD. Aksum inherited the advantageous

7 Saheed A. Adejumobi, *The History of Ethiopia* (Westport, CT: Greenwood, 2007), p.5.

This Egyptian rock stella tells the story of two brothers, Nebsu and Amenhotep, who journeyed to the lands of Punt. (Photo courtesy of L'Orientale/Boston University Investigations at Mersa/Wadi Gawasis, Egypt)

trading location that gathered together the interior's products and exported them in exchange for the luxury items produced in both the Roman Empire and later the Byzantine Empire.[8] Semitic immigrants from the Arabian peninsula, many of them Jewish, helped establish the Aksumite Kingdom and propel it to a level of prosperity far surpassing the earlier Ethiopian kingdom of Da'amat.[9] Aksumites spoke and wrote using Ge'ez, a language that plays a role in Ethiopia similar to that of Latin in the West. The port city of Adulis served as a significant hub for merchants and traders from the Mediterranean sailing from the Byzantine Empire, India, and Persia, and uninterrupted access to Adulis drove Aksumite foreign policy.[10] Ensuring maritime access through the Red Sea was as important 1,500 years ago to the Aksumites as it is to the major world powers in the twenty-first century. What is today the modern state of Ethiopia began as a group of independent and autonomous provinces which paid tribute to the *negusa nagast*, the title given to the King of Aksum.[11] The *neguse* was the term used to designate the ruler of the autonomous regions that proclaimed loyalty to Aksum.

Trade and commerce linked Ethiopia with merchants in India, Egypt, Rome, Persia, and Ceylon. Many goods were traded along these crucial routes, which were responsible for the rise of the great empires of antiquity. The primary trade goods included:

> elephant tusks and tortoise shells, plus rhinoceros horn, hides and skins, various kinds of incense and fragrant gums, dyes, aromatic woods, spices of many kinds, precious stones and pearls, live exotic animals and slaves. In return traders offered cloth and several kinds of clothing, olive oil and wine, axes, adzes and other tools of iron, copper, and bronze, pottery, drinking cups, gold and silver objects (made for the king "in the shapes of the country") and glassware (perhaps beads).[12]

Of all the products and goods to come out of Ethiopia, none is as well known as coffee. While Ethiopians refer to both the bean and the drink as *buna*, the Arabic term is *qahwa*, while the Turkish call it *kahve*, from which the name in various other languages originated.[13] The abundance of coffee beans and other

8 David W. Phillipson, 'Aksum in Africa', *Journal of Ethiopian Studies*, 23 (November 1990), p.55.
9 George A. Lipsky, *Ethiopia* (New Haven, CT: Hraf Press, 1962), p.7.
10 Marcus, *A History of Ethiopia*, p.9.
11 Huntingford, *Historical Geography*, p.61.
12 Henze, *Layers of Time*, p.12, note 18.
13 Henze, *Layers of Time*, p.12, note 26.

resources, and Ethiopia's position along the trade route from India to Egypt and the Roman Empire, helped spur the development of the first great Ethiopian kingdoms of Da'amat and Aksum. The "Erythraean Sea" was the ancient name for the Red Sea and the western expanse of the Indian Ocean, to include the Persian Gulf, through which the Classical world received spices, incense, and other luxury goods from Somalia, Arabia, the Horn of Africa, India and the Far East.[14] The importance of these maritime trade routes to the people of India, Africa, and Europe would grow over time with the increase in the types and quantities of available trade goods. Ethiopia, lying as it does astride these trade routes, would see its fortunes rise and fall in direct proportion to its access to the coastal cities such as Adulis through which these trade goods moved.

Slaves were among the most important trade goods that travelled from the Horn of Africa to Asia and Europe. The first-century Roman naturalist and philosopher Pliny mentioned the vast quantities of slave exports from the Aksumite port of Adulis, "and the *Periplus of the Erythraean Sea* reports on the shipment of slaves from the ports of the Gulf of Aden".[15] Describing the territory lying in the vicinity of Adulis and the inland city of Aksum, a merchant in the first century AD recorded:

> Opposite Mountain Island, on the mainland twenty stadia from shore, lies Adulis, a fair-sized village ... and the first market for ivory. From that place to the city of the people called Auxumites there is a five days' journey more; to that place all the ivory is brought from the country beyond the Nile ... Practically the whole number of elephants and rhinoceros that are killed live in the places inland, although at rare intervals they are hunted on the seacoast even near Adulis. These places, from the Calf-Eaters to the other Berber country, are governed by Zoscales, who is miserly in his ways and always striving for more, but otherwise upright, and acquainted with Greek literature.[16]

The *negus* Zoscales is believed by some scholars and historians to have been in the line of Ethiopian kings established by Menelik I. However, others assert that he was merely a local *negus* who maintained control over a province in the Kingdom of Aksum. Zoscales helped establish Aksum's regional dominance, and by the third century AD the Persian prophet Mani wrote, "there are four great kingdoms on earth: the first is the Kingdom of Babylon and Persia; the second is the Kingdom of Rome; the third is the Kingdom of the Aksumites: the fourth is the kingdom of the Chinese."[17] Clearly, Aksum was among the great empires due to its advantageous position along the Red Sea trade routes. Trade between Aksum and the Mediterranean world had exposed Ethiopians to Christianity, a new religion that had steadily acquired new followers in the lands administered by the Roman Empire.

---

14 Phillips, 'Punt and Aksum', p.446.

15 Giulia Bonaci, 'Revisiting Slavery and the Slave Trade in Ethiopia', *Northeast African Studies*, Vol. 17, No. 2 (2017), p.8.

16 Wilfred Schloss, trans., *The Peryplus of the Erythraean Sea: Travel in the Indian Ocean by a Merchant of the First Century* (New York: Longmans, Green & Co., 1912), p.23.

17 Henze, *Layers of Time*, p.22.

In the third century, the Aksumite court began to discuss the political and economic benefits that adopting Christianity as the official religion might confer upon the kingdom.[18] In approximately 340 AD the Aksumite king Ezana, "previously a worshipper of gods identified with such Greek deities as Zeus, Poseidon, and Ares", converted to Christianity.[19] In one of the most momentous events in the history of the Western world, the Roman Emperor Constantine had converted to Christianity in 312. Ezana may have converted to Christianity to win Rome's favour and integrate Aksum into the wider Roman and Mediterranean political and economic sphere.[20] His conversion continues to generate interest among scholars; exactly when and why did he adopt the Christian faith, and to what end? While contemporary scholars debate these questions, it is widely agreed that by the fourth century, the Aksumites had managed to extend their domination over the many different ethnic groups of what is today known as Ethiopia.[21] Christianity would become intrinsic to Aksumite (and later, Abyssinian and Ethiopian) identity. So extensive was Aksum's power that when the Roman Empire began to decline in the third century AD, Aksum became the dominant (in fact, the only) Christian state, maintaining control over the lucrative trade routes which continued to boost Aksum's already well-developed economy.[22]

As Aksum's trade routes flourished and the kingdom prospered, coinage became a means to assert the empire's status among the other regional powers. Aksum's emperors took full advantage of their coins to display their power and wealth. Aksum used coins both for international and domestic trade, coins which today can be found throughout the Horn of Africa. Aksumite coins have also been unearthed in India, a testament to the expansive trade carried out by Ethiopian merchants.[23]

As Aksumite power increased and the kingdom expanded its borders, Christianity became an integral part of the culture and political system. The Christian church in Askum depended upon the Coptic Christian church of Egypt for its guidance in matters of faith and orthodoxy. In about the year 500, a travelling group of monks known as the "Nine Saints" arrived in Ethiopia from Egypt. After establishing their monasteries, the Nine Saints translated Aksum's sacred books into Ge'ez, developed a distinct Ethiopian liturgy, and most importantly, propagated the Monophysite theology, which would remain a central element of Ethiopian Christianity until the present day.[24] Monophysites believed that Jesus Christ had only a divine nature, a position contrary to that established at the Council of Chalcedon in 451 – the Diophysitist position – which proclaimed that Jesus was both divine as

18 Marcus, *A History of Ethiopia*, p.7.

19 Stuart Munro-Hay, *Aksum: An African Civilization of Late Antiquity* (Edinburgh: Edinburgh University Press, 1991), p.13.

20 Alessandro Bausi (ed.), *Languages and Cultures of Eastern Christianity: Ethiopia* (London: Ashgate, 2012), p.31.

21 Munro-Hay, *Aksum*, p.11.

22 Phillips, 'Punt and Aksum', p.451.

23 Henze, *Layers of Time*, p.31.

24 Dale H. Moore, 'Christianity in Ethiopia', *Church History*, 5 (September 1936), p.276.

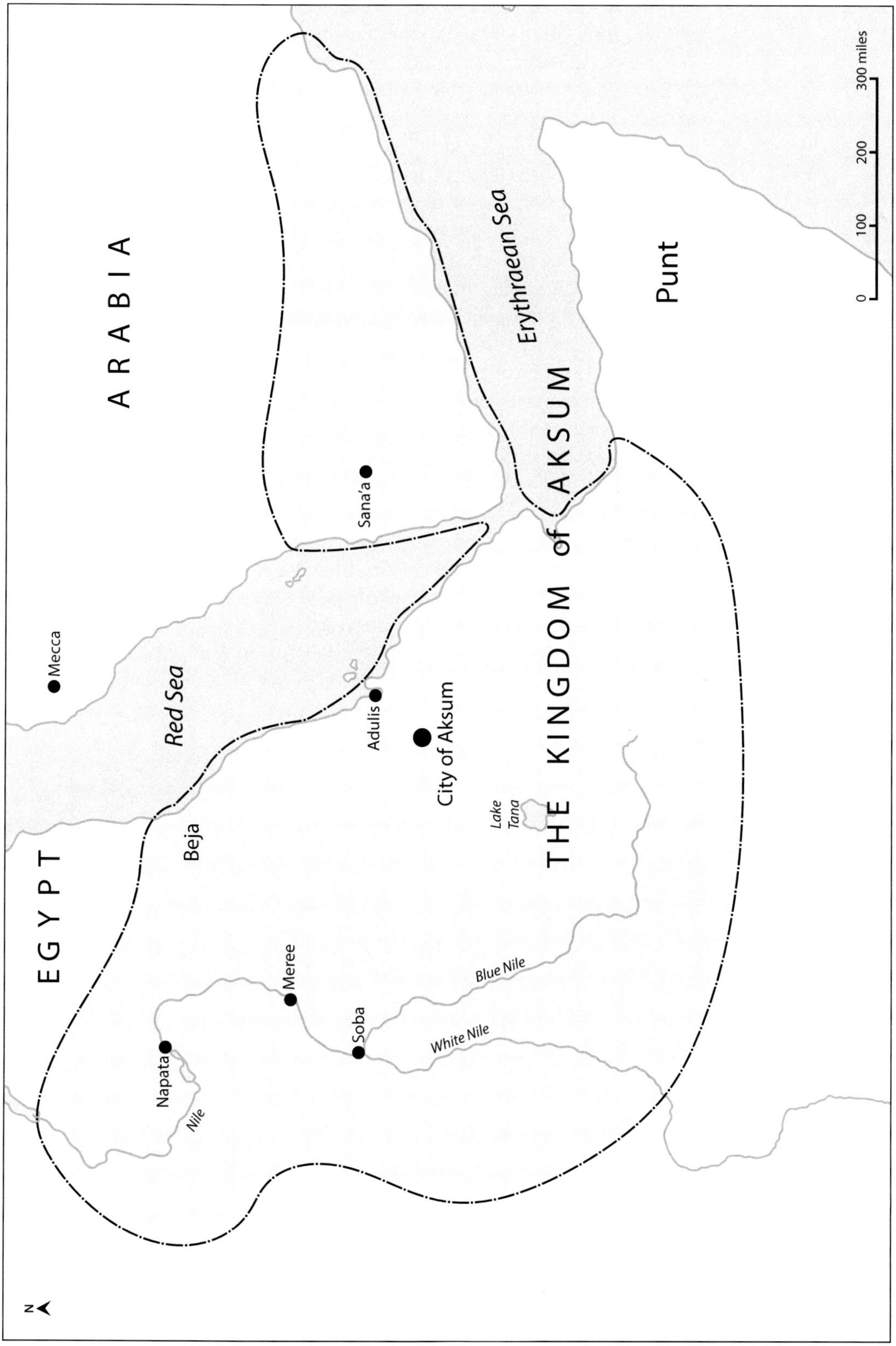

The Ethiopian Kingdom of Aksum in about 500 AD. Aksum encompassed land in Africa and on the Arabian Peninsula by this time. The port city of Adulis lies a few days journey north-east of Aksum on the Red Sea. The land of Punt lies further to the south-east.

well as human. Adhering to Monophysitism would complicate Ethiopia's relations with Rome and with other European powers in the future.

In the sixth century an Ethiopian army, in conjunction with forces from the Byzantine Empire, defeated a Jewish army led by Dhu'Nawas in Arabia. For centuries after that, the Ethiopian Aksumite Kingdom straddled the Red Sea, incorporating territory in both Africa and the Arabian peninsula.[25] Ethiopia went to war against the Jewish kingdom in Arabia to maintain its position of economic superiority in an early example of the interrelationship between religious faith and economic interest. This military expedition to Arabia also represents the first example of the Christian Ethiopians appealing to fellow Christians (in this case, the Byzantines) for help in subduing a foe that threatened Ethiopia's trade and security. Both the Ethiopians and the Byzantines benefitted from this joint military expedition to Arabia. Nearly 1,000 years later, Ethiopia would seek assistance from Christian Portugal when Imam Gurey's army invaded in 1529.

The Kingdom of Aksum dominated the Ethiopian highlands. The nomadic peoples settling in the lowlands to the south-east and south-west suffered through harsher summer seasons, lower rainfall, and more frequent droughts. The competition for arable land and sustainable water supplies would be a recurring theme throughout the centuries as bands of lowland nomads attempted to penetrate the highlands. There was a crucial link between highland and lowland, which would persist through the centuries, and this was salt. The lowlands possessed salt deposits, and the salt was formed into blocks and traded throughout the Horn of Africa, transported by camel, mule and horse over the trade routes throughout the lowlands,

The ruins of Aksum. The once-great empire declined after the Persians gained control of the lucrative Red Sea trade routes. (Photo from the collection of Jones Ofuasia, pictured in the image)

25 Lewis H. Gann and Peter Duignan, *Africa and the World* (New York: University Press of America, 2000), p.154.

into the highlands' cities, and to the Red Sea ports, such as Adulis for trade to India and Egypt. However, when the Zoroastrian Persians conquered southern Arabia in about the year 570, adding maritime control of the Red Sea trade to their already established supremacy in the Indian Ocean, Ethiopia's economic fortunes began to decline.[26] Within 50 years of Persia's conquest of southern Arabia a new religion appeared on the Arabian Peninsula, which would change the course of history.

The Rise of Islam

The prophet Muhammad's pilgrimage from Mecca to Medina in the year 622 marks the beginning of the Islamic calendar. Over the next few years Muhammad's small group of followers spread the new religion throughout Arabia. Some of Muhammad's followers made their way across the Red Sea to Ethiopia as refugees in the aftermath of the violent struggle against Arab clans, which resisted Islam, resulting in several clashes such as the Battle of Badr (624) and the Battle of the Ditch (627). Ethiopia would be the first Christian nation to encounter Islam directly, and the Ethiopian people accepted these Muslim refugees willingly and treated them well.[27] As a result of this kindness, Muhammad directed that Ethiopia be left in peace so long as the Ethiopians never took up arms against Islam.[28] Despite this amicable beginning, the relationship between Islam and Christianity in Ethiopia would be exceptionally violent in later centuries.

Within a few years after the prophet Muhammad's death in 632, Palestine and Egypt were brought under Islamic control. Within 100 years of his death, Islam had spread west across North Africa (the Maghreb) and into Spain and Portugal. To the east, the Persians were converted, and Islam made its way to India. A major force propelling the spread of Islam was trade, and Islam's advance occurred most rapidly along the principal trade routes that had been in place since ancient times, such as the Red Sea routes, which connected East and West. The Ethiopian Kingdom of Aksum faltered and declined as Muslim control over the Red Sea prevented Ethiopian shipping from maintaining the crucial cultural and economic ties with the Mediterranean world and the Indian Ocean that had allowed Ethiopia to flourish. Ethiopian merchant ships had ventured to most of the known world over the preceding centuries, but were no longer able to do so once the Red Sea was no longer under their control. A ninth-century Chinese text stated that the people of Berbera, a port city on the Horn of Africa in modern-day Somalia not very far from the port city of Zeila, "do not eat any cereals but they eat meat".[29] If

26 Phillips, 'Punt and Aksum', p.455.

27 Mukerrem Miftah, 'Key dimensions in Abyssinia-Ottoman relations in the sixteenth and seventeenth centuries: a critical review of literatures', *Journal of Pan African Studies*, Vol. 10, no. 1, (2017), p.268.

28 Abraham Demoz, 'Moslems and Islam in Ethiopic Literature', *Journal of Ethiopian Studies*, 10 (January 1972) p.1.

29 Herbert S. Lewis, 'The Origins of the Galla and Somali', *The Journal of African History*, Vol. 7 (1966), p.30.

the Chinese knew this much about Berbera's inhabitants, they most likely had also traded with the Ethiopian Aksumite Kingdom. These lucrative trade routes were jeopardised once Islam surrounded Ethiopia by the late ninth century. Egypt's conversion to Islam was a further blow to Ethiopia, as their church relied upon the Egyptian Coptic Christian church for the appointment of bishops. Islam's advance cut Ethiopia's communication "to the north and east; the new faith was destined in later centuries also to spread to the south and west, thus rendering Ethiopia's isolation almost complete, a Christian island in a Muslim sea".[30] Once culturally, economically and spiritually connected to the wider Mediterranean world, Ethiopia falls from the historical record as Islam surrounded it, placing it far out of the European field of view for many centuries.

Ethiopia suffered as Islam prospered. The eighteenth-century British historian Edward Gibbon wrote:

> encompassed on all sides by the enemies of their religion [Islam], the [Ethiopians] ... had almost relapsed into the savage life. Their vessels, which had traded to Ceylon, scarcely presumed to navigate the rivers of Africa; the ruins of Aksum were deserted, the nation was scattered in villages, and the emperor, a pompous name, was content, both in peace and war, with the immovable residence of a camp.[31]

Such was Ethiopia's condition for centuries – hemmed in by Islam and cut off from contact with Europe, India, and China. Multiple factors led to Aksum's decline, and Islam's rise should not be considered the only cause of Aksum's plight. The movement of nomadic people into Aksumite territory weakened the power of the *negus*. The pagan religious elements that these people brought with them moulded Ethiopian Christianity into a unique form, different even from the Egyptian Coptic Christianity from which it emerged. These various peoples who migrated into the Ethiopian highlands were inheritors of the Aksumite tradition; they spread the Ge'ez language and their form of Christianity deep into the interior, setting in motion the process of fusion, which produced the modern Ethiopian nation.[32]

The rise of Islam and the decline in trade through the Red Sea, which would soon be dominated by the Persians – who had taken control of Yemen in 570 and converted to Islam in 651 – hastened Aksum's downfall.[33] However, King Ezana's conversion to the Christian faith would have lasting repercussions throughout eastern Africa. Although Christianity had flourished during the sixth century, various upheavals plagued the Ethiopian church from the seventh until the thirteenth century. While Aksum declined politically, its Christian church hierarchy survived the ruin in a manner similar to the

30 Richard Pankhurst, *An Introduction to the Economic History of Ethiopia* (London: Sidgwick & Jackson, 1961), pp.55–56.

31 Edward Gibbon, *The Decline and Fall of the Roman Empire*, vol. 56 (New York: Peter Fenelon Collier, 1899), p.584.

32 J. Spencer Trimingham, *Islam in Ethiopia* (London: Oxford University Press, 1952), p.49.

33 Adejumobi, *The History of Ethiopia*, p.13.

Roman Church's survival after the collapse of the Roman Empire in Western Europe in the fifth century. A resurgent Christianity would galvanise Ethiopian kings in the centuries following Aksum's collapse. The Ethiopian military was structured so that the kings could use military force to bring recalcitrant provinces back under Christian control. The battle to restore Christianity led to a more robust and efficient military machine, and the church and state would work hand in hand over the following centuries to salvage what could be saved from Ethiopian civilisation and carry it forward.

The Struggle to Restore Christian Ethiopia

With Aksum's collapse, the Solomonic succession of Ethiopian kings was temporarily interrupted. In the power vacuum that followed the rise of Islam and the fall of Aksum, a pagan queen named Judith led a revolt which occupied and destroyed Aksum in the tenth century, wiping out nearly all traces of Christianity. Judith was:

> a pagan, a lapsed Christian, a Jew, an Agaw or a Beja, and as a subordinate of the Emperor who rebelled to lead a pagan resurgence against Christianity. She is credited with a lust to destroy by fire and sword churches, monasteries, buildings and everything that symbolized Christian and imperial power and is often called Esato in Amharic, a name derived from the word for fire. She is said to have killed the emperor, ascended the throne herself, and reigned for forty years. Accounts of her violent misdeeds are still related among peasants in the north Ethiopian countryside.[34]

The impact of Judith's reign, paganism in general, and the continued spread of Islam led to a dissolution of the Christian orthodoxy that had prevailed in the Ethiopian Church, further separating it from Egypt's Coptic Church, and even more so from the Roman Catholic Church.[35]

As Christianity struggled to survive in post-Aksumite Ethiopia, Islam thrived in lowland provinces to Ethiopia's south and south-east. The Ethiopian provinces of Shoa and Sidama and the lands surrounding the city of Harar saw many of their inhabitants convert to Islam. The Sultanate of Ifat and the territory around Lake Zway in the Ethiopian lowlands' western reaches also witnessed enthusiastic conversions to Islam. Much as Christianity had co-opted pagan practices in the Roman Empire, Aksum's ancient pagan shrines were transformed into Christian sanctuaries in order to ensure that Ethiopia's unique brand of Christianity could attract new members who might otherwise be tempted to become Muslims. The new faith:

> was a cult deeply steeped in mythology both pagan and Judaic. Its ritual and hagiography, its literature and ecclesiastical organization, show the originality of this native Christian cult against many of whose indigenous practices such

34 Henze, *Layers of Time*, p.48.
35 Moore, 'Christianity in Ethiopia', p.277.

St George tapestry in Aksum. Saint George is the patron saint of Ethiopia. Often pictured in battle or slaying the dragon, George has been Ethiopia's patron since the fourth century. (Photo from the collection of Jones Ofuasia)

> as polygamy, the Church of Alexandria was to struggle in vain throughout the centuries. At the same time the creative reaction of the Abyssinians to Christianity enabled them to assimilate it naturally and cling to it tenaciously, whilst the symbolical status of the Church in the divinely ordained monarchy enabled the State to rise again and again triumphant over the vicissitudes of fortune.[36]

Christianity would be a significant element of the Ethiopian kings' attempt to restore the state's power. In the tenth and eleventh centuries, after recovering from Judith's pagan revival, Ethiopia forged a new path, part of which is exemplified by the magnificent churches hewn from rock in the town of Lalibela. The Ethiopian king Lalibela ordered the construction of churches that were carved from solid rock. He intended to build a new Jerusalem meant to replace the holy city which was captured by Islamic forces in 1187. The Lalibela River was renamed the River Jordan to complete the town's transformation into the new Jerusalem. Construction on these churches began around 1180, and most of the 11 churches were completed within a quarter-century. With the Muslim occupation of Jerusalem, Christians wishing to visit the Holy Land were often turned away. Lalibela offered an alternative to Jerusalem, and pilgrimages to visit the churches have continued from the twelfth century until the present day. Lalibela, along with Aksum, was the holiest site in Ethiopian Christianity.

Much like Christian rulers in Europe, such as Charlemagne, Ethiopian kings spread Christianity by the sword, forcibly converting people who

36 Trimingham, *Islam in Ethiopia*, pp.54–55.

The church of Abba Libanos. This is the only one of the churches to have the roof and the ground level still attached to the main rock structure. Legend holds that it was carved on one night by King Gebre Mesqel Lalibela's wife, Meskel Kebra, who was assisted by angels. (Photo from the collection of Mikael Muehlbauer)

The Church of St George (Amharic: Beta Giyorgis). This church, commissioned by King Gebre Mesqel Lalibela, was carved downward into volcanic rock over the course of a quarter-century. As an infant, Gebre Mesqel was surrounded by a swarm of bees but was not harmed. The name "Lalibela" means "the bees recognise his sovereignty". The church of Beta Giyorgis is considered to be the eighth wonder of the world. (Photo from the collection of Mikael Muehlbauer)

had previously held to animist or other beliefs.[37] However, confrontation with Islam would present a more serious challenge than that posed by Ethiopia's more peripheral people's pastoral religions. With a powerful Islamic presence in Egypt, Ethiopia could only hope to expand to the south, in the direction of the much weaker lowland sultanates. As a result, conflict with the small Muslim kingdoms along Ethiopia's southern border intensified. The ethnic and religious tension in the Horn of Africa between Ethiopia and the peoples of present-day Somalia has continued ever since. However, the beginnings of this contest were more than merely a religious quarrel between the Christian Ethiopians and the Muslims who inhabited the small coastal states. Access to land and sea trade routes fuelled the fighting; land routes to Egypt, the salt trade, and the lucrative sea routes to the Red Sea and thence to the Indian Ocean. Both the land and sea routes were heavily travelled, and Ethiopian control of these routes would lead to renewed economic prosperity. The struggle to regain access to the trade routes and restore Christianity's place in Ethiopia was of paramount concern throughout the twelfth and thirteenth centuries. The Ethiopian military would play a vital role in both pursuits.

37 Adejumobi. *The History of Ethiopia,* p.14.

Marco Polo and Ibn Battuta

The Venetian explorer Marco Polo transited Arabia on his return trip from the Orient to Venice in 1288, when Ethiopian kings were consolidating their power. His journal includes an account of Ethiopia, which included descriptions of its warriors. Although this account is likely second-hand, he wrote that the Ethiopians were "excellent soldiers, and they go on horseback, for they have horses in plenty. Well they may; for they are in daily war with the Soldan of ADEN, and with the Nubians, and a variety of other nations."[38] Marco Polo is almost certainly referring here to the Muslim inhabitants of the lands to Ethiopia's south-east when he wrote "variety of other nations". Polo described Ethiopia's people and landscape, including the animals and game to be found there. He recorded:

> I have still some particulars to tell you of the same province. It abounds greatly in all kinds of victual; and the people live on flesh and rice and milk and sesame. They have plenty of elephants, not that they are bred in the country, but they are brought from the Islands of the other India. They have however many giraffes, which are produced in the country; besides bears, leopards, lions in abundance, and many other passing strange beasts ... for instance, they have ostriches ... and plenty of beautiful parrots, with apes of sundry kinds, and baboons and other monkeys that have countenances all but human. There are numerous cities and villages in this province of Abash [Abyssinia, or Ethiopia] and many merchants, for there is much trade to be done there. The people also manufacture very fine buckrams and other cloths of cotton. There is no more to say on the subject, so now let us go forward and tell you of the province of Aden.[39]

Polo's description of Ethiopia's actual location contributed to the widespread confusion and ignorance among Europeans about much of the world's geography outside of Europe. He wrote, "Abash [Ethiopia] is a very great Province, and you must know that it constitutes the MIDDLE INDIA, and it is on the mainland."[40] The distinction between Africa and India was vague in most Europeans' minds in the thirteenth century. To most Europeans, Ethiopia and India were simply territories in "the Orient". Marco Polo's journey also took him through the port city of "Aden", which would appear at first glance to be in modern-day Yemen. However, Richard Pankhurst believes that Polo was actually somewhere in the African Sultanate of Adal and not the port city on the Arabian Peninsula in Yemen, even though Polo used the name "Aden".[41] It could be that instead of Aden, Polo is referring to Adal, or maybe the port city of Zeila. Marco Polo described this town, sharing his observations that:

---

38 Marco Polo and Rustichello of Pisa, *The Travels of Marco Polo*, Volume 2.

39 Polo, *The Travels of Marco Polo*.

40 Polo, *The Travels of Marco Polo*.

41 Richard Pankhurst, *The Ethiopian Borderlands: Essays in Regional History from Ancient Times to the End of the Eighteenth Century* (Lawrenceville, NJ: The Red Sea Press, 1997), p.19.

> You must know that in the province of ADEN [Adal], there is a Prince who is called the Soldan. The people are all Saracens and adorers of Mahommet, and have a great hatred of Christians. There are many towns and villages in the country. This Aden is the port to which many of the ships of India come with their cargoes, and from this haven the merchants carry the goods a distance of seven days further in small vessels. At the end of those seven days they land the goods and load them on camels, and so carry them a land journey of 30 days. This brings them to the river of ALEXANDRIA, and by it they descend to the latter city. It is by this way through Aden that the Saracens of Alexandria receive all their stores of pepper and other spicery, and there is no other route equally good and convenient by which these goods could reach that place.[42]

By the early 1300s the Muslim states along Ethiopia's southern border had merged into what is known as the Kingdom of Zeila, centred primarily around the small states of Ifat, Dawaro, Bali, and Adal. These small states competed with one another for control of the lucrative regional trade routes, and they rarely cooperated with one another in matters of economics or defence. Competition for hegemony between the Muslim sultanates to the south of the Ethiopian highlands resulted in violent warfare. The endemic conflict in this region was not only between lowland Muslims and highland Christians. The Sultanate of Ifat absorbed the entire Kingdom of Showa at the close of the thirteenth century; the power vacuum left by the fall of Showa led to Christian migration into the area during the time Marco Polo would have been transiting the region, with churches and monasteries built over the following centuries.[43]

In about the year 1330, roughly three decades after Marco Polo travelled through Arabia and possibly through the Horn of Africa region, the Muslim adventurer and chronicler Ibn Battuta travelled to the port city of Zeila, which served as the point of entry for trade coming into the area, and into and out of Ethiopia. He described the town as "the dirtiest, most disagreeable, and most stinking town in the world".[44] Considering that fresh fish and camel meat were staples of the trade upon which the region depended, it is not surprising that the town lacked fresh air. From Zeila, Ibn Battuta travelled along the African coast by ship to the port city of Mogadishu. Although Ethiopian ships still sailed the Red Sea, Muslim ascendancy kept the Christian traders in check. Ethiopia's economy stagnated in the centuries after the Islamic conquest of nearly all the territory surrounding Ethiopia. Ibn Battuta's journey through the Horn of Africa would likely not have included any stops in Ethiopia, which was not as actively engaged in trade and merchant activity as it had been centuries earlier.

---

42 Polo, *The Travels of Marco Polo*.

43 Deresse Ayenachew, 'A historical overview of the Wärǧəḥ Muslim community in the Christian highland of Šäwa', Afriques <http://afriques.revues.org/1944> accessed 22 Oct 2020.

44 Ross E. Dunn. *The Adventures of Ibn Battuta: A Muslim Traveler of the Fourteenth Century* (Berkeley, CA: University of California Press, 1986), p.122.

Chapter 2

Christian Ethiopia Restored

Ibn Battuta's visit to the Horn of Africa coincided with a return to stability within Ethiopia. Christianity returned to its former ascendancy, literature flourished, and the Amharic language proliferated throughout Ethiopia, taking its place alongside Ge'ez. Amharic would be the vernacular language of Ethiopia, with Ge'ez continuing in use among the learned classes and the church hierarchy. To keep the people's energy focused on the continuing restoration of the Ethiopian kingdom, the kings led continuous military campaigns against Islamic states such as the Sultanate of Ifat, one of the member states of the Kingdom of Zeila, to the south-east of Ethiopia. The Sultan of Ifat launched what historians consider to be the first major *jihad* against Ethiopia, successfully defeating Ethiopian forces in a series of battles.[1] The Ethiopian king Amda Seyon (r. 1314–1344) resisted the *jihad*, engaging in a conflict that featured savage fighting marked by religious overtones between Muslims and Christians. He faced the dual threat of *jihad* and paganism, as Christianity in Ethiopia during this time still existed side by side with a plethora of animistic and outright pagan beliefs that had continued to thrive in Ethiopia since the time of Queen Judith's rebellion. Ethiopian Christian churches were attacked and destroyed, and monks faced persecution and even death at the hands of other Ethiopians who still adhered to ancient beliefs. Amda Seyon consolidated Christian control in many parts of the kingdom. Together with the Ethiopian church's leading bishop (the *Abuna)*, it linked the provinces' military control with the requirement to protect the churches and clerics.[2] This institutional reform was a significant step in the effort to restore the church's power.

Amda Seyon's 30-year reign began in 1314. *The Glorious Victories of Amda Seyon* chronicles his war against the Islamic forces, which had merged into the Kingdom of Zeila and had consolidated political control of most of the lowland territory adjoining the Red Sea. Written almost certainly by a church hierarchy member, as these Ethiopians were the most literate, the *Glorious*

1 I.M. Lewis, 'The Somali Conquest of the Horn of Africa', *The Journal of African History*, 1 (1960), p.222.

2 Taddesse Tamrat, 'A Short Note on the Traditions of Pagan Resistance to the Ethiopian Church (14th and 15th Centuries)', *Journal of Ethiopian Studies*, 10 (January 1972), p.140.

Victories is a classic of Ethiopian literature. Amda Seyon's military campaign began in 1329. Marching against the forces of Ifat, he faced a Muslim force of approximately 20,000 infantry and 15,000 cavalry.[3] The Ethiopian mindset was one of impending victory as the *Chronicle* recounts:

> As for us, we have heard and we know from the Holy Scriptures that the kingdom of the Moslems, established for but seven hundred years, shall cease to be at the proper time. But the kingdom of the Christians shall continue till the second coming of the Son of God, according to the words of the Holy Scripture; and above all (we know) that the kingdom of Ethiopia shall endure till the coming of Christ, of which David prophesied saying "Ethiopia shall stretch her hands unto God."[4]

Amda Seyon's forces joined in battle against the Muslim army under the leadership of Sabradin in February 1329 and defeated them "through the power of God".[5] Throughout the spring and summer of 1329 and for the next three years, Amda Seyon faced a succession of Muslim armies, defeating each one in turn. His reign ended with the Ethiopian highlands mostly back under Christian rule. The nomadic pastoralists of the lowland periphery were firmly kept in their place, and their ability to launch further attacks against Ethiopia was substantially reduced. These pastoralists were by now almost exclusively Muslims. Christian Ethiopia gained undisputed supremacy under Amda Seyon's leadership, and he is considered by many scholars and historians to have been nothing less than a military genius. The powerful striking force that he created revolutionised warfare in the Horn of Africa, introducing a level of efficiency and ferocity that changed the relationship between highland Christian and lowland Muslims. Ethiopia was a centralised state, able to move its forces over interior lines and flexible enough to move against any one of the smaller lowland sultanates individually before reforming in the highlands and replenishing supplies and forces before striking again. The Muslim states, on the other hand, were not centralised but dispersed. These states "were not well organised; mobilisation was difficult, they had little power of resistance, and were liable to sudden collapse".[6] Without a leader able to transcend these challenges, the lowland sultanates had to endure the regular Ethiopian incursions.

Ethiopian Military Organisation

Warriors were the central figures in the Ethiopian Christian kingdom, which was for all practical purposes a warrior society. Two ethnic groups, the Amhara and the Tigray, formed the majority of Ethiopia's population, two groups that embodied a warrior ethos. Military values of loyalty, courage,

3 G.W.B. Huntingford, trans., *The Glorious Victories of Amda Seyon, King of Ethiopia* (Oxford: Clarendon, 1965), p.20.
4 Huntingford, *Glorious Victories*, p.59.
5 Huntingford, *Glorious Victories*, p.59.
6 Trimingham, *Islam in Ethiopia*, p.68.

and honour carried over into Ethiopian religion, art, literature, and the economy.[7] As Ethiopia's centre of power moved further to the south, away from Islamic Egypt, new ways of maintaining control of the state were required. In 1270 the king Yekunno Amlak had "established himself near Ankobär, on the eastern escarpment of Showa, to defend the highlands from incursions by the Muslim lowland pastoralists".[8] From that time forward, the Ethiopian capital was not located in a city or in a fixed location. Instead, it was located in a moving court, composed of royal officials, merchants, artisans, and regiments of soldiers charged with protecting the king and the royal household. The *Çäwa* (pronounced kawa, meaning "earth") military regiments protected this moving court, known as the *katama*.[9] Soldiers were not the only members of this travelling court. Camp followers of many different kinds also accompanied the army and the king. The *katama* was much like a moving city, described by Portuguese observers in the fifteenth century as follows:

> the aforesaid number of Troops … makes an extraordinary great Camp, by reason the other People that follow Multitudes the Army are far more numerous than the Soldiers, and each following the Baggage very much; and this is because they commonly go to War with their whole Families, Wives and Children, and the Queen herself goes; and there is need of many Women to make their … daily Food … also their Wine; and all these Hangers on, with the Merchants and other Followers, amount to so great a number, that where there are 100,00 Soldiers, there never are less than 30,000 Souls, and if the Emperor be there 100 or 200,000.[10]

In the centre of the *katama* was the large, round tent of the chief. Surrounding this tent, representing the centrality of Christianity to the state, were the tents for the holy ark. Commanding officers of the infantry forces were in another outer ring, which were encircled by the tents of the cavalry. Common soldiers, labourers, wives, and families formed the furthest ring of the camp.[11] By the sixteenth century, "when documents on historic Ethiopia became relatively accurate and plentiful, no signs of a permanent capital existed".[12] This moving capital and the accompanying military organisation, trained *Çäwa* regiments supplemented by peasant levies, surrounded by multitudes of followers, merchants, and families, would last for the next few centuries.

Ethiopian warriors, whether members of the *Çäwa* regiments or not, aspired to the ideals of *gwäbäznet*, or masculine aggressiveness and hardiness. Ethiopian soldiers have been noted for their endurance, stemming from

7 Thomas P. Ofcansky (ed.), *Ethiopia: A Country Study* (Washington DC: Library of Congress, 1993), p.270.

8 Merid W. Aregay, 'Military Elites in Medieval Ethiopia', *Journal of Ethiopian Studies*, Vol. 30 (June 1997), p.41.

9 Deresse Ayenachew, 'Evolution and Organisation of the Çäwa Military Regiments in Medieval Ethiopia', *Annales d'Éthiopie*, 29 (2014), p.84.

10 Fr. Balthazar Tellez, S.J., *The Travels of the Jesuits in Ethiopia* (London: Knapton, 1710), p.57.

11 Donald N. Levine, *Wax and Gold* (Chicago: University of Chicago Press, 1972), p.75.

12 Ronald J. Horvath, 'The Wandering Capitals of Ethiopia', *The Journal of African History*, Vol. 10, No. 2 (1969), p.213.

their mountain homes, many of which are perched on elevations over a mile high. They "climb mountains with ease, march rapidly for distances under heavy pack with light rations, and sleep on a rock".[13] Ethiopians thus made fine soldiers and were also versed in horsemanship. Those who observed these soldiers in camp or in training or on the battlefield noted that "they are strong, endure hunger and thirst beyond belief, and with little influence can brook any sort of weather".[14] Imperial duties and responsibilities were founded upon these warrior traditions and characteristics, from Aksumite times to the present day. Ethiopian kings kept the country united, whether opposing upstart religious zealots like Judith or facing the Muslim armies surrounding the kingdom. Great emperors were the ones who repulsed invasions, conquered new land, and subjugated pagans, forcing them to accept Ethiopian Christianity.

Amda Seyon established an army with two basic elements. The first and most powerful element was a strike force closely attached to the royal court. This force was the king's central army and could be called to battle at short notice. Second, in times of national or local crisis, the king could summon the local militias from the provinces, such as Tigray, Amhara, Gojjam, and Gondar, and all the other provinces of the Christian kingdom. Local chiefs oversaw these militias, and it was these chiefs that led their forces from the front and commanded their troops' unwavering loyalty. When committed to punitive expeditions or conquering new territory, the king often transferred overall control to these sub-commanders. However, when the king was present with the army, he had total control, and victory or defeat rested solely on his leadership and ability. Another element of the Ethiopian army consisted of troops recruited from frontier areas newly conquered by the king. However, many of these troops were prisoners of war forced into service to Christian Ethiopia.[15]

As far back as Aksumite times, the army and the nation's social organisations were pyramid-shaped structures with the emperor at the pyramid's apex as the supreme military leader. The Ethiopian army was led by warlords who came from within the pyramid-like structure of Ethiopian society. At each level of command, the military drew troops from three sources. Each warlord:

> from the emperor to a minor noble, had a standing corps of armed retainers that varied in size according to the leader's importance. Many landholders also served several months each year in the local lord's retinue in lieu of paying taxes. Most troops, however, came from the mass of able-bodied adult freemen, clergy alone excepted, who could be summoned by proclamation.[16]

13 Donald Levine, 'The Masculinity Ethic and the Spirit of Warriorhood in Ethiopian and Japanese Cultures', *International Journal of Ethiopian Studies*, Vol. 2 (Summer/Fall 2005–2006), p.164.

14 Job Ludolphus, *A New History of Ethiopia*, Translated by J.P. Gent (London: 1684), p.217.

15 Taddesse Tamrat, *Church and State in Ethiopia: 1270–1527.* A Thesis submitted for the degree of Ph.D. in the University of London (February 1968), p.173.

16 Ofcansky, *Ethiopia: A Country Study*, p.271.

Amda Seyon created a large and well-organised army designed to rule the empire and expand its borders. The king maintained undisputed overall control of the military, deciding when to employ forces against neighbouring provinces or to quell Muslim or pagan uprisings. Although the army maintained a pyramid structure, there was no direct line of authority from the king down to the lowest common soldier. Instead, it was a group of mutually independent contingents commanded by numerous officers of equal rank, each responsible to the king himself. This arrangement "made the king the sole master of his forces and the emergence of a warrior leader with sufficient influence in the army to challenge the king's position was quite impossible".[17] The military force created by Amda Seyon allowed the king to either reimpose his will on a recalcitrant Christian province or engage in subjugating and incorporating Muslim or pagan regions into the larger Ethiopian Christian kingdom. However, one shortcoming in the Ethiopian military's composition was in its diverse ethnic groups and religion. Yekunno Amlak's army, which campaigned against Ethiopia's Muslim neighbours, was itself composed of many Muslims from the subjugated sultanates such as Ifat.[18] Even Tigrayan and Amharan soldiers often did not work together effectively. This diversity would threaten the Ethiopian army's ability to operate against a motivated and determined adversary.

From the earliest days of Aksum through to the sixteenth century, an Ethiopian soldier was armed with spears, bows and arrows, and daggers. Cavalry, as well as infantry, carried shields and spears. Two spears were the usual battlefield array for Ethiopian infantry; one short spear that resembled a javelin was thrown from a distance. A longer spear would be used for the inevitable hand-to-hand fighting, which was the way battles at the time were decided.[19]

The Ethiopian system was efficient, and victory on the battlefield demonstrated that the military organisation met the kingdom's needs. Throughout the centuries, this organisation remained unchanged following Amda Seyon's reign up to Imam Gurey's invasion in 1529. The Ethiopian military took the field in much the same fashion against the Italians in the nineteenth and twentieth centuries.

By the fourteenth century, Mohammed's seventh-century plea to the Muslims in the Horn of Africa to treat the Ethiopians well was long since forgotten, and internecine conflict would take on a ruthless, pitiless character. In addition to increasing the size of the Ethiopian army, Amda Seyon introduced new techniques in its organisation and training, which were superior to anything that the Muslim armies of the small, lowland states could achieve.[20] Over the next 200 years nomadic incursions into

17 Tamrat, *Church and State in Ethiopia*, p.179.

18 Richard Pankhurst and Andreu Martínez d'Alòs-Moner, 'Military Units and Organization', in Merid Aregay *et al.* (eds.), *Encyclopedia Aethiopica*, Vol. 5 (Wiesbaden: Harrassowitz Verlag, 2003), p.431.

19 Merid Aregay, 'A Reappraisal of the Impact of Firearms in the History of Warfare in Ethipia (c. 1500–1800)', *Journal of Ethiopian Studies*, 14 (JANUARY 1980), p.98.

20 Mohammed Hassen, 'Reviewed Work(s): Ethiopia and the Red Sea: The Rise and Decline of the Solomonic Dynasty and Muslim-European Rivalry in the Region by M. Abir', *Northeast*

the highlands prompted punitive reprisals from Ethiopia, in a cycle that would continue into the sixteenth century. However, despite the outward perception that Ethiopia was now unified under the banner of Christianity, by the end of Amda Seyon's reign Islam had been firmly established in the Ethiopian highlands.[21] While Muslims and Christians lived as neighbours in the highlands, the reprisals launched by Ethiopia's kings against the lowlands effectively kept the Muslim states under control. The reprisals also increased the discord and distrust between Ethiopian Christians and Muslims and planted in the lowlanders' hearts and minds a yearning for revenge against the highland kingdom.

In 1415, Ethiopian king Yeshaq I defeated Muslim forces under Sultan Sa'd ad-Din. The growing Sultanate of Adal absorbed parts of the conquered Sultanate of Ifat, while Ethiopia occupied the remainder of Ifat. Thus, the Sultanate of Adal became the focal point for Muslim power among the lowland states south and east of the Ethiopian border.[22] The year 1415 also saw the first Portuguese conquest in Africa when over 40,000 Portuguese soldiers landed on the Moroccan coast and captured Ceuta. A momentous year, 1415, marked the Ethiopian victory over the Muslim Sultanate of Ifat and the beginning of Portuguese involvement in Africa.

King Zara Yaqob (r. 1434–1468) employed the Ethiopian military in much the same manner as Amda Seyon and Yeshaq I. His primary objectives resembled those of all Ethiopian kings from the time of Aksum – ensuring stability within the highland kingdom and securing the trade routes leading to Massawa and Zeila, port cities that had eclipsed Adulis in importance to the Ethiopian economy.[23] As the Sultanate of Adal continued to cause trouble along the south-eastern border, Zara Yaqob led punitive expeditions into the lowlands. Ethiopian chronicles describe Sultan Badlay of Adal (r. 1432–1445) as the "accursed and rebellious son of Satan, enemy of righteousness who opposes the religion of Christ, far removed from God, separated from the glory of the Son, and deprived of the gift of the Holy Ghost ... This rebel son of the viper, seed of the snake, son of a barbarian, from the origins of Satan."[24] The struggle culminated at the Battle of Egubba (1445), where, according to the chronicles, Zara Yaqob personally killed Sultan Badlay "and dispatched pieces of his body throughout his domain to admonish potential dissenters".[25] But more than just "potential dissenters" noticed the overwhelming Ethiopian victory. The Mamluk Sultan of Egypt acted in defence of his Islamic brethren to the south of Ethiopia, ordering the Christian patriarch of Alexandria to be tortured in retaliation for Badlay's execution and dismemberment.[26] Zara

African Studies, Vol. 6, No. 3 (1984), pp.62–63.

21 Ahmed, 'Historiography of Islam in Ethiopia', p.16.

22 Ulrich Braukämper, 'Islamic Principalities in Southeast Ethiopia Between the Thirteenth and Sixteenth Centuries (Part 1)', *Ethiopianist Notes*, Vol. 1, No. 1 (Spring 1977), pp.29–30.

23 Matteo Salvadore, *The African Prester John and the Birth of Ethiopian-European Relations, 1402–1555* (London: Routledge, 2016), p.44.

24 Demoz, 'Moslems and Islam', p.8.

25 Salvadore, *The African Prester John*, p.44.

26 Thomas P. Ofcansky and David H. Shinn, *Historical Dictionary of Ethiopia* (Lanham, MD: Scarecrow Press, 2004), p.412.

Yaqob still faced Islamic threats to both the north (the Mamluk Egyptians) and south (the Sultanate of Adal). The savagery between the Christian highlands and their lowland Islamic neighbours showed no signs of abating and would only increase in intensity as Adal continued to challenge Ethiopian hegemony in the Horn of Africa. Having restored stability to the kingdom, Zara Yaqob constructed his residence at Debra Berhan, "and during his stay in that locality, he toiled at strengthening the institutions of the kingdom", which included constructing a royal residence "surrounded by a strong wall, such as had never been built by any of his predecessors".[27] Ethiopian Christians also believe that during this time, Zara Yaqob obtained a piece of the True Cross of Christ and placed it in a church built atop Amba Gesen, about 100 miles north of Debra Berhan.

In 1456, three years after the great city of Constantinople fell to Ottoman forces, Pope Callixtus III sent a letter to King Zara Yaqob, whom the Pope thought to be the legendary Prester John, seeking to ally against Islam. Since the middle of the twelfth century, nearly 100 years before Marco Polo's travels, European Christians held firmly to the legend of a priest-king named Prester John, who reigned over a realm of fabulous wealth and power somewhere in the Orient. Letters from this king had apparently been received by the Byzantine emperor, describing "lands with extraordinary features – such as crystal-clear rivers of emeralds flowing from Paradise, massive amounts of gold, monstrous animals, enchanted castles, the fountain of youth and, later, by one interpolation of the letter, proximity to the Ten Lost Tribes of Israel and, at the edge of his kingdom, the Garden of Paradise."[28] As tempting as the description of his kingdom's wealth and glory might have been, finding Prester John and joining an alliance with him offered the chance for Christianity to achieve ultimate victory over Islam.

Liberating Jerusalem from Mamluk Egyptian control was at the forefront of Pope Callixtus III's demand, but keeping pressure on the Ottomans to forestall any further advances into the Balkans was another reason to ally with Ethiopia.[29] However, as Ethiopia returned to stability and prosperity, Ethiopian kings had little desire to go to war with Mamluk Egypt. Still subordinate to the Egyptian Coptic Christian Church, which continued to thrive under the Mamluks (along with a Jewish community in Egypt), Zara Yaqob and his immediate successors sought reproach and accommodation with Egypt. Joining with European Christian states in a crusade against Islam, even with the lofty goal of liberating the holy city of Jerusalem, was not in Zara Yaqob's interest. He was content with a secure northern border, which would allow him to concentrate on pacifying the troublesome small sultanates and principalities on the southern border, states such as Adal. Besides, the city of Lalibela had served as a substitute for pilgrims who were

---

27 Richard Pankhurst, *The Chronicle of the Emperor Zara Yaqob (1434–1468)*, online, see bibliography for URL.

28 Andrew Kurt, 'The search for Prester John, a projected crusade and the eroding prestige of Ethiopian kings, c.1200–c.1540', *Journal of Medieval History* (2013), p.2.

29 Verena Krebs, 'Crusading Threats? Ethiopian-Egyptian Relations in the 1440s', in *Croisades en Afrique Les expeditions occidentales a destination du continent africain, XIlle–XVIe siecles*, Benjamin Weber (ed.), (Toulouse: Presses Universitaires du Midi Meridiennes, 2019), p.245.

The fabled empire of Prester John. By the sixteenth century, Europeans had come to believe that this Christian king reigned in the Orient. His wealth and his armies offered the potential to tilt the balance of power against the rising tide of Islam. (Public Domain)

unable to visit the Holy City of Jerusalem, so the desire to free Jerusalem was not as intense to Ethiopian kings as it was to the kings of Christian Europe.

Both Ethiopians and Muslims believed God was on their side throughout the conflicts that plagued the Horn of Africa in the fourteenth and fifteenth centuries. Religion and commerce drove the competition between Ethiopia and the Muslim states along her southern and eastern borders. Christianity and Islam competed in a zero-sum game for control over trade routes and commodities. The ideological crux of the struggle between the Muslims and the Christians could be summed up in brief:

> Each wanted to win this lucrative area in the name of their God, for their followers. Each condemned the other as "infidels", and each invoked the help of God for its just cause. The need to maintain commercial links in time established a modus vivendi of ideological co-existence, which did not preclude stepping into the activities of winning supporters from the camp of the other, which in turn was the cause for the drawing of swords in the name of God, spreading the word of God and destroying the force of evil. "… If you have killed ten Christians, then I will kill among your side a thousand Muslims, and if you kill a thousand, then I will kill many thousands."[30]

This mindset was part of the repetitive cycle of conflict and violence which characterised Muslim–Christian relations in the Horn of Africa.

30 Mohammed Hassen, '*The Oromo of Ethiopia, 1500–1850: With Special Emphasis on the Gibe Region*', PhD Diss., University of London, School of Oriental and African Studies (1983), p.12.

Ethiopian kings restored Christianity to its position of dominance by the close of the fifteenth century. With stability at home and external enemies subdued, Zara Yaqob's widow, Queen Eleni, followed a conciliatory policy regarding the Muslim states along Ethiopia's borders in the 1490s, such as Adal. Queen Eleni was born a Muslim, which contributed to her ability to bring some calm to the relationship between highland Christian Ethiopia and the lowland Muslim states. Queen Eleni was well-versed in Christian theology, and she was the author of two religious works, "one on the Laws of God, and the other on the Holy Trinity and the Purity of St Mary".[31] She also sponsored the translation of Greek and Arabic religious texts into Ge'ez. In daily life she was kind and pious, keeping the fasts prescribed for monks and nuns. Following Amda Seyon's and Zara Yaqob's decades of punitive raids against states such as Ifat and Adal, a period of peace ensued. For the time being, Ethiopia was not moving aggressively towards Adal, and vice versa. This state of affairs would soon change.

The First Portuguese Mission to Ethiopia

In 1487, King John II of Portugal (r. 1481–1495) sent an emissary, Pero da Covilhão, on an exploratory voyage to India. His goal was to reconnoitre the east, and if possible to find the fabled kingdom of Prester John. Portuguese explorer Henry the Navigator (1394–1460) envisioned an alliance with Ethiopia to secure Portuguese access to the Asian spice trade and open doors to the messianic vision of defeating Islam and destroying the holy cities of Mecca and Medina.[32] Disguised as a Muslim merchant, Pero da Covilhão travelled overland from Portugal to Cairo (the sea route from Portugal to India had not yet been discovered), then across the Arabian Peninsula to Aden. Like other Christian merchants, priests, and travellers, he was no longer able to use the overland road through Constantinople since it had been captured by the Ottoman Sultan Mehmet II's army in 1453. From Aden on the southern end of the Arabian Peninsula, he travelled by sea to India but was unable to find Prester John's kingdom. He then left India for Ethiopia in the early 1490s, arriving by ship on the African coast at Zeila and travelling inland to search again for Prester John's court. European Christians had long stigmatised black Africans, but Renaissance conceptions of race were flexible, and "perceptions of race were expanding and ambivalent".[33] Prester John's location in Africa did not present any issues that conceptions of race would complicate. Although slaves were brought from Africa into Europe in large numbers, these were mostly from the west coast and were often sold to Europeans by other Africans. Ethiopians were not involved in the slave trade with Europe, although slavery had been practiced in Ethiopia and the Horn of Africa continuously from the time of Aksum. By the fourteenth

31 Rita Pankhurst, 'Tayitu foremothers: Queen Eleni, Queen Sabla Wengel and Bati Del Wanbara', *Proceedings of the 16th International Conference of Ethiopian Studies*, 1 (2009), p.53.

32 Kurt, 'The Search for Prester John', p.10.

33 Kurt, 'The Search for Prester John', p.8.

century, Ethiopia was a hub for the slave trade, managing the movement of slaves from the Red Sea to the Indian Ocean and into the Ottoman Empire.[34] Although slavery was a key economic component of many of the nations on the African coast, this fact did not dissuade Christians from believing that Prester John's kingdom was still likely in this part of the world.

As communication between Europeans and Ethiopians increased, in places like Rome and Jerusalem, "fertile soil was available for the sowing of the Prester John myth in Africa".[35] Prester John offered Christians hope, and by the sixteenth century many had begun to believe that he was somewhere in or near India or possibly in Africa. As recounted earlier, the distinction between India and Africa in the mind of the average European was vague. Most Christians believed that Prester John was somewhere in the Orient, but exactly where that might have been could not be ascertained with any precision. Pero da Covilhão truly thought that he had found Prester John in Ethiopia. Arriving at the royal court, da Covilhão was welcomed and became an influential advisor to the Ethiopian king Eskender, who ruled Ethiopia from 1478-1494. Queen Eleni was also present in the court as a trusted adviser to King Eskender.

Pero da Covilhão had difficulty convincing both King Eskender and Eleni that an alliance with faraway Portugal would offer many benefits to Ethiopia, regardless of how Portugal might benefit from the arrangement. Times would change, however, and as tensions rose along Ethiopia's southern border in the early 1500s, the Ethiopian court reassessed its foreign policy. An alliance with Portugal might offer mutual benefits after all. As Portuguese explorers made their way up the east coast of Africa in the early sixteenth century, the Ethiopian court also watched as the Ottomans simultaneously extended their control south from Anatolia into Arabia and the Red Sea. It was apparent to Eleni that an alliance with Portugal would suit Ethiopia, as "the entire region would soon find itself embroiled in an epochal conflict aptly referred to as history's first world war".[36] Eleni's foresight to seek an alliance with Portugal is one of the most critical and consequential political decisions in Ethiopian history.[37] One can compare her foresight to that of George Washington, who knew that the American colonies needed to align themselves with France in order to be able to challenge Britain on the seas. Ethiopia had no navy and no way to defend its own borders from maritime incursion. Forging an alliance with the Portuguese would offer Ethiopia the opportunity to accomplish political and military objectives that they would not be able to do on their own.

---

34 See Abdussamad H. Ahmad, 'Ethiopian Slave Exports at Matamma, Massawa and Tajura, c. 1830–1885', in *The Economics of the Indian Ocean Slave Trade in the Nineteenth Century*, ed. William Gervase Clarence-Smith (New York: Routledge, 2013), pp.93–102. Cited in Giulia Bonaci, 'Revisiting Slavery and the Slave Trade in Ethiopia', *Northeast African Studies* Vol. 17, No. 2 (2017), p.9.

35 Kurt, 'The Search for Prester John', p.8.

36 Salvadore, *The African Prester John*, p.108.

37 R.B. Serjeant, *The Portuguese off the South Arabian Coast* (Beirut: Libraire du Liban, 1974), p.9.

Pero da Covilhão finally convinced Eleni to contact King John II, requesting Portuguese assistance in keeping the Sultanate of Adal and other small Muslim states from encroaching on Ethiopian territory and hampering trade out of Ethiopia. Acting as regent after Eskender's death, Eleni continued to pursue an appeasement policy, not acting aggressively towards the Muslim states as had Ethiopian leaders in past decades, such as Amda Seyon. However, Pero da Covilhão had convinced her that an alliance with Portugal would be in Ethiopia's best interest, and she finally sent an emissary to Lisbon. Not only did Ethiopia stand to benefit from an alliance with Portugal, but Portugal stood to gain a foothold in the Red Sea, a base from which they could harass Ottoman shipping. When Portuguese king Manuel I (r. 1495-1521) received a letter from Queen Eleni of Ethiopia in 1509, Prester John's existence in Africa seemed to have been affirmed.[38] Queen Eleni's letter of 1509 was the first correspondence received in Lisbon from Ethiopia. Surrounded by a resurgent Islam, Christian Ethiopia faced increasing peril. An alliance with the powerful Portuguese might be just what was needed to keep further Islamic incursions into the Christian highlands in check.

Although the Portuguese king received Queen Eleni's letter in 1509, the mission that she requested would not arrive in Ethiopia until April of 1520. There was still a great deal of confusion among average Europeans, and even among many in the ruling classes, as to where places such as "Ethiopia" and "India" actually were. The Italian journeyer Ludovico de Varthema contributed to this confusion when he recorded his travels from Rome to Egypt, Arabia, and India between 1502 and 1509. He visited "Ethiopia" on his return journey back to Europe. He considered all the Portuguese possessions in Africa to be part of Ethiopia, including Mozambique, Malindi, and Mombasa. Varthema wrote that "from what I have seen of India and Ethiopia, it appears to me that the king of Portugal, if it pleases God, and he has been victorious as he has been hitherto, I think that he will be the richest king in the world".[39] De Varthema does not appear to have visited Ethiopia proper. Still, his suggestion that Africa's entire south-east coast was "Ethiopia" indicates that in the early sixteenth-century European mind, Ethiopia encompassed much of the known African continent and even the Indian subcontinent.

The Portuguese mission that finally arrived in Ethiopia in 1520 included Father Francisco Alvarez and Dom Rodrigo da Lima. Father Alvarez's record of the Portuguese mission to Ethiopia, published in 1540, was the first accurate account of Ethiopia available to the few Europeans literate enough to read it. The mission visited the rock-hewn churches at Lalibela and met with the *bahrnagash*, the ruler of the northern Ethiopian

38 Jesse Sargent, 'Following in Jesuit Footsteps: British Expeditions to Ethiopia in the Early Victorian Era', pp.31–58. In *Encounters between Jesuits and Protestants in Africa*, eds. Robert Aleksander Maryks and Festo Mkenda S.J. (Leiden: Brill, 2018), p.36.

39 Ludovico de Varthema, *The Travels of Ludovico Di Varthema in Egypt, Syria, Arabia Deserta and Arabia Felix, in Persia, India, and Ethiopia, 1503 to 1508*. Translated by John Winter Jones (London: Hakluyt Society, 1863), p.296.

Qalhat was a great trading post on the Arabian Sea visited by fabled travellers Marco Polo, Ibn Battuta, and Chinese explorer Zheng He in the thirteenth, fourteenth, and fifteenth centuries, respectively. Ludovico de Varthema almost certainly visited the city in the early sixteenth century. The vibrant city went into decline, probably due to an earthquake as the city sits on the Qalhat fault. By the sixteenth century the centre of trade moved to Muscat, although Alfonso de Albuquerque captured the remains of Qalhat for Portugal in 1507. Qalhat was the second city of the Kingdom of Hormuz ruled by Bibi Maryam during the early fourteenth century. She built a mosque visited by Ibn Battuta, who commented on its beauty. Little is left of Qalhat, with its now silted harbour, except the ruins of Maryam's tomb, which once had a dome. The ruined tomb has become a part of the coast of Oman visually, with its stark beauty of buff-grey stone hills set off by contrasting blues of sea and sky. (Photo and caption by Grant Rhode)

provinces that today compose the nation of Eritrea. The *bahrnagash* was an important political figure; he was effectively the leader of the Ethiopian maritime forces made up primarily of trading vessels, but he also commanded some troops who could be employed as part of the Ethiopian military in times of crisis.

Queen Eleni's son, Lebne Dengel, had ascended the Ethiopian throne in 1507, shortly after Eleni had requested Portugal's assistance. The young king did not believe that an alliance with Portugal served Ethiopia's interests. His pride did not lend itself to entering an alliance with the Portuguese, a faraway people who practiced a much different form of Christianity to the Ethiopian Monophysite variety. To the members of the Portuguese delegation, Lebne Dengel was Prester John, and his Christian kingdom was the long-sought-after ally in the struggle against Islamic expansionism. It appeared that Prester John was less interested in the Portuguese than the Portuguese were in him. Unable to agree to an alliance with Lebne Dengel (Prester John), the Portuguese expedition left Ethiopia and returned home in 1526.

The Portuguese Empire

Like Ethiopia, Portugal has a rich history within which Christianity and Islam have had a lasting influence. Islam spread into Iberia in 711 AD, essentially adding large parts of Spain and most of Portugal to the Umayyad Caliphate. For nearly five centuries *Al-Andalus,* the Arabic name for Portugal and Spain, was Islam's westernmost territory. In 1249, in the Algarve city of Silves known as the "Baghdad of the West", Christian forces defeated the last Muslim stronghold in Portugal, and the few remaining Muslims who were captured were killed. The Portuguese had driven Islam from their soil. A bitter hostility would mark all future encounters between Portuguese troops and Muslim soldiers - the "bitter hereditary enemies of the Cross" - whenever and wherever they would meet.[40] In 1385 the House of Aviz was established as the ruling dynasty of independent Christian Portugal, a small nation hemmed in by the mountains and the sea, with a zeal for spreading the Christian faith.

The Portuguese under the House of Aviz had much in common with the Ethiopians, who had restored Christianity to their nation and had developed a military machine designed to crush the Islamic armies along Ethiopia's borders, which occasionally challenged Ethiopian Christian hegemony.

Even a partial history of the European age of exploration is outside of the scope of this book. However, Portugal's voyages of discovery and search for the kingdom of Prester John are essential elements in the Ethiopian–Adal War's outcome. The Portuguese general, admiral, explorer, and statesman Alfonso de Albuquerque (1453-1515) envisioned a global strategy that

Ruins of a tenth-century Muslim fishing village, Algarve coast, Portugal. Five centuries of Islam left an indelible mark on Portuguese culture, cuisine, and art. The Arabic word *inshallah*, or "God willing", found its way into the Portuguese language as *oxala*, or "I hope". (Photo by Robin Shaw)

40 John Laband, *Bringers of War: The Portuguese in Africa during the Age of Gunpowder and Sail from the Fifteenth to the Eighteenth Century* (London: Frontline, 2013), p.5.

would allow Portugal to control the spice trade and vanquish global Islam. Portuguese expansion into the Indian Ocean had been well underway since Vasco da Gama rounded the Cape of Good Hope. Gama departed Portugal on 8 July 1497, a day "chosen by astrologers as auspicious", replete with "parades, pageantry, and intense religious fanfare, similar to earlier Crusades".[41] His expedition arrived in India in May of 1498. The experience of one of the first Portuguese sailors to come ashore in India sums up the entire Portuguese overseas enterprise, illustrating both the religious and economic dimensions. Upon stepping foot in India, this sailor "was accosted by two Spanish-speaking Tunisians ... they asked him: 'What the devil has brought you here?' to which he replied: 'We have come to seek Christians and spices.'"[42] The search for Christians and spices was indeed in full swing, and in order to find both, the Portuguese established trading posts in India at Cochin (1505), Goa (1510), and Hormuz (1515) in the Arabian Sea. Over the next decade they would add Bombay (Mumbai) and Diu (1535) along the Indian coast. The *Estado da India* was established in 1505 with its capital at Cochin, with Francisco de Almeida as its first viceroy. In 1510 the capital moved to Goa, and it was from here that Portugal managed its affairs east of the Cape of Good Hope to include the Indian Ocean and the Red Sea. Fleets known as the *Armadas da India* maintained communication between India and Lisbon. The main objective of this maritime empire was trade.[43] Spreading the Christian message and fighting Islam wherever it could be found were also priorities, and Albuquerque would dutifully serve in both the economic and religious capacities. While the Portuguese had also sent exploratory voyages to the west, reaching Brazil in 1500, economic opportunities in the east, including India, Japan, China, and Africa, far outweighed the advantages to be gained by competing against the Spanish, who had established themselves as the premier European power in the western hemisphere.

Four primary motives drove Portuguese expansion and exploration: first, a crusading zeal against the Muslims; second, the desire for Guinea gold; third, the quest for Prester John; and fourth, the search for Oriental spices.[44] Summarising these objectives, most scholars and historians would conclude that the desire to replace the Venetians as the primary distributors of Asian trade goods and joining Prester John's Christian Empire in the east in an attack on the Islamic world from the rear were the most important motives for Portuguese eastward expansion at the turn of the sixteenth century.[45] Separating the economic from the religious elements which drove

41 S.M. Ghazanfar, 'Vasco da Gama 's Voyages to India: Messianism, Mercantilism, and Sacred Exploits', *Journal of Global Initiatives: Policy, Pedagogy, Perspective*, (13) 2018, p.21.

42 C.R. Boxer, *The Portuguese Seaborne Empire in Asia, 1415–1825* (London: Hutchinson, 1969), p.37.

43 Ujjayan Bhattacharyay, 'The Portuguese Maritime Strategies and Options in the Eastern Indian Ocean Region (1515–1526)', *Proceedings of the Indian History Congress*, Vol. 57 (1996), p.263.

44 Boxer, *Portuguese Seaborne Empire in Asia*, p.18.

45 Andrew C. Hess, 'The Ottoman Conquest of Egypt (1517) and the Beginning of the Sixteenth-Century World War', *International Journal of Middle East Studies*, Vol. 4, No. 1 (Jan 1973),

the Portuguese voyages of discovery and conquest is difficult. The Vatican contributed to the zeal with which explorers set out from Portuguese ports en route to convert, conquer, and barter. Pope Nicholas V's *Romanus Pontifex*, written in 1454, encouraged the seizure of territory held by Islam. *Romanus Pontifex* provided the divine sanction that justified messianic exploration aimed at "universalising" Christianity, converting heathens, and bringing about the apocalypse, a prelude to the reigning "end-of-the-world" theology.[46] The Portuguese decision to join forces with Prester John, whom they believed Pero da Covilhão had found in Ethiopia, was an early sign that Portugal was becoming more than just a European power and was ready to operate on a larger stage. The Portuguese would soon be the masters of most of the African coast, from the Cape of Good Hope at the southern tip of the continent up the east side of Africa to modern-day Somalia and considerable areas of India and Arabia.[47]

By 1509 the Portuguese had wholly subjugated the Muslim states along the coast of East Africa, together with the islands of Zanzibar, Pemba, and Mafia. Arab power in south-east Africa was shattered.[48] To ensure their supremacy in the Red Sea and the Indian Ocean, the Portuguese fought several wars against adversaries who threatened their trade routes from Portugal to India. The Portuguese thrust into the Indian Ocean can be considered in a sense "the logical culmination and triumph of Christendom's anti-Muslim thrust", which began with their victory over Islam at Silves in 1249 and the liberation of Christian Portugal.[49]

From the 1505 battle and siege of Cochin on India's western coast to the Portuguese–Mamluk naval war of 1505-1517, the Portuguese were able to use military force throughout the sixteenth century to establish trade routes and ensure their economic dominance in the spice trade. Portuguese naval technology and armament proved superior to that of their rivals. The establishment of a string of coastal bases along the African coast facilitated trade and resupply of the fleets sent from Portugal to the Red Sea and further into the Indian Ocean. Although these bases along the African coast were mostly inaccessible to Portugal's enemies, the Muslim powers that lined the East African coastline were likewise inaccessible to the largely maritime-based Portuguese forces.[50] During King Manuel I's reign, the drive to extend Portuguese trade to the east and to join forces with the kingdom of Prester John drove the Portuguese to the Red Sea in much greater numbers. Albuquerque was the first European ship captain to enter the Red Sea, launching an unsuccessful attack on the port of Aden in 1513. He planned the conquest of Aden as a part of the global plan to establish Portuguese bases in Asia. But the 1513 attack failed due to the strong walls which surrounded the port city, effectively keeping the

p.60.

46 Ghazanfar, 'Vasco da Gama 's Voyages', p.17.

47 Pankhurst, *Economic History*, p.73.

48 Serjeant, *The Portuguese off the South Arabian Coast*, p.14.

49 Serjeant, *The Portuguese off the South Arabian Coast*, p.2.

50 Marshall G.S. Hodgson, *The Venture of Islam: Conscience and History in a World Civilization* (Chicago: University of Chicago Press, 1974), p.21.

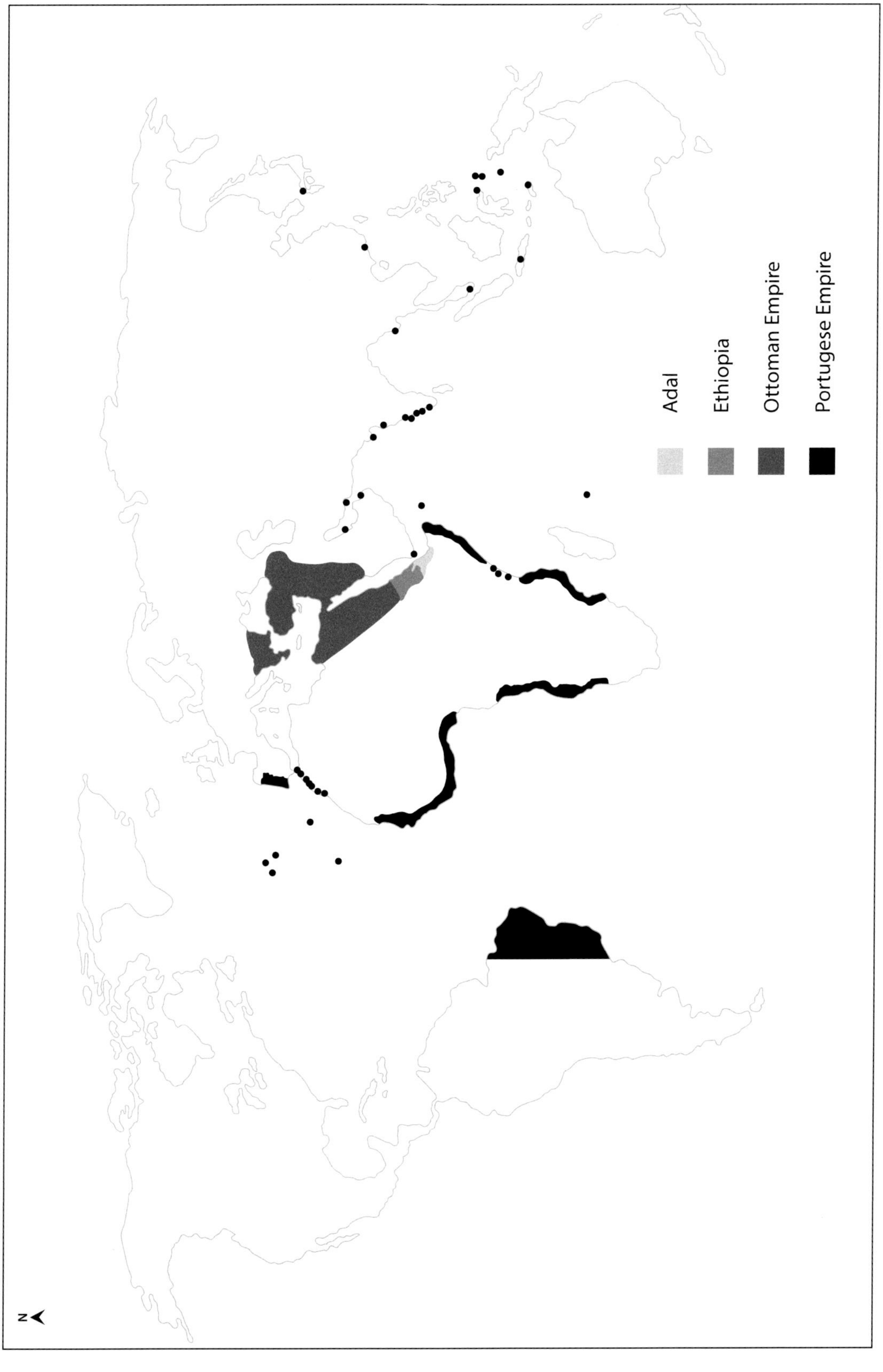

The Portuguese Empire, Ottoman Empire, Ethiopia, and the Sultanate of Adal in approximately 1520. Portugal's global reach is evident, but the Ottoman Empire's central location posed a threat to Portuguese maritime interests.

aggressive Portuguese attackers at bay.[51] Capturing Aden was a key element in controlling the Red Sea, which was the gateway to Islam's holiest cities and the destination for all Muslims making the Hajj. Among many of Portugal's leading soldiers, including Albuquerque, destroying Islam's holy sites had been a goal ever since the liberation of Silves in 1249.

In 1526 Francisco Alvarez and Rodrigo da Lima, members of the Portuguese expedition which had been sent to Ethiopia, arrived home in Portugal. While they were still in Ethiopia trying to arrange an alliance against Islam, Ethiopian king Lebne Dengel proclaimed that he would lead Ethiopia to war against the lowland sultanates, specifically the Sultanate of Adal. Many of his senior advisors disagreed with this idea, and "the Archbishop and the clergy, considering his young age, tried to dissuade him, threatening him with excommunication, but he refused to stay and left for the campaign".[52] Lebne Dengel's campaign led to Adal's total defeat. A general sense of relief took hold among the Ethiopians, believing that the endemic warfare between high and lowland peoples, and hence between Christian and Muslim, was over. There was no need to invite the Portuguese back to Ethiopia. Hailed as a hero:

> King [Lebne Dengel] went from Debre-Libanos to Yerer. Again the people of Ethiopia began to sing and dance [in his honour], and they gave him the name of Dawït [after the biblical king David]. There had never been such happiness and rejoicing. As time went by, the King was filled with conceit. He also began to teach the soldiers to parade.[53]

Lebne Dengel's pride and self-righteousness alienated him from his people and rekindled the resentment towards the highland Christians in the hearts of the Muslims inhabiting the lowland states. He had decided against an alliance with Portugal at an inopportune time. Having defeated an army from Adal, he would soon face a vengeful new leader from that small lowland sultanate who would change the course of Ethiopian history.

The Sultanate of Adal

The Sultanate of Adal was a multiethnic Muslim state in the Horn of Africa during the medieval period, from approximately 1415-1576.[54] The first

---

51 Rui Manuel Loureiro, 'Portas do Estreito: The ports of the Red Sea and the Gulf of Aden according to 16th century Portuguese iconographic sources', *Orientierungen Themenheft* 2013, p.131.

52 Reidulf K. Molvaer, 'The Tragedy of Emperor Libne-Dingil of Ethiopia (1508–1540)', *Northeast African Studies* New Series, 5, No. 2 (1998), p.25. Molvaer translated a history of Ethiopia written by Aleqa Tekle-ïyesus, an ethnic Oromo brought up and educated in Gojjam. Only a few copies of this history are available in Ethiopia. Aleqa wrote using "familiar" pronouns and verbal forms when describing Lebne Dengel's actions, and he does not hide his shortcomings. Aleqa Tekle-ïyesus died in 1936 at the age of 68. According to Margaux Herman, the original of this manuscript is kept in the hands of Wudu Fänta who lives in the town of Debra Marqos.

53 Molvaer, 'The Tragedy of Emperor Libne-Dingil', p.26.

54 Mohammed Hassen Hinika, 'The Genealogy and Ethnic Identity of Ahmed Ibn Ibrahim Al-Gazi (Gragn) of Ethiopia: A Historiographical Reappraisal', *East African Journal of Social Sciences and Humanities*, Volume 2, (2017), p.22.

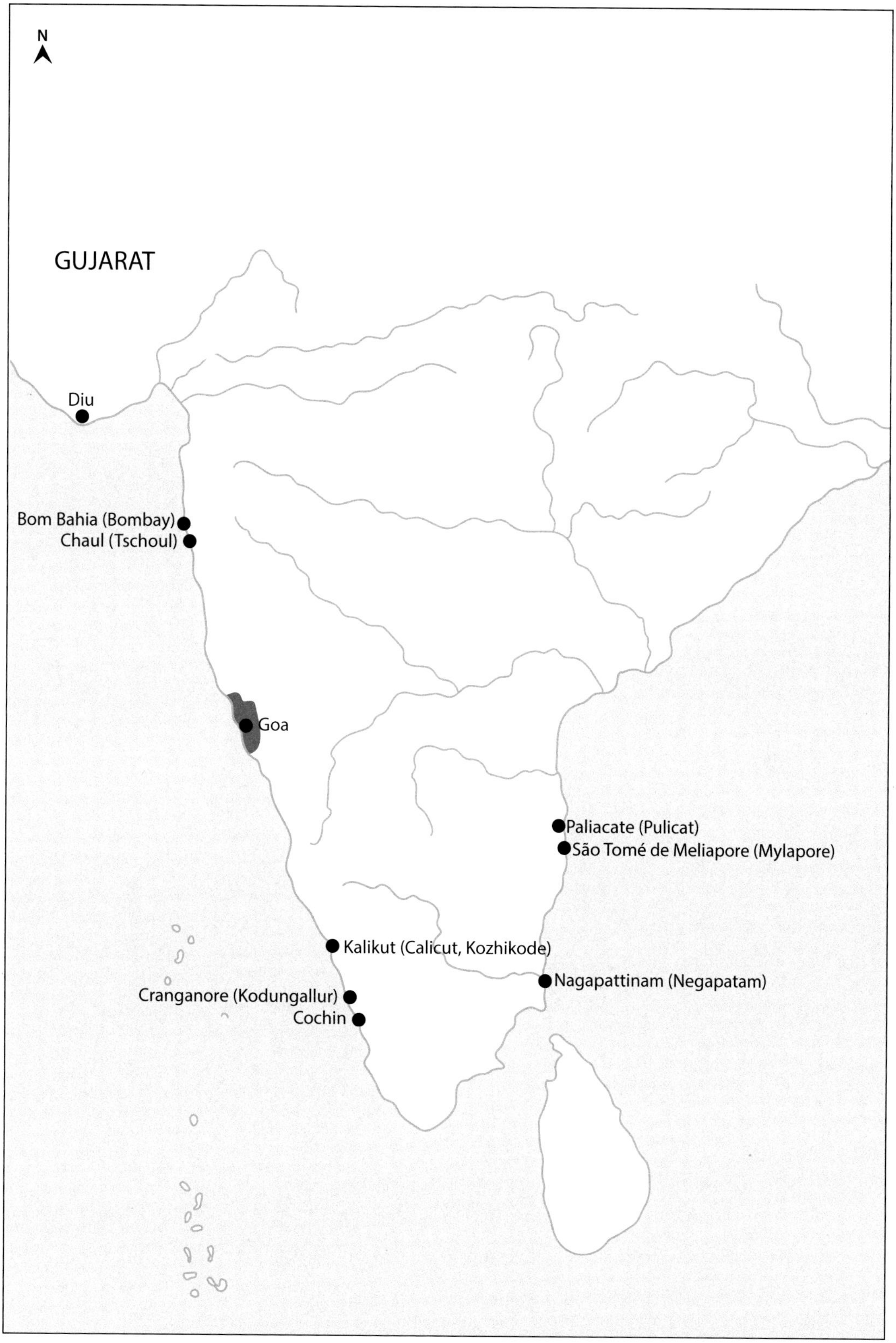

The Portuguese *Estado da India* in the sixteenth century.

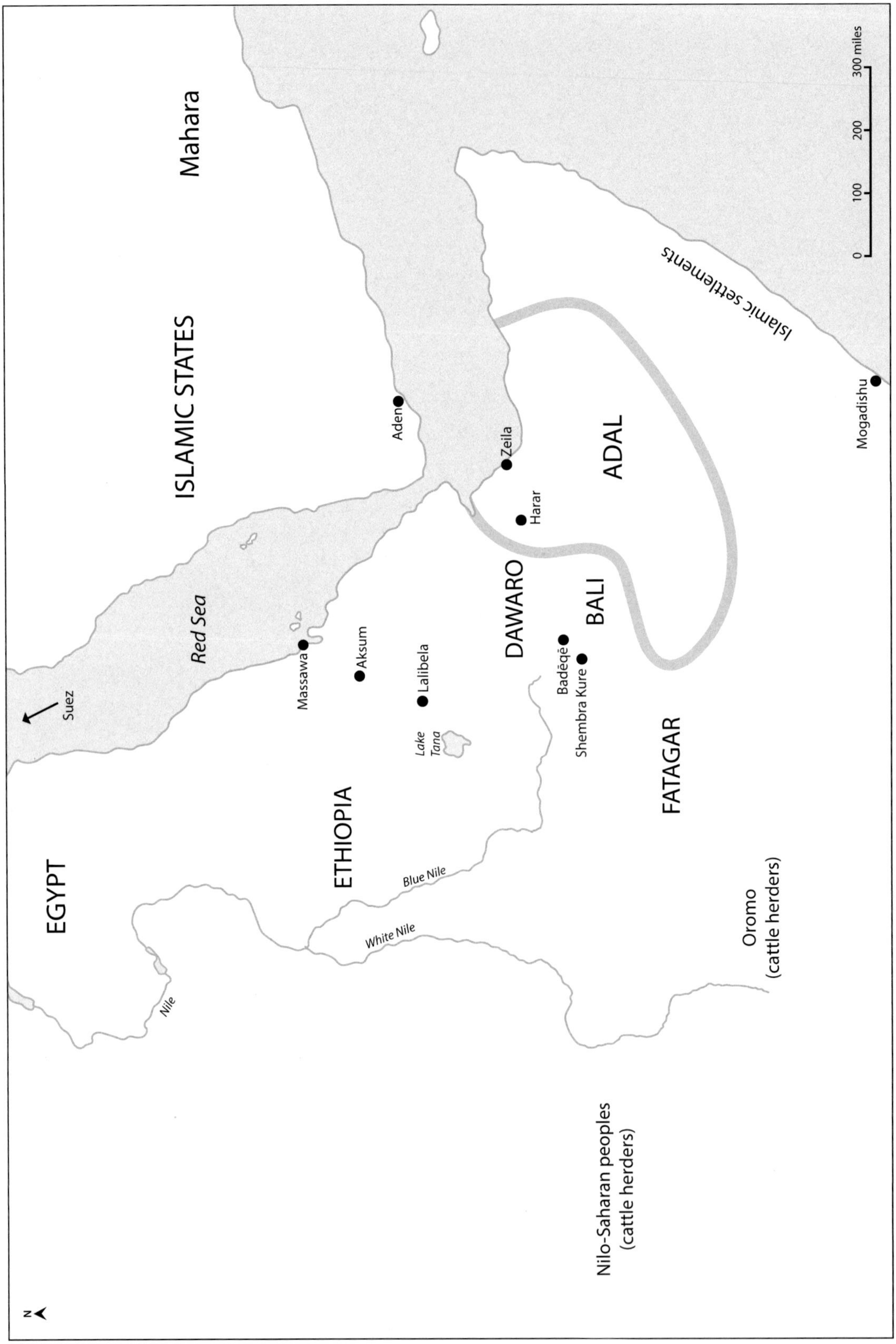

The Horn of Africa in the year 1500. Fatagar, Bali, and Dawaro were lowland provinces ruled by Ethiopia. The locations of Shembra Kure and Badēqē are conjectural.

mention of the Sultanate of Adal appears in the chronicles of the Ethiopian king Amda Seyon. Composed primarily of ethnic Somalis and Afaris, they "lived largely as pastoralists and spoke languages belonging to the East Cushitic branch of the Afroasiatic language family".[55] Most of the people living in this region had migrated south from Egypt and across the Red Sea into Africa over the preceding centuries, mostly following the established trade routes. Relations between the Afar and Ethiopia can be traced as far back as the era of Aksumite dominance over the port city of Adulis on the Red Sea coast in the fifth and sixth centuries AD. The Afar people successfully resisted many incursions into their territory, including attacks by the Ethiopian highlands' Tigrayan people.[56] As a result of Amda Seyon's punitive campaigns against the lowland Muslims, Christian control over the territory to the south and south-east of Ethiopia was secure. Unlike many of the ethnic groups which had been forcefully included in the Ethiopian kingdom over the last 1,000 years, repeated Christian victories over the lowland Muslims "failed to impose its religion and language on the overwhelming majority of the conquered peoples".[57] The lowland people maintained their Islamic faith and their distinct identity despite years of suffering at the hands of Ethiopian armies and kings. The Sultanate of Adal became the focal point for satisfying the desire for revenge, which had not been dormant since Amda Seyon's fourteenth-century conquests.

Adal territory consisted of what today covers Somalia, south-eastern Ethiopia, Djibouti, and Eritrea. Just as the kingdoms, sultanates, and principalities along both shores of the Red Sea had done for millennia, Adal engaged in a robust trade in slaves, ivory, salt, and other goods with the Arabians, Indians, Egyptians, and probably the Chinese. Just as the Kingdom of Aksum relied on the port city of Adulis, and Ethiopia in the fifteenth century relied on Massawa, Adal's commerce depended upon the port of Zeila. Relations between Ethiopia and Adal were rarely healthy, and Ethiopian king Zara Yaqob launched expeditions against Adal more than once in the fifteenth century, consistent with the pattern of highland–lowland conflict that permeated relations between Christians and Muslims in the Horn of Africa.

Historic cities in the region, such as Berbera, Zeila, and Harar, "flourished with mosques, shrines, courtyard houses, and cisterns during the kingdom's Golden Age".[58] A European observer noted that:

> the kingdom of Adel (as they say) is a large kingdom, and extends over the Cape of Guardafuy, and there in that part another ruler subject to Adel. Amongst the Moors they hold this King of Adel for a saint, because he always makes war upon

55 Donald N. Levine, 'A Revised Analytical Approach to the Evolution of Ethiopian Civilization', *International Journal of Ethiopian Studies*, Vol. 6 (2012), p.49.

56 Yasin Mohammed Yasin, 'Political History of the Afar in Ethiopia and Eritrea', *Africa Spectrum*, Vol. 43, No. 1, Horn of Africa (2008), p.44.

57 Hassen, 'Ethiopia and the Red Sea', p.63.

58 Levine, 'Revised Analytical Approach', p.49.

> the Christians … This Kingdom of Adel borders upon the kingdoms of Fatagar and Xio, which are kingdoms of the Prester John.[59]

This king who "always makes war upon the Christians" was Ahmad ibn Ibrahim al-Ghazi, or Ahmed Gurey. The observer accurately noted that the Ethiopians (Prester John) ruled over these lowland states, requiring tribute and collecting taxes, but the people were allowed to continue to practice Islam.

Ahmed Gurey was born in the vicinity of Zeila in 1506. Zeila was the same busy trading port through which Ibn Battuta had travelled nearly 160 years before Gurey's birth. A pious Muslim, Gurey's form of Islam was nevertheless tempered by the realities of commerce.[60] Little is known of his youth, although Ethiopian author Aleqa Tekle-ïyesus tells a story of his birth. Aleqa wrote that Gurey's mother travelled into Ethiopia to deliver Adal's required tribute to the Ethiopian king. This tribute consisted of "90 white mules, 50 golden puppies, and 2,300 fatted sheep and goats"[61] After a long journey to deliver the tribute to the church at Debre Libanos, a journey into the heart of the Christian highlands, Gurey's mother became involved in various mischievous affairs, eventually leading to her entering a convent and becoming pregnant by a monk. Once this became known, the monk was beaten to death by his compatriots for defiling the church. She returned to Adal, where Ahmed Gurey was born in 1506. Aleqa wrote that when Gurey was a young man his mother exclaimed to him in anger, "If you are a man, you will revenge your father's blood."[62] This account must be weighed against other historical accounts of Gurey's youth and his desire to conquer Ethiopia. It should not be taken as the definitive explanation of the motive behind his *jihad*, nor should it be considered an accurate portrayal of his youth or of his mother. Other sources claim that Gurey's father was the Muslim Ibrahim el-Ghazi and that both father and son were common soldiers in the Adal army and were both of Somali ethnicity. Ahmed Gurey married Bati Del Wanbara, a prominent woman who would not likely have been betrothed to someone of dubious lineage as described in the Ethiopian account.

Firearms were introduced into Arabia by the Ottomans roughly in the year 1515. With control of the Red Sea in Ottoman hands, firearms made their way from Arabia to the port city of Zeila, unmolested on the waterways by the Portuguese fleet, which had been unable to operate against the Ottoman navy in the Red Sea effectively. Once in Zeila, firearms were acquired by Muslim forces, which continued to wage low-intensity warfare against Ethiopia. The acquisition of firearms by the coastal Muslim states, including Adal, drastically changed the balance of power between Muslim

59 Fr. F. Alvarez, *Narrative of the Portuguese Embassy During the Years 1520–27*, ed. and translated by Lord Stanley of Alderley (London: The Hakluyt Society, 1881), p.346.

60 Marcus, *A History of Ethiopia*, p.31.

61 Molvaer, 'The Tragedy of Emperor Libne-Dingil', p.27.

62 Molvaer, 'The Tragedy of Emperor Libne-Dingil', p.28.

and Ethiopian forces.[63] Adal's capital moved from the coast north-westerly into the interior, closer to Ethiopia. From this and other cities and towns within the Sultanate of Adal, Ahmed Gurey would launch his conquest of Ethiopia. However, average troops armed with sixteenth-century firearms rarely provided an advantage over well-trained and motivated troops armed with the traditional weapons of spear, shield, and sword. Unless troops equipped with firearms "were properly drilled and supported, they generally suffered defeat when attacked by determined cavalry or infantry".[64]

While the Ottomans and Portuguese battled over maritime supremacy in the Red Sea and beyond, Adal and other small states and kingdoms sought to expand their territory, defend their borders, and seek revenge for the brutal punitive raids that the Ethiopians had launched against them over the last two centuries. For Adal and all of the Muslim communities along the African coast, from the southern tip at the Cape of Good Hope up to the Ethiopian coastline, "the Christian discovery of the Cape route was a calamitous disaster, and at the close of the fifteenth century the great age of Muslim culture there was brought to a rude and abrupt close".[65] The Portuguese brought an end to Islam's golden age when they crossed the southern tip of Africa and established a series of coastal forts on territory which for centuries had been flourishing, prospering Muslim communities engaged in trade with India and Asia. Describing the savagery encountered by the inhabitants of this part of the world, Italian traveller Ludovico de Varthema recalled hearing that, "In [1502] the ships of the Sultan of the Franks [Portuguese] made their appearance in the sea between India and the island of Hormuz. They seized seven vessels and murdered most of the crews."[66] The Portuguese demonstrated both their desire to break into the trading structures already established and their vehement opposition to Islam wherever it was encountered anywhere in the world.

As the Sultanate of Adal rose to become the most prominent of the small Muslim enclaves along the Red Sea coast, the Ethiopian military faced organisational and logistical issues that would hamper its ability to defend the kingdom. Whether it be Tigray, Amhara, or one of the many other provinces that composed the Ethiopian kingdom, the king's home province provided the bulk of the troops that made up the army's infantry component. When on the attack, these troops could be assembled before launching an offensive. But it was not always easy to assemble the troops at a moment's notice to defend the kingdom. In addition, following Amda Seyon's victory over the Sultanate of Ifat in the fourteenth century, the practice of recruiting troops from the king's home province resulted in a lack of consistent training and doctrine, as every few years a new cadre of soldiers appeared in the Ethiopian army's ranks. However, the sheer size of the Ethiopian army often compensated for any deficiencies in cohesion, training, and morale. For example, after assuming the Ethiopian throne in 1507, King Lebne Dengel's

63 Whiteway, *Portuguese Expedition to Abyssinia*, p.xxii.

64 Aregay, 'A Reappraisal', p.113.

65 Serjeant, *The Portuguese off the South Arabian Coast*, p.11.

66 De Varthema, *The Travels of Ludovico Di Varthema*, p.61, note 1.

army was composed primarily of soldiers from Gondar, his home province.[67] Newly crowned, Lebne Dengel led this army straight into the heart of Adal in July 1517, crushing the Muslim force which took the field against him just as Zara Yaqob had done at Egubba in 1445. While Lebne Dengel succeeded in keeping the lowland states under Ethiopian control, these states remained restive and did not willingly accede to Ethiopian dominion. The attempted integration of these Muslim territories into the Christian Ethiopian kingdom would prove troublesome. These "colonies of an alien faith proved a great weakness to the country [Ethiopia] in withstanding the onslaughts of [Gurey]".[68] The Sultanate of Adal would soon emerge under Ahmed Gurey's leadership as the most significant challenger to these punitive raids that the Ethiopians had yet encountered. The balance of power in the Horn of Africa was about to change.

The First Jihads

Perhaps not since Islam spread like wildfire through Arabia and North Africa in the seventh and eighth centuries had the spirit of *jihad* been unleashed as it was in the Horn of Africa in the early 1500s. Islam was on the march again, and:

> *jihads* were popular in the 15th and l6th centuries. One of these was the *jihad* of the Ottoman Turks in Hungary. Another was the *jihad* of the Safavid Persians in the Caucasus. After a long period of quiescence, the armies of Islam were again on the move against the Christian world, as they had not been since the 7th century. If Turks and Persians were advancing the frontiers of Islam elsewhere, why should Arabs not penetrate Ethiopia?[69]

For descriptions of the first years of the campaign, we must rely solely upon the *Futuh Al-Habaša*, written by Arab Faqih. Before launching his assault on Ethiopia, Ahmed Gurey first had to deal with opposition within the ranks of his fellow Muslim commanders from neighbouring sultanates and principalities. The lowland sultanates engaged in constant disputes amongst themselves over trade and access to arable land, making Ethiopia's job of keeping them subservient much easier. Gurey's task was to try to unite the lowland people behind a common cause, and this he did by combining Islamic piety with the prospect of revenge for centuries of Ethiopian raids and the expectation of increased profit from trade. To get the people motivated to pursue these objectives, Gurey launched a series of military campaigns, described by G.W.B. Huntingford as "preliminary raids into Ethiopia which

---

67 Asa J. Davis, 'The Sixteenth Century Jihad in Ethiopia and the Impact on its Culture (Part Two): Implicit Factors Behind the Movement', *Journal of the Historical Society of Nigeria*, Vol. 3 (December 1964), p.121.

68 Frederick A. Edwards, 'The Conquest of Abyssinia', *The Asiatic Quarterly Review & Quarterly and Colonial Record.* 3rd Series, Vol. XIX, 37 & 38 (Jan–Apr 1905), p.329.

69 Martin, E.G., 'Mahdism and Holy Wars in Ethipia Before 1600', *Proceedings of the Seventh Seminar for Arabian Studies* (1974), p.113.

took place before the real invasion began".[70] In 1525 Gurey launched what is considered his first actual *jihad* into the lowland provinces, nominally under Ethiopian overlordship, which included Dawaro, defeating the Ethiopians in pitched battle not far from Harar. Arab Faqih recounts:

> They joined forces at a place called Aqam - it was a mighty river with copious water - and the Muslims drew up their battle lines. The infidels unaided by God, did likewise, and mobilised their infantry and their cavalry. The Muslims attacked them in a single wave. The fighting was intense, the battles hard fought, with choking dust, hero joining with hero. At that time all that could be heard was the thud of sword against leather shield.[71]

It is interesting to note in this description of the fighting that there are no sounds of firearms mentioned, nor is there any reference to the inevitable smoke which would have clouded the battlefield if firearms were used in any capacity. This is not to imply that there were no firearms at all anywhere within Ahmed Gurey's army, but the firearms themselves were not the key element in the early Muslim victories over their Ethiopian foe. Ahmed Gurey's Adal warriors enjoyed battlefield success due to superior training, morale, and dedication to their leader.

Ahmed Gurey's route of march into Christian territory corresponded roughly to the established trade routes that carried goods back and forth from the lowland coastal cities into the Ethiopian highlands.[72] The battle described by Arab Faqih was a decisive Muslim victory, but Ahmed Gurey would not pursue the defeated Ethiopian army and instead returned to Adal to shore up his forces for further *jihad*. A second *jihad* into Ethiopia ended with no contact between the Muslim and Christian armies. Gurey's subordinate commanders decided to return to their homeland as they did after the first *jihad*. Arab Faqih recorded that Gurey "wept bitter tears" and ordered one of his commanders to march into Ethiopia with 100 cavalry and 2,000 infantry.[73] This force did find the Ethiopian army and took from it additional captives and many mules. The Muslims then returned to Adal, bringing an end to the second *jihad*. A third small *jihad* followed, but it was not until the fourth *jihad* was launched that Ethiopia's actual conquest can be considered to have begun in earnest. In 1528, Gurey:

> made preparations for Abyssinia [Ethiopia] for the *jihad* for the sake of the Most High God. The imam equipped his soldiers and his army, and all the tribes. He sold the gold and the silver jewelry of his wives and the furnishings of his house in order to provide the tribes and the soldiers with weapons of war, keeping nothing

70 Huntingford, *Historical Geography*, p.122.

71 Šihab ad-Din Ahmad bin Abd al-Qader bin Salem bin Utman. *Futuh Al-Habaša: The Conquest of Abyssinia [16th Century].* Translated by Paul Lester Stenhouse (Hollywood, CA: Tsehai Publishers and Distributors, 2003), p.11.

72 Pankhurst, *Ethiopian Borderlands: Essays*, p.221.

73 Šihab ad-Din, *Futuh Al-Habaša*, p.29.

> back for himself - may God forgive him, for he hoped only for the reward held out by the Most High God that he might dwell in the paradise of delights.[74]

Assembling his forces, and having been proclaimed an imam, Gurey crossed into Ethiopia when his wife was just about to give birth. Gurey's commanders quarrelled over her presence with the army, so she was sent home, where she gave birth to a son. At this time, Gurey also divided his army into three columns, each of which raided into Christian territory; Gurey's column reaching as far as Antukyah, which would be the site of a major battle a few years later. No major battles were fought, but the Muslim troops gained valuable information about the terrain over which they would travel in the coming years, and were also able to determine that the Ethiopian army was not standing at the ready to resist any further incursions into the highlands.

74 Šihab ad-Din, *Futuh Al-Habaša*, p.45.

Chapter 3

The Ethiopian–Adal War: Imam Gurey Triumphant

The conquest of Ethiopia began as a continuation of the struggle between the Ethiopian Christian kingdom and the small Muslim sultanates and principalities to Ethiopia's south and south-east. Amda Seyon and Zara Yaqob had subdued the sultans of these states in the previous centuries. Occasionally, an uprising of one of the sultanates would lead to further conflict with the powerful Ethiopian kingdom. However, to attribute the *jihad* to nothing more than a desire to spread Islam into Christian Ethiopia would disregard other powerful motives for the war. Political unity was lacking among the Muslim states that lined the Horn of Africa, and Ethiopian military excursions into these small states had become routine. By 1529 Imam Gurey had successfully leveraged centuries of frustration over subservience to the Christian kings of the Ethiopian highlands. Irredentist movements among the lowland pastoralists may have also been a motivating factor behind Gurey's decision to continue his attacks into Ethiopia.[1] If this was a factor, it is unlikely that Muslim pastoralists sought to inhabit the highlands, although many had been forcibly removed from more fertile land over the centuries of Ethiopian punitive raids. Still, the desire to move north into territory under direct Ethiopian control probably motivated many non-Christians to challenge Ethiopian control of the fertile highland provinces. A further motivating factor leading to a desire to launch a military assault into the fertile Ethiopian highlands may have been that famine had plagued the lowlands in the 1520s.[2]

Adal Military Organisation

The lowland provinces shared Islam but little else. Competition for access to the lucrative Red Sea trade routes and dynastic struggles ensured that the small sultanates south and east of Ethiopia remained as opposed to each

1 Lewis, 'The Somali Conquest', p.223.
2 Martin, 'Mahdism and Holy Wars', p.111.

other as they were to the highland Ethiopian kingdom. Imam Gurey's first task was to rally the sultanates to a single cause; it was a difficult task and took years to accomplish. He spent over a year subjugating the lowland tribal groups through both military campaigns and adept diplomacy. He succeeded in creating a new type of army, one that might be capable of taking on the Ethiopian military. This army was an improvement over anything seen before in the lowlands, due primarily to its superior organisation.[3] He also compelled rival warlords to cooperate, no small achievement in the hardscrabble lowlands. He promised riches, both spiritual and temporal, to any of them who survived the coming clash with the Christian Ethiopian army.[4]

Imam Gurey's new military organisation was based on an army divided into three main groups. The first group was the *Malassy*, his personal bodyguard. This elite force was under Gurey's direct command. It was composed of only one or two main ethnic groups so that a common language would ensure effective communications. The ability to issue clear and effective orders, and have those orders be clearly understood, had been a challenge that Muslim armies faced when dealing with the Ethiopians. The Ethiopian army may have been composed of troops from many different provinces, but they spoke the same language, and there was thus less difficulty distributing orders no matter how many tens of thousands of troops took the field. The *Malassy* was highly disciplined, thoroughly trained, and above all mounted on strong horses and well-armed with the finest weaponry from Arabia. These men were also given shields from India and swords from throughout the North African Maghreb. The *Malassy*'s ranks were increased by Arab preachers and mercenaries who now flocked to Adal to join this force. Within Gurey's new army:

> The Arab preachers fueled the ideological base for *jihad*, prepared written slogans on the standards carried by each wing [of the army] and raised the morale of the fighters, while the firearms of the Arab mercenaries provided an additional weapon which the Muslim force had lacked in the previous wars. This crack force, with which the Imam policed the surrounding hostile tribes and attacked the Christian armies, faithfully carried out his will.[5]

The second wing of this new force was composed entirely of Somali nomads, all commanded by Imam Gurey's brother-in-law. The third wing was composed of troops from Afar and Harla, and to ensure their loyalty and maintain their morale, their hereditary leaders commanded them. The Imam held regular meetings with the commanders of the three wings, discussing military matters. Unlike the Ethiopian kings, who tended to oversee their military with absolute authority, he listened to the commanders' strategic and tactical suggestions and recommendations. Gurey provided separate flags for the three wings of his force, banners that were lavishly embellished with religiously inspired slogans meant to keep the spirit of *jihad* alive and

3 Hassen, 'The Oromo of Ethiopia', p.33.
4 Richard Reid, *Warfare in African History* (New York: Cambridge University Press, 2012), p.54.
5 Hassen, 'The Oromo of Ethiopia', p.33.

well in his army. During every battle, the wings were arrayed with one on the right and left, the *Malassy* in the middle, and the Imam leading them from the front rank. The *Malassy* provided support to both wings at the crucial moment and prevented the troops from abandoning the field.[6] Included within Gurey's army were groups of soldiers armed with firearms, these weapons being available for purchase throughout the Red Sea ports following the Egyptian defeat by the Ottomans in 1517. Firearms had not proliferated widely in the Horn of Africa, but they would play a role in the fighting between Ethiopia and Imam Gurey's army.

By the time Imam Gurey began his military campaign in earnest against Ethiopia, the Ethiopian military was deployed in the same manner as it had been for the preceding centuries. *Çäwa* regiments and troops from Lebne Dengel's home province of Gondar composed the core of the Ethiopian army. Accompanying the army were the *etcahge* or the superior monks of the Debra Libanos monastery.[7] These elite members of society did not necessarily fight in the front rank, but their presence served to raise the fighting troops' morale. The entire *katama* court moved with the army, which presented a formidable sight. While the Ethiopian army's organisation had not changed for centuries, new equipment had likely appeared in the ranks. Lebne Dengel probably purchased firearms and small cannons to outfit some parts of the Ethiopian army, just as Imam Gurey had done. However, the cavalry was Ethiopia's elite arm, and "most of [Lebne Dengel's] money was spent on equipping his cavalry units with horses from Egypt and, no doubt from the same region, swords, lances, helmets with and without visors, cuirasses, coats of mail and protective coverings for the horses".[8] The Ethiopian cavalry was the army's pride, and it would be called upon to defend the kingdom from Imam Gurey's invaders.

While the Ethiopian army was formidable in size, it lacked adequate logistical support. It could not rely on outside supply sources, unlike their Adal enemy, who benefitted from their proximity to the Red Sea port of Zeila though which flowed arms and material that could be used to resupply and sustain the army. Ethiopian indigenous production could not provide weaponry at a rate fast enough to replace heavy losses, which is one reason that for the past decades, Ethiopian kings chose to conduct quick, punitive raids when seeking to subdue their Muslim neighbours rather than engage in prolonged campaigns. The Portuguese diplomat Francisco Alverez reported to Lisbon that although the Ethiopians possessed a plentiful supply of shields, spears, lances, and "many bows and arrows", they were otherwise poorly equipped. They had at most "a few swords, a handful of long and narrow coats of mail, which the Portuguese considered of inferior quality, two swivel guns, a small quantity of helmets, which had been obtained from the mission, and a mere fourteen muskets which had recently been purchased from the Turks".[9] Other Portuguese sources at the time recorded that:

6 Hassen, 'The Oromo of Ethiopia', pp.33–34.
7 Davis 'Sixteenth Century *Jihad*', p.121.
8 Aregay, 'Military Elites', p.55.
9 Pankhurst, *Economic History*, p.159.

> the Emperor, when he gathers all his Force, brings into the Field 30 or 40,000 Men, 4 or 5,000 of them Horse, the rest Foot. Of the Horse about 1,500 are sizeable, and some of them very fine and strong. About 7 or 800 of these Horse wear Coats of Mail and Head-Pieces, all the rest both Horse and Foot, have no other Arms than have been said above.[10]

Even if not adequately armed to face a determined foe, Ethiopia's geography leant itself to providing numerous defensive positions if attacked. Mountain fortresses dotted the highlands, known as "ambas", most have a flat top and "a surface that is sometimes contracted in area and sometimes extends to several square miles; there is usually an ample water supply with space to grow the food of the garrison and give pasture to their flocks and herds".[11] These ambas would be the scenes of many hard-fought battles in the coming years.

The elite Ethiopian cavalry participated in most military campaigns and was well suited to operations in the lowlands' flat terrain. Foot soldiers made up the bulk of the army and formed the standard attack formation. This formation was invariably "a crescent-shaped mass of foot soldiers in which both wings advanced to outflank and envelop the enemy's defences. Once engaged, the individual soldier was the army's basic fighting unit, and a final charge to bring the enemy to hand-to-hand combat usually decided a battle."[12] The resulting clash of sword and spear-wielding infantry left many casualties on both sides of the battlefield, and "mutilating slain enemies and abandoning the wounded and dead on the battlefield were accepted practices".[13]

There was little compassion shown between adversaries. Battlefield command was exercised right at the front, even if the *negusa nagast* was not present in the front rank, as he was often in the rear echelon during pitched battles, unlike Imam Gurey. Leadership, especially among powerful nobles, "was intensely personal, and commanders at all levels led their men in combat. Success or failure often depended on the leader's fate; upon his death, whole armies frequently scattered and fled."[14] The Ethiopian army would take the field against Imam Gurey in precisely the fashion thus described, just as it did with resounding success against Muslim infidels at Egubba in 1445.

Skirmishes between Imam Gurey's force and the Ethiopian army were frequent in the first weeks of the invasion in the spring of 1529. Arab Faqih describes the events that led up to the Battle of Badēqē – the first major clash since Aqam between Imam Gurey's forces of *jihad* and the Ethiopian army. Badēqē is not an identifiable location, like many of the places named in the historical record.[15] Prior to the actual battle, King Lebne Dengel ordered his troops to allow Imam Gurey's forces to enter the city of Badēqē. He would further allow them to burn down the churches and the monastery, and

10 Tellez, *Travels of the Jesuits in Ethiopia*, p.57.

11 Whiteway, *Portuguese Expedition to Abyssinia*, p.xxiii.

12 Ofcansky, *Ethiopia: A Country Study*, p.271.

13 Ofcansky, *Ethiopia: A Country Study*, p.271

14 Ofcansky, *Ethiopia: A Country Study*, p.271.

15 Huntingford, *Historical Geography*, p.121. Huntingford explains that 'there is a wealth of topographical information in the *Futuh al Habasa*, but it is not possible to identify all the names mentioned in it.'

One of the many ambas which cover the Ethiopian landscape. This one is approximately 60 miles east of Lake Tana. (Photo by Jean-Claude Latombe)

then when they were distracted with these tasks, the Ethiopian army would attack. However, the Ethiopian commanders could not coordinate their actions, leading to a half-hearted assault on the Adal troops pillaging in Badēqē. The description of the fighting indicates a violent clash; the ferocity intensified by the motivation to bring *jihad* to Ethiopia. Arab Faqih recounts the Muslim commander Abu Bakr having his right hand shattered in the fighting, but "the Muslims tied it up for him, and it was as good as if nothing ever happened. This was one of the graces of *jihad*."[16] Ethiopian troops also fought bravely, as Arab Faqih also records an Ethiopian commander named Aron had a spear thrust into his mouth, and even though "the shimmering point emerged under his ear, the [Ethiopian] sat firmly in his saddle".[17] These descriptions of violent battlefield encounters recur throughout Arab Faqih's account of the war. Athough the Ethiopian army gave a valiant account of itself at Badēqē, ultimately Imam Gurey rallied his commanders and his troops, driving the Ethiopian force back.

Included in Lebne Dengel's army at Badēqē were archers who used poisoned arrows. Arab Faqih wrote that these archers, the Maya people, unleashed thousands of arrows against the Muslim forces, arrows which Imam Gurey ordered his troops to collect off the ground rather than let the Maya get hold of their previously fired arrows and possibly use them again. After the Ethiopian forces retreated from Badēqē, the Muslim army

16 Šihab ad-Din, *Futuh Al-Habaša*, p.63.
17 Šihab ad-Din, *Futuh Al-Habaša*, p.63.

used the arrows as kindling for the fires over which they roasted the meat of captured cattle. Once Badēqē was burnt and pillaged, the Ethiopian army retreated to the north, to the city of Barara. The course of events at this point is unclear. Was Barara an ancient Ethiopian capital city, or was it the location of the *katama*, the moving camp which served as the capital? Either way, the Ethiopian army was unable to stop Imam Gurey's further advance into Christian territory.[18] The next encounter between his forces and Lebne Dengel's Ethiopian army took place at Shembra Kure (meaning The Swamp of Chickpeas) on approximately 11 March 1529.[19] It is this battle which historians most often use to denote the beginning of the Ethiopian–Adal War.

The Battle of Shembra Kure

Hoping to avoid a repetition of the Battle of Egubba, Imam Gurey assembled his army and marched forth to meet the Ethiopians on the field of battle. According to Arab Faqih, Imam Gurey's Muslim army was composed of 560 horsemen and about 12,000 infantry, armed with sabres and many archers. The Ethiopian army deployed a cavalry force whose numbers were "beyond counting" and deployed their infantry in seven battle lines, according to Arab Faqih in *The Futuh Al-Habaša*. King Lebne Dengel distributed the finest weapons to his troops - "Davidic suits of mail, helmets of king Sabur, Egyptian sords, and spears of Katt".[20] Arab Faqih's description of the Ethiopian army was supplied by a Christian soldier who joined Imam Gurey's army and embraced Islam after the Battle of Shembra Kure.[21] No accurate number has been identified for the Ethiopian army at Shembra Kure, but it is logical to assume that the Ethiopians were probably able to muster at least twice as many soldiers as the army of Adal.

Advancing in their characteristic crescent-shaped formation, the Ethiopians seized the initiative over their Muslim foes, just as had been the pattern over the last few centuries when these armies met in the field. The battle began in much the same way many of the punitive campaigns against recalcitrant Muslim armies had been waged for centuries, with the sheer weight of numbers giving the Ethiopians an edge. During the battle, fought

18 Contemporary archaeological exploration has made great progress in uncovering many of Ethiopia's medieval cities and fortifications. Richard Pankhurst and Hartwig Breternitz stated that "Neither Barara nor Badēqē could be identified by this survey. None of the located sites can be assumed with certainty to be either of the two cities." ('Barara, the Royal City of 15th and Early 16th Century (Ethiopia), Medieval and Other Early Settlements Between Wechecha Range and Mt Yerer: Results from a Recent Survey', *Annales d'Ethiopie* 24, (2009), p.228). However, expeditions led by Dr Marco Vigano have uncovered convincing evidence that Barara was in fact one of Ethiopia's leading cities in the centuries prior to the Ethiopian–Adal War.

19 Paul Stenhouse, the editor of the *Futuh al Habasa*, suggests that the battle took place on 11 March 1529. Other sources vary by up to six months on either side of this date.

20 Šihab ad-Din, *Futuh Al-Habaša*, p.78. Spears of Katt are sought after-weapons – a type of spear described in note 281 on page 78 as either an Indian spear, or perhaps just an 'excellent' or 'choice' weapon.

21 Aregay, 'A Reappraisal', p.101.

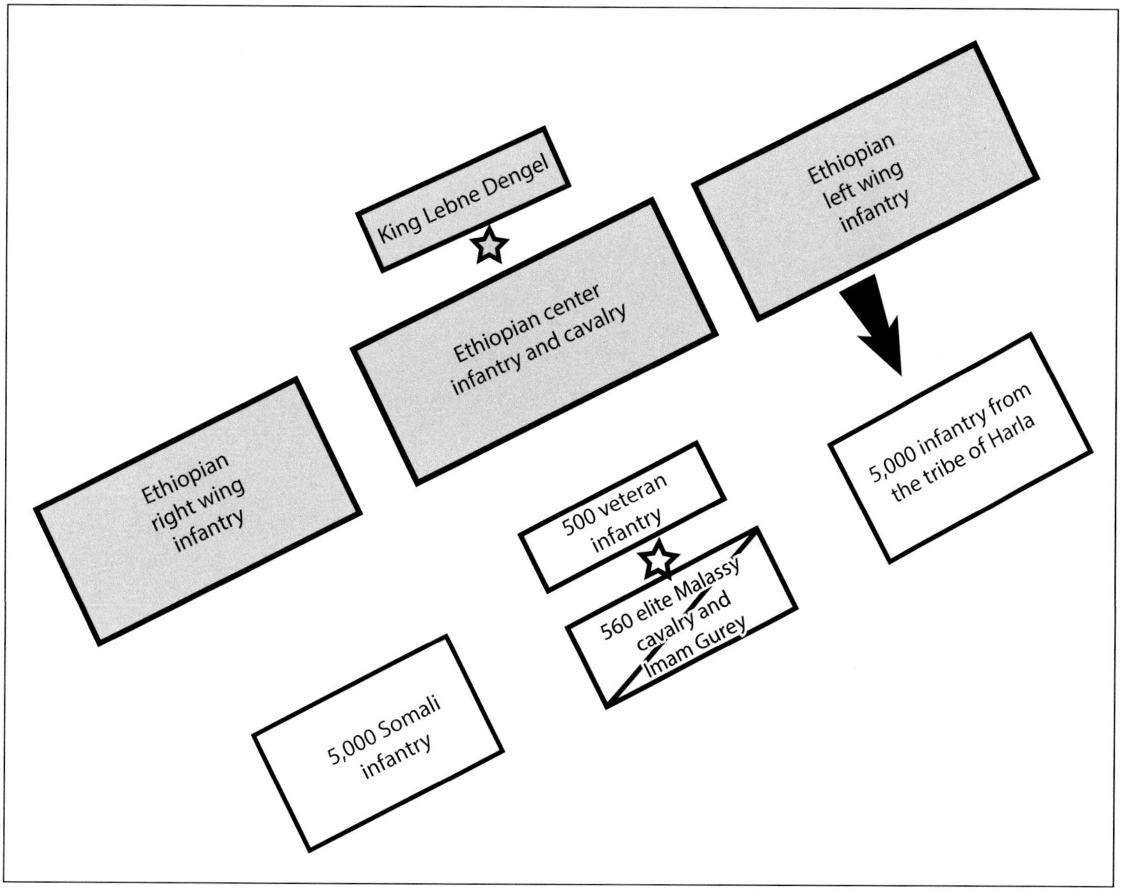

The Battle of Shembra Kure. While Imam Gurey led his army from the front rank, King Lebne Dengel remained at the rear of his army.

near the Mojo river in the rolling plains where the lowlands began to rise into the mountainous highlands, Lebne Dengel's Ethiopian infantry initially overwhelmed Imam Gurey's troops. As the Ethiopians advanced, they were sheltered from the sun by a cloud, while Imam Gurey's troops were exposed to the sun's heat. But Arab Faqih claims that in response to the prayers of the Imam, the cloud passed from over the Christians' heads, settling firmly in place above the heads of the Muslim warriors, providing shelter from the heat. Sensing divine intervention on behalf of their foe, the Ethiopians desperately charged forward, pushing the Muslim army's left wing back, nearly causing their entire line to collapse. Throwing their javelin at the run and then closing in hand-to-hand combat with the spear and dagger, the Ethiopians demonstrated the ferocity for which they were known. The Adal troops absorbed the shock of the Ethiopian surge but could not withstand the weight of their numbers.

Falling back, Gurey's forces struggled to maintain their discipline, certain that if they routed from the field in disorder, they would be hunted down and killed. Pursued by the Ethiopians, most of the Somali troops from the left wing were slaughtered. The Ethiopians then drove the right wing of the Muslim army into the centre, where Imam Gurey and his entourage of *Malassy* were fighting bravely against the Ethiopian cavalry. There the fight became desperate, assuming the savage character of the close-quarter

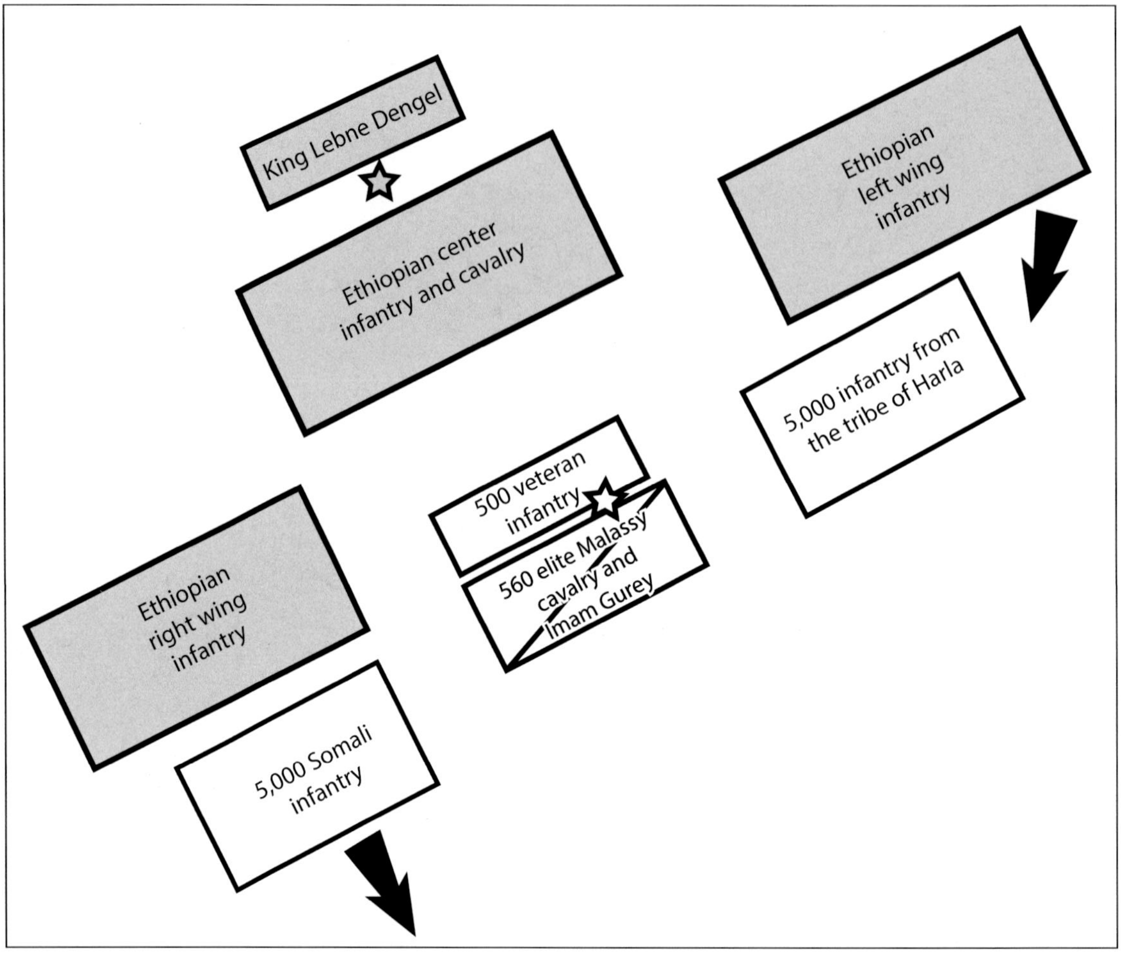

The Ethiopian army has pushed back both wings of the Muslim force. The outcome appears to be reminiscent of the many encounters between Ethiopian and Muslim armies since the era of Zara Yaqob and Amda Seyon. However, Imam Gurey had motivated his troops to stand and fight regardless of the odds. His *Malassy* cavalry would soon overwhelm the elite Ethiopian cavalry, forcing the Ethiopian army to retreat in disarray.

combat for which battles between the highland Christians and lowland Muslims were noted. Once the armies joined in hand-to-hand combat there was no overall battle plan, the crescent-shaped formation having done its job of getting the troops into contact on terms favourable to the Ethiopians. Each Ethiopian warrior hoped to use the engagement as an opportunity to display his martial skills.

From Aksumite times until the sixteenth century (and even into the twentieth century, as would be demonstrated against the Italian invasion), the Ethiopian warrior ethic "took the form of a cult of the hero" in which "personal bravery, not discipline, training, honour, or self-sacrificing loyalty, was the paramount virtue in warfare".[22] The Muslim infantry nearly gave way to what seemed at the time to be the *coup de grâce* delivered by the Ethiopian cavalry, which far outnumbered Imam Gurey's *Malassy* troops. Although heavily outnumbered, the Muslim cavalry resisted bravely, hamstringing the Ethiopian horses and using their swords with great effect against the Ethiopian riders. While firearms were likely present in the Muslim ranks at

22 Levine, 'The Masculinity Ethic', p.169.

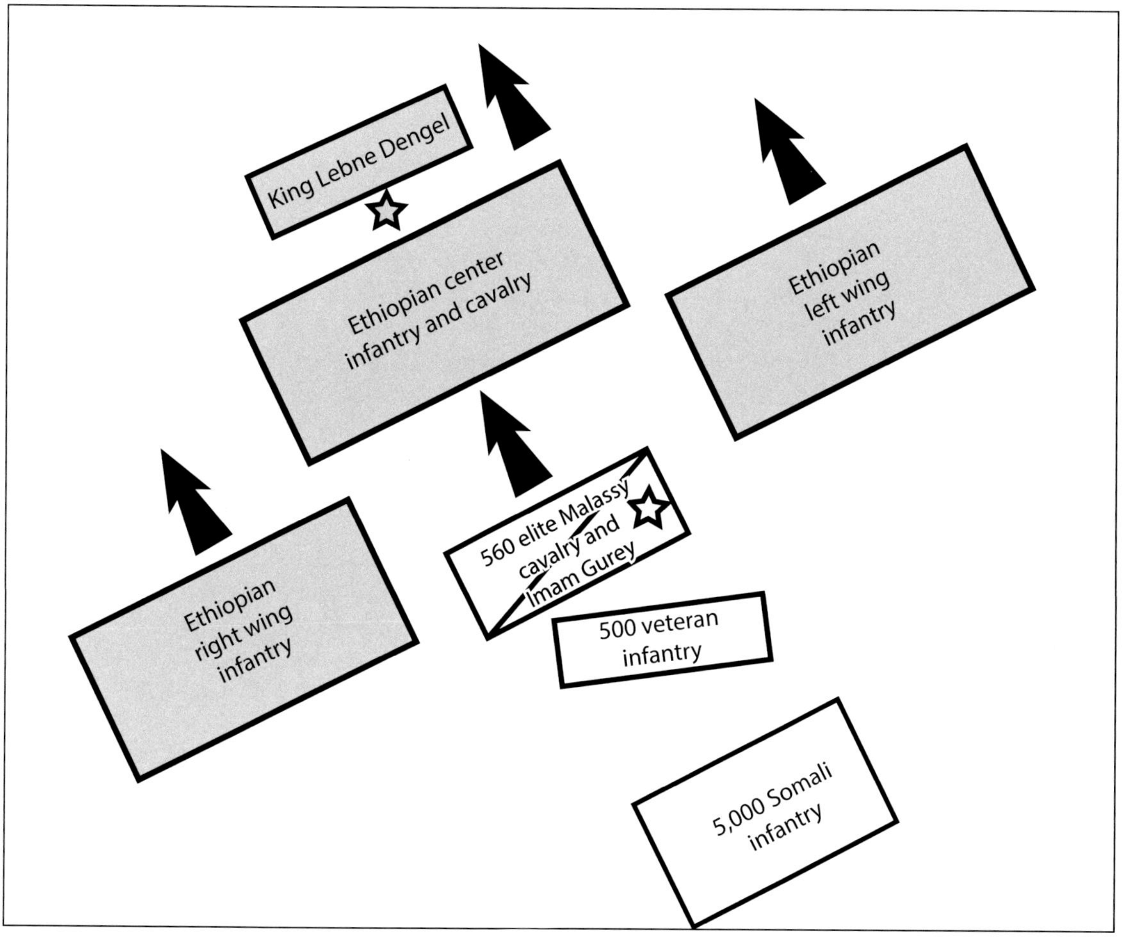

Imam Gurey had been at the forefront of the fighting from the beginning of the battle. The Ethiopian army, however, did not see their king until they fled past him in headlong retreat. The Ethiopians suffered a stunning and unprecedented defeat at Shembra Kure.

Shembra Kure, it was the *Malassy*, the elite force, which Imam Gurey had created, which swore loyalty to him alone, and which facilitated his rise to power that won the day. The *Malassy* were well disciplined, and it was their bravery and valour, and "not with firearms, that Imam Gurey won the first decisive victories against the Christians".[23] Muslim losses numbered nearly 5,000. At the end of the fateful day, the Ethiopians were thrown back and ultimately fled the field. Thousands of soldiers were dead. More than 10,000 Ethiopian troops from Tigray were killed. Many of their commanders also perished – an irreplaceable loss which prompted Ethiopian king Lebne Dengel to retreat back into the highlands.

Lebne Dengel's poor relationship with his commanders and the low esteem in which he was held by his army, and by the Ethiopian people in general, are other factors that explain the Ethiopian defeat at Shembra Kure. His "cruel temperament, his greed, and the harsh exploitation of his subjects" failed to motivate his troops in the same way that Amda Seyon and Zara Yaqob had inspired previous generations of Ethiopia's warriors.[24]

23 Hassen, 'Ethiopia and the Red Sea', p.64.

24 Aregay, 'A Reappraisal', p.98.

Worse, Lebne Dengel's presence on the battlefield did nothing to inspire his troops, precisely the opposite of what Imam Gurey's was able to instil in his smaller though much more effective army. During the battle, Lebne Dengel remained in the rearguard. Also complicating matters for the Ethiopian army were the petty jealousies that had arisen between commanders from different provinces.[25] Troops from Gojjam, Tigray, and Amhara may have fought well enough together, but their leaders had lost the ability to effectively coordinate their actions for fear that one ethnic component of the army might outshine another. The Battle of Shembra Kure is likely the first time Ethiopian forces faced an adversary equipped with firearms. However, other factors account for their defeat. Low morale, overconfidence in the Ethiopian ranks, and the determination shown by Imam Gurey's elite *Malassy* cavalry are more compelling reasons for the Muslim victory than their possession of firearms. Gunpowder weapons would play a more important role in this war's outcome in later years, but at Shembra Kure, other factors were at play.

In the two centuries since Amda Seyon's military reorganisation, the cavalry had been the pride and the elite arm of the Ethiopian army. Its destruction at Shembra Kure reduced King Lebne Dengel's ability to resist further incursions by Imam Gurey. He never recovered from this setback, and "the only decision he made and kept was never to face Ahmad again and risk being killed or captured".[26] Without his cavalry, he had no other choice.

Unfortunately for Imam Gurey, he was unable to exploit his victory immediately. His two infantry wings were composed of regular troops fielded by his subalterns and pastoral irregulars along for the *jihad*. Traditionally, "pastoralist hordes preferred surprise raids, hit and run attacks and day or night ambushes".[27] The Battle of Shembra Kure was not the type of fighting to which most Muslim troops were accustomed. Thus, the momentum gained by their spectacular victory was not exploited to the fullest, and many of Imam Gurey's troops went home. After this hard-won victory, the Imam returned to Adal.[28] Here he regrouped, assembled reinforcements, and motivated his commanders and troops for further *jihad*.

To an observer at the time in the immediate aftermath of Imam Gurey's victory at Shembra Kure, the battle might have appeared as the latest in the centuries-old struggle between the Christian Ethiopians of the highlands and the Muslim inhabitants of the lowland fringes to the south and east. Few would have suspected that Ethiopia would face a continued onslaught. Traditionally, Muslim forces would attack their Ethiopian rivals during Lent, when the Christians would be fasting and hence physically less able to withstand a military campaign's rigours.[29] Large battles between armies drawn up in formal battle lines were rare. Surprise attacks and ambushes were the usually preferred tactics of the lowland troops along the Ethiopian periphery, making the Ethiopian defeat at Shembra Kure even more shocking to King

25 Reid, *Warfare in African History*, p.54.
26 Aregay, 'Military Elites', p.56.
27 Aregay, 'Military Elites', p.53.
28 Edwards, 'Conquest of Abyssinia', p.333.
29 Aregay, 'Military Elites', p.53.

Lebne Dengel. Christian forces in Ethiopia had suffered their worst defeat in recorded history at their Muslim neighbours' hands. Muslim fortunes were on the rise elsewhere against Christian adversaries: while Imam Gurey was celebrating his victory at the Battle of Shembra Kure, a large Ottoman army was at the gates of Vienna, threatening the very heart of Christian Europe.

Having won a complete victory over his Ethiopian adversary, Imam Gurey could not keep his troops focused on continuing the advance into Christian territory. Many of his captains and their men were content to load up their loot and return home. He would need an army that was willing to do more the just seek revenge for the campaigns waged by Ethiopian kings such as Amda Seyon and Zara Yaqob against the lowland Muslim states. While his elite *Malassy* troops were loyal to him, he would need to ensure that the entire army maintained a higher standard of loyalty, similar to the *Malassy*, putting the difficult demands of *jihad* and permanent conquest over that of plunder and short-term gain.

Shortly after the victory at Shembra Kure, Imam Gurey and 30 of his *Malassy* horsemen were separated from the main Muslim army. The *Futuh Al-Habaša* does not give an exact location or date for the events which follow. Still, Arab Faqih wrote that upon reaching a river where they stopped to water their horses, this small group spotted a large detachment of the Ethiopian army. Sensing that they were trapped, Imam Gurey and his companions "were convinced that their Judgment and their Resurrection would occur in this place".[30] Facing over 600 Ethiopian cavalry and a larger force of infantry, Imam Gurey led his small force valiantly. For a few hours, the Muslims engaged in hand-to-hand combat against overwhelming odds, and as with any of the battles in this war, violence was the order of the day. One of Gurey's horsemen dealt an Ethiopian commander a fatal blow, which "severed his head from his body", and according to Arab Faqih, "God thrust his soul into Hell."[31] At the end of the battle Imam Gurey's troops held their ground, routing the Ethiopian force, led by Ras Baniyat. After this victory, clearly brought about by Allah's good graces, Imam Gurey "resolved to settle down in the land of Abyssinia [Ethiopia] and conquer it."[32] Ras Baniyat had tried to overwhelm Imam Gurey's small force, but instead he provided a catalyst for Gurey's further conquest into Ethiopia, leading to the Imam's determination to exterminate the Christian kingdom in the Ethiopian highlands. His troops were not quite ready for such an expedition, and the main Muslim army had already returned home laden with horses, gold, slaves, and other booty in tremendous quantity.

Now determined to subdue all of Ethiopia, Imam Gurey replenished the army's supplies, which he could easily acquire from the port city of Zeila. Further excursions into Bali and Dawaro occupied his army throughout 1530 and 1531. The campaign against the province of Bali netted more slaves, many of whom were pressed into service in the Muslim army,

30 Šihab ad-Din, *Futuh Al-Habaša*, p.97.
31 Šihab ad-Din, *Futuh Al-Habaša*, p.97.
32 Šihab ad-Din, *Futuh Al-Habaša*, p.100.

which included the elite *Malassy* cavalry, and 12,000 infantry.[33] Following many days of pillaging and burning, the province of Bali and Dawaro were reduced to ashes. After subjugating these provinces and removing them from Ethiopia's control, Gurey's army stood prepared to launch a seventh *jihad* (according to Arab Faqih's count) into Ethiopia proper. Boasting seven new cannons and a reinforced contingent of Somali foot soldiers, Gurey marched to the north, intent on destroying Lebne Dengel's army. The path to the Ethiopian highlands was open to the marauding Adal forces, and numerous monasteries and religious sites were pillaged and destroyed.

The Battle of Antukyah

Imam Gurey marched northwards into the Ethiopian highlands, determined to completely subjugate Christian Ethiopia. He broke from the tradition of raiding by embarking on a prolonged campaign, the objective of which was to integrate Ethiopia into the community of Muslim nations known as the *Dar al-Islam*. From 1531 onwards, Imam Gurey's army would be composed of more than just his elite *Malassy* cavalry and the Somali and Harla tribal soldiers from Adal. He would be reinforced with infantry and cavalry from throughout the Horn of Africa region and beyond. His army was joined by troops and individual soldiers from Arabia, including Mahra, and from other parts of the Islamic world from as far away as Morocco.[34]

Learning that the Muslim army was entering Ethiopia, Lebne Dengel ordered a ditch to be built close to the border with Dawaro. This somewhat unrealistic move failed to slow Imam Gurey, and at Antukyah in February 1531, an Ethiopian army under the command of Eslamu manoeuvred to block Imam Gurey's northward advance. Arab Faqih claimed that Eslamu had assembled 6,000 cavalry and 100,000 infantry, outnumbering Imam Gurey by 8 to 1.

Eslamu was confident that he would lead his army to victory over Imam Gurey's invasion force, stemming the tide of this powerful onslaught and restoring Christianity to the subjugated southern provinces such as Bali. Eslamu's force was composed of many Christian warriors from Bali who had fled from Imam Gurey's troops after Bali was overwhelmed, its people given the choice of converting to Islam or perishing. These determined warriors gave Eslamu hope that a great victory was at hand. Imam Gurey's cavalry scouted out the Ethiopian positions at Antukyah, revealing that Eslamu had concealed a portion of his force on a hill to the east of his main force at Antukyah. This Ethiopian flanking force was commanded by Abit, an Ethiopian general described by Arab Faqih as "a tyrant" who wrote a letter to Imam Gurey after the battle of Shembra Kure which read in part "battle is a matter of give and take … God was guiding you at the battle of Shembra

33 Edwards, 'Conquest of Abyssinia', p.335.

34 Amélie Chekroun and Bertrand Hirsch, 'The Muslim-Christian Wars and the Oromo Expansion: Transformations at the End of the Middle Ages (*c*. 1500–*c*. 1560)'. In S. Kelly (ed.), *Companion to Medieval Ethiopia and Eritrea*, 2020, p.336.

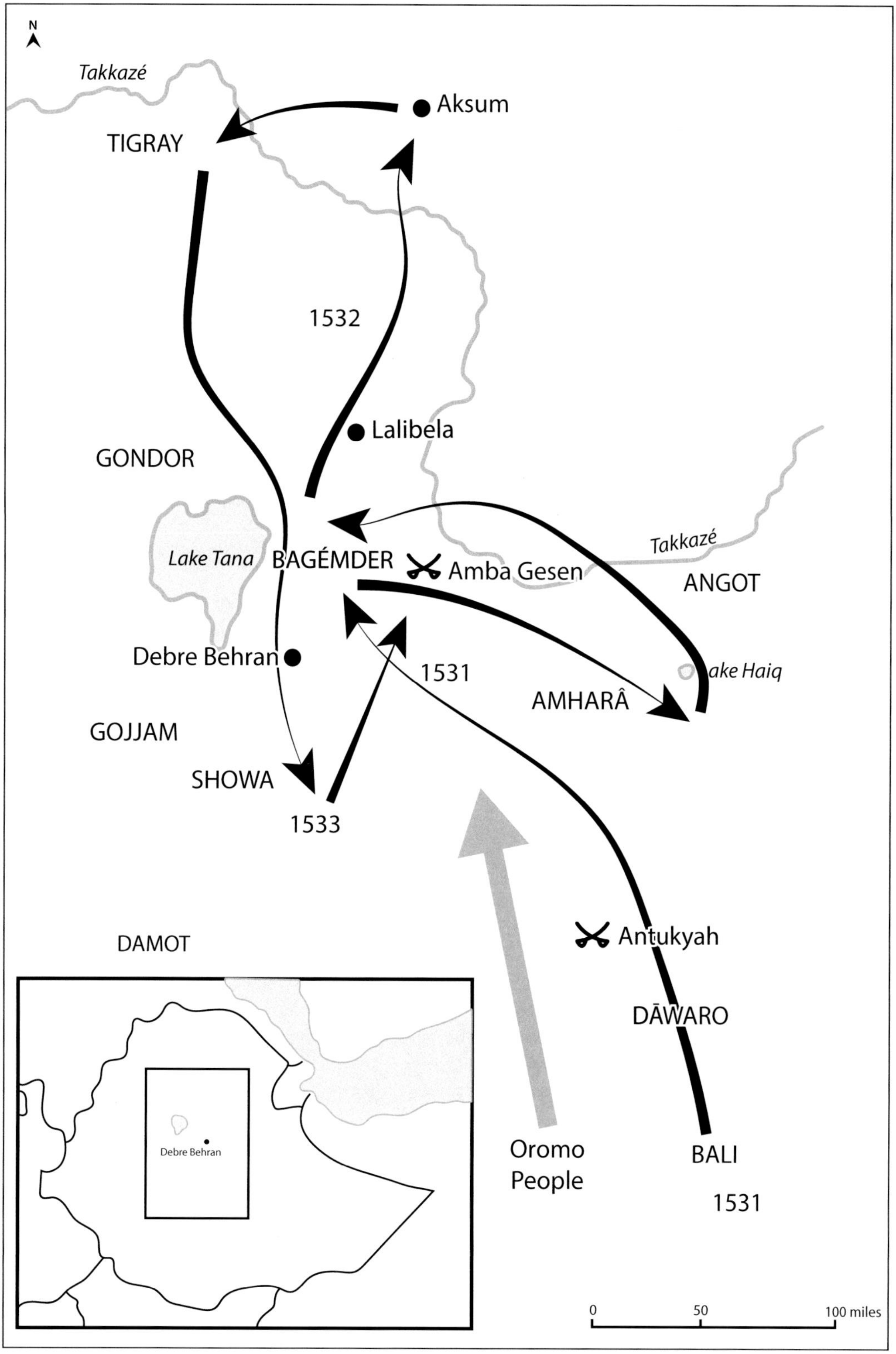

Gurey's campaign to subjugate the Ethiopian highlands between 1531 and 1533. This map was created by Dr Amélie Chekroun, 2013, but is modified to show only the main avenues of advance into the Ethiopian highlands.

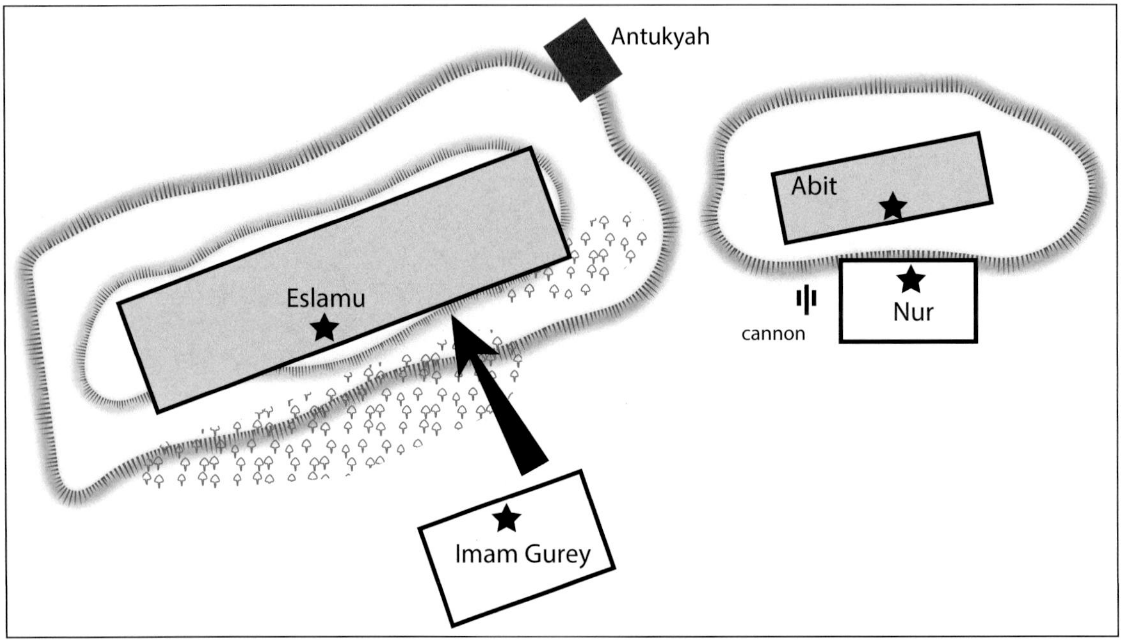

The Battle of Antukyah. Ethiopian generals Eslamu and Abit established strong defensive positions in mountainous terrain but could not hold their ground against Imam Gurey's motivated troops, who employed a single cannon to great effect.

Kure when you killed our men and scattered our heroes. Now leave us. Be content with what you have done to us, otherwise God will destroy you as he destroyed the village of Lot. Do not give in to vanity."[35] Imam Gurey may have been amused by Abit's letter, but at Antukyah, it appeared that Abit was prepared to make the Imam pay for his vanity.

In order to avoid falling into Eslamu's trap and allowing Abit's concealed force to threaten his right flank, Imam Gurey sent one of his own sub-commanders named Nur with a force to confront Abit head-on. Battle was joined, and a general engagement lasted throughout the morning and into midday. Arab Faqih recorded that after Imam Gurey pitched his tent, "sometimes it was the Muslims who charged against the idol-worshippers [the Ethiopians] and other times it was the idol-worshippers who charged against the Muslims. And this went on tirelessly until the end of the time for the afternoon prayer."[36] The Ethiopian troops from Bali were noted on that day as having displayed remarkable courage and resilience. Repeatedly charging Nur's force, the Balians "fell upon them from above and pushed them as far as where the Imam was".[37] Imam Gurey ordered his troops not to advance against the Balians, and for a few hours, the fighting died down. Instead of continuing to try to ascend the mountain and engage the troops from Bali directly, Imam Gurey called forth one of his cannons. The cannon was manned by troops from Mahra on the Arabian peninsula who had joined Imam Gurey's army only a few months earlier.[38]

35 Šihab ad-Din, *Futuh Al-Habaša*, p.133.
36 Šihab ad-Din, *Futuh Al-Habaša*, p.135.
37 Šihab ad-Din, *Futuh Al-Habaša*, p.135.
38 Aregay, 'A Reappraisal', p.111.

The terrain gradually rising into the highlands, close to the likely site of the Battle of Antukyah. (Author's photo)

Advancing against the Balian positions, the cannon and a small group of selected cavalrymen, accompanied by some Moroccan archers who also had joined the *jihad*, drove the Balians from the heights. Seeing Abit's flanking force fleeing the field, Imam Gurey's main army advanced against Eslamu. Arab Faqih described the violence and the courage which characterised the fighting:

> As for what happened to Hussain al-Gaturi, who was among those who charged the [Ethiopians]: when he did so they overwhelmed him, and surrounded him. Finding him in their midst, they pelted him with javelins, and threw three javelins at his horse which fell with him, and they hamstrung it. They struck him in the right thigh with a spearhead which emerged from the other side. The spearhead fell out. He returned safely to his companions, and recovered. Darkness separated the two groups and each returned to his own place. The Imam went back to his tent, and [the Muslims] rejoiced at the victory.[39]

Arab Faqih wrote that the Muslims employed only a single cannon at Antukyah. Was this enough to force nearly 100,000 Ethiopian warriors out of their hilltop positions? Or did Ethiopian morale collapse throughout the day? Perhaps a general strategic paralysis infused the highest levels of command in the Ethiopian army, starting with King Lebne Dengel himself, who was still in hiding during the Battle of Antukyah. Whatever the cause of the Ethiopian retreat from their commanding positions at Antukyah, nothing is known of what Lebne Dengel did with his small arsenal of firearms which he had accumulated since the early 1520s. It is likely that "either from the lack of balls, powder or shooters, they were not used anywhere".[40] Lebne Dengel's reliance upon foreign craftsmen for court luxuries may have come at the expense of bringing trained gunsmiths to Ethiopia in the early years of his reign. Imam Gurey had taken the time to integrate gunpowder weapons into his arsenal. Even a single cannon had an impact at Antukyah. Eslamu's force was dispersed, and Christian casualties during and after their retreat reached

39 Šihab ad-Din, *Futuh Al-Habaša*, p.137.

40 Aregay, 'A Reappraisal', p.111.

nearly the same level as those suffered at Shembra Kure.[41] At Antukyah, gunpowder weapons had proven to be a decisive addition to Gurey's army.

Continuing his pursuit of the Ethiopian king and his army, Imam Gurey moved north-west into the highlands. On 20 April 1531 Adal troops burnt down the city of Debra Berhan, the city in which Ethiopian king Zara Yaqob had built his personal residence over 100 years earlier, in an act of retribution that must have satisfied the lowland warriors whose ancestors had suffered humiliating defeats centuries earlier at the hands of Zara Yaqob and Amda Seyon.[42] In July Gurey sent a force of 300 horsemen to Debra Libanos, one of Ethiopia's holiest sites, and Gurey's mother's destination when she accompanied the tribute delivery party into Ethiopia years earlier, at least according to the Ethiopian account of his youth. The monks and worshippers tried to dissuade the Muslims from burning the church and monastery, but they were unsuccessful. One of their holiest churches in flames, "the monks emulated one another in throwing themselves into the fire, like moths against a lamp".[43] Many other churches, monasteries, and monks would meet a similar fate in the coming months.

Following their defeat at Antukyah, and in the weeks and months that followed as Ethiopian forces continued to retreat throughout the countryside, the Ethiopians abandoned eight small cannons, even though they were not actively pursued by Muslim forces.[44] This inexplicable act further reinforces the idea that either the Ethiopians lacked the supplies or the training to operate the cannons effectively, or perhaps their morale was so low that they

The terrain in the vicinity of Amba Gesen in the province of Begemeder. The small village would have looked the same in 1531 as it does in this picture. It is not surprising that the retreating Ethiopian army would have abandoned its cannons. Carrying heavy artillery pieces and cannonballs would not be an appealing prospect in mountains such as this. (Photo by Jean-Claude Latombe)

41 Edwards, 'Conquest of Abyssinia', p.336.
42 Molvaer, 'The Tragedy of Emperor Libne-Dingil', p.30.
43 Edwards, 'Conquest of Abyssinia', p.339.
44 Aregay, 'A Reappraisal', p.111.

did not think the cannons would help turn the tide against Imam Gurey's forces. With their morale well past the point of collapse, Lebne Dengel's beleaguered Ethiopian army was in no condition to stand and fight anywhere.

The Battle of Amba Gesen

After taking control of most of southern Ethiopia and establishing Muslim governors in each of the provinces, Imam Gurey prepared to complete Ethiopia's conquest and finally deliver the land and its people into the *Dar al-Islam*. Advancing to the north-west after their victory at Antukyah, the Muslim army learned that the Ethiopian royal family and much treasure was hidden away in a hilltop fortress and church known as Amba Gesen in the province of Begemeder. On about 23 November 1531, a few days march ahead of Imam Gurey's main army, a Muslim captain named Garad Ahmusa led a small force up the steep slopes and caught the Ethiopian guards sleeping around their fires. These guards awoke and drove the Muslims back down the hillsides with rocks and stones. Once Imam Gurey learned of this setback, he decided to join Garad Ahmusa at Amba Gesen. This news reached Ethiopian king Lebne Dengel, and he hurriedly sent three generals with as many troops as he could muster to Amba Gesen. Only soldiers on foot could ascend the heights of the amba; horses and cannon were useless in this harsh terrain. A desperate struggle ensued, marked by bitter and determined resistance on the part of the defending Ethiopians. The lure of gold and treasure motivated Garad Ahmusa's force which was still waiting for Imam Gurey's main force to arrive. The fighting lasted throughout the day, at the end of which the Ethiopian force retreated. Sensing a chance to destroy the final remnants of the Ethiopian army, the Muslims pursued.

Battle was joined again as the pursuing Muslim forces caught the retreating Ethiopians. Again, the Ethiopians withdrew, only to be caught a second time. Twice more the Ethiopian relief force retreated, but it was a trick. Determined to stand and fight, on the fourth time that the armies clashed the Ethiopians overwhelmed Garad Ahmusa's army. The severed heads and captured horses were presented to King Lebne Dengel, who rejoiced that the sacred church at Amba Gesen had remained in Christian hands.[45] Amba Gesen was a rare Ethiopian victory, but it was not enough to compel Lebne Dengel to emerge from seclusion and rejoin the Ethiopian army in the field against Imam Gurey.

45 Edwards, 'Conquest of Abyssinia', pp.342–343.

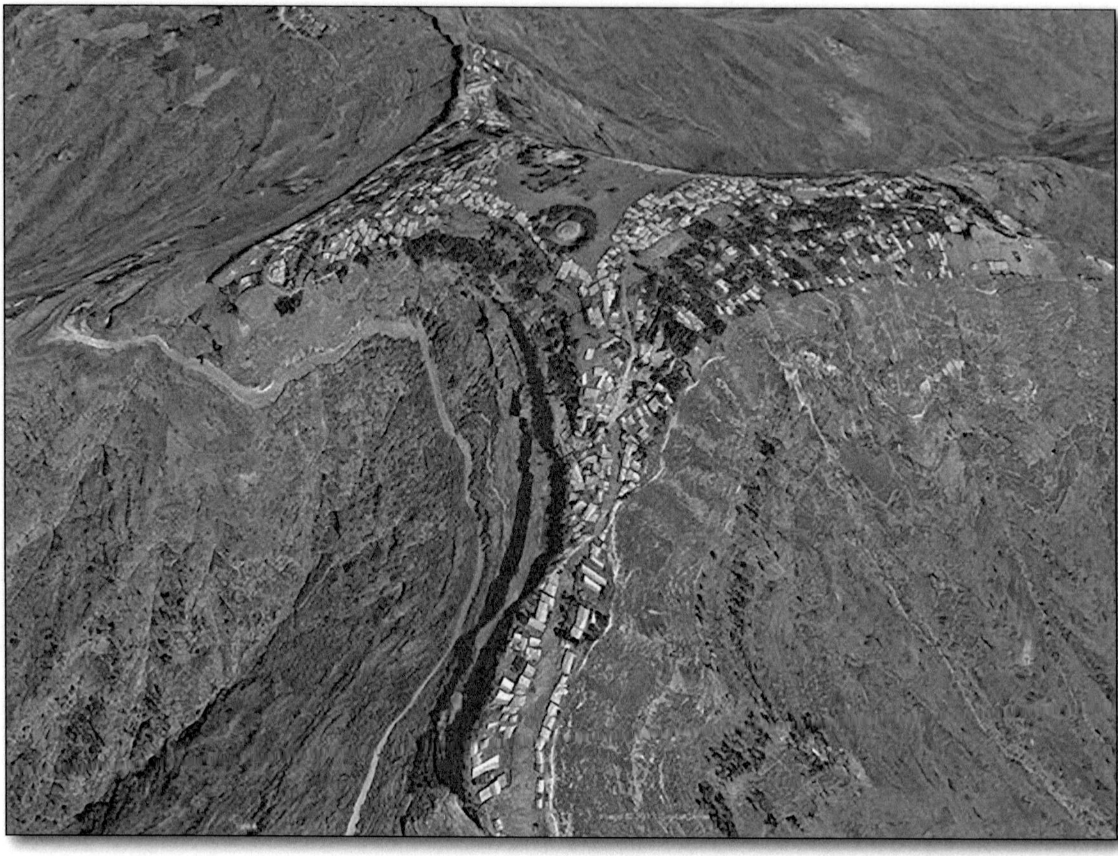

Aerial view of Amba Gesen. The cross-shaped mountain was chosen by King Zara Yaqob as a suitable location to store the True Cross. Its rugged hillsides provided strong defence against attack, and the Ethiopian defenders withstood attacks in 1531 and 1533. Imam Gurey finally captured it in 1537. (Photo by Jean-Claude Latombe)

The Conquest of the Highlands

Throughout 1532, Imam Gurey's forces:

> came again, and on the 7 November, he burnt down [a church] where there were 300 (church) scholars. On the 8 November he burnt down Gennete-Gïyorgïs. On 10 November he burnt down the main church of Abune (Bishop) Gebre-Mariyam. On 11 November, he burnt down Debre-Dimah, the monastery of Abba Anbessa. On 12 November, he burnt down Debre-Gelïla, the main church of the Icchegé, where there were 450. On 15 November he burnt down Mekane-Sillasé, the main church of the King. On 17 November, he burnt down Welde-Negodgwad. On 21 November, he burnt down Debre-Kïrubél. On the 23 November, he burnt down Atronse-Mariyam. On 24 November, he burnt down Gol, the main church of Abba Beselote-Mïkaél, the Icchegé. On 25 November, he burnt down the church of Mariyam at Éndros. On 28 November, he burnt down Ta'ika-Mengist, and on 29 November Debre-Sirha-Mariyam. Debre-Sirha-Mariyam had a [monastic] community of 640. Many clergy died. One hundred one monks took the tabot (sacred altarpiece) 45 and the holy vessels and vestments ("holy property" of a church) and ran (or were chased) away.[46]

46 Molvaer, 'The Tragedy of Emperor Libne-Dingil', p.31.

Lalibela and its 11 rock-hewn churches lay in the path of Imam Gurey's northward advance. Whether or not it was actually plundered is a matter of historical debate. Arab Faqih does not describe an assault on the churches, but two centuries later, Scottish traveller James Bruce wrote that "the town was burnt, and with it many of the richest churches in Abyssinia - Hallelujah, Banquol, Gaso, Debra Kerbe, and many others."[47] Whether the churches were burnt or not, the looting and pillaging and the fact that the Muslim army lived off the land wherever they went in Ethiopia spoiled the landscape. Gurey's troops "seem to have been like a flight of locusts in the country, destroying everything, producing nothing. Their sojourn of a year in Tigray so impoverished the country that their provisions were exhausted."[48] Lebne Dengel remained unwilling to face Imam Gurey in open battle, and so the depredations continued unabated.

While pursuing remnants of the Ethiopian army, Imam Gurey's forces captured Lebne Dengel's son Minas, and his two cousins. Expressing empathy and compassion, Imam Gurey's wife, Bati Del Wanbara, insisted that Minas be spared from execution. Unlike the savagery committed by both sides in this war over the last few years, she displayed a degree of compassion, which resulted in Minas being sold into slavery, a rare instance of good fortune. The cousins were made into eunuchs, not executed, although perhaps they would have preferred to have been. Both Christian and Muslim accounts at the time attest to Bati Del Wanbara's kindness.[49]

By the end of 1532 Imam Gurey established his camp at Debra Berhan in Showa, which became the centre of his new power. As news of Imam Gurey's conquest spread, Christians in Rome, according to an English account, printed the following notice about Ethiopia:

> Not without reason do we weep, when we call to mind the Captivity of our Brethren, our country laid waste, Our Temples Burnt, Our Books and Our Sanctuaries consum'd with Fire, and the profanation of our Monasteries by that wicked and impious Grainus, a Companion for Goats, a Persecutor and invader of the Sheep, from Wagaci, to the Red Sea.[50]

European Christians learned of Lebne Dengel's plight (in their mind he was still Prester John), but they could do little to save him. Imam Gurey had nearly achieved complete victory over his Ethiopian Christian foes, although unbeknown to him at the time, the plea to come to the aid of Ethiopia's persecuted and oppressed people would be answered over the course of the next few years.

In the early spring of 1533, Imam Gurey again decided to capture Amba Gesen. Having failed to do so two years earlier, his forces and commanders were ready to adapt their tactics in order to finally capture the royal family

47 James Bruce, *Travels to Discover the Source of the Nile: In the Years 1768, 1769, 1770, 1771, 1772, and 1773* (London: Ruthven, 1790), p.164.

48 Edwards, 'Conquest of Abyssinia', p.352.

49 Whiteway, *Portuguese Expedition to Abyssinia*, p.xxxiv.

50 Ludolphus, *A New History of Ethiopia*, p.221.

and the enormous treasures stored in the churches atop the amba. The mountain could only be ascended by means of ladders, and once these were in place the Muslim army laid siege to Amba Gesen throughout May and June of 1533. The first line of Ethiopian entrenchment was captured, followed the next day by the fall of the second line of forts which ringed the rising terrain. A large iron cannon and two smaller cannons were employed against the fortifications remaining between Imam Gurey's army and the top of the amba. These cannons were manned by Gujarati troops from India. Imam Gurey encouraged his troops forward as they attacked the last Ethiopian forts on Amba Gesen. However, King Lebne Dengel had positioned a cannon atop Amba Gesen, along with troops from the far northern province of Tigray. The cannon was manned by Arab mercenaries who had been taken in by the Ethiopian army, perhaps by choice, or perhaps as prisoners. Arab Faqih recalled the names of these two apostates, writing that "one was called Hasan al-Basri, and the other was Abd Asfar Turki. They used to recite the Quran, but then they apostatised and became Christians. May God curse them."[51] Amba Gesen was thus defended not only by troops and priests hurling stones from the heights but by cannons and matchlock muskets.[52] With gunpowder weapons deployed by both sides for the first time in the war, "the fighting lasted the whole day; stones and rocks fell on the [Muslims] like hail, though, we are told, none of them was hit. At last, realizing that the place was not to be captured, the Imam ordered his men to give up the siege, and his army withdrew to Angot."[53] The Ethiopians had again prevailed at Amba Gesen.

In less than two years, between 1531 and 1533, Imam Gurey's army had subjugated the southern provinces such as Bali and Fatagar, the provinces of Begemeder, Amhara, and Tigray, and the coastal region in present-day Eritrea. By the end of 1537, Muslims controlled a large majority of the Christian territory, including a number of key regions.[54] However, by 1538 Imam Gurey's army began to decline in fighting strength and motivation. Several of his leading generals had died in the battles since Shembra Kure. Of greater consequence were a plague and famine in Tigray in 1539, "which wiped out over half of the forces with which he had started the invasion."[55] Having campaigned for over a decade, Imam Gurey's army was a shadow of its former self. Almost all his soldiers were captured Ethiopians, and thus Christian converts to Islam. The only remaining Muslims were his wife Bati Del Wanbara, "some of his *Malassy* companions and their sons, and the 40 Ottoman mercenaries who were left out of the 200 that had deserted sometime after Shimbra Kure."[56] Most of his Somali, Afari, and other foot soldiers from the lowlands had returned home, likely thinking that their *jihad* was successfully concluded. Others perhaps lost their motivation for

51 Šihab ad-Din, *Futuh Al-Habaša*, p.180. Paul Stenhouse, in note 775 on page 180, notes that one of the apostates was likely from Basra, the other a Turk.

52 Aregay, 'A Reappraisal', p.111.

53 Edwards, 'Conquest of Abyssinia', pp.345–346.

54 Amélie Chekroun and Bertrand Hirsch, 'The Muslim-Christian Wars and the Oromo Expansion', p.337.

55 Hassen, 'The Oromo of Ethiopia', p.35.

56 Aregay, 'Military Elites', p.56.

further *jihad*. While many Christian Ethiopians fought in Gurey's army, when he advanced into Tigray and threatened the holy city of Aksum, two "Turks" who had left Gurey's army and converted to Christianity "helped the Ethiopians acquire muskets and cannons" which allowed the defenders of Amba Gesen and the churches of Aksum to put up stiff resistance.[57] It was not enough, and Gurey's army of former Ethiopian Christians destroyed the ancient church of St Mary of Zion, along with most of the rest of the city. The church of St Mary of Zion had been built in 372 AD and was one of the earliest Christian churches in all of sub-Saharan Africa. Contained inside its sacred space was the Ark of the Covenant, which Ethiopian Christians believe had been brought to Ethiopia over 1,000 years earlier. The Ark is said to have been saved from destruction and was moved to a different location within Ethiopia just before Imam Gurey's army destroyed the church.[58]

In 1539, as the conquest of Ethiopia seemed to be nearing completion, the eldest son of Lebne Dengel and Sabla Wengel, Fiqtor, was killed.[59] As a result, Lebne Dengel's second son, Gelawdewos, would eventually succeed to the throne unless he too was found and killed.

An unintended result of the fighting and the destruction of the Ethiopian military was the Oromo people's great migration into the Ethiopian highlands.[60] Traditionally opposed by the Ethiopian army's full might, once this army was shattered and dispersed, the Oromo began to settle into formerly Christian provinces. Regardless of the outcome of Imam Gurey's invasion, the Oromo's presence would permanently change the nature of the Ethiopian state. While Imam Gurey struggled to maintain a disciplined fighting force, it appeared that his goal of conquering Ethiopia had been achieved. Arab Faqih's *Futuh Al-Habaša,* his account of the conquest of Abyssinia, ends with Imam Gurey comfortably established along Lake Tana's shores. A suitable place to end the history, Faqih himself probably believed that Christian Ethiopia had been wiped from the map, subjugated, and converted to Islam for perpetuity.

Prisoners, Slaves, and Cross-Cultural Diffusion

Throughout the first decade of the Ethiopian–Adal War, tens of thousands of Ethiopian soldiers were captured, as were many Ethiopian citizens, whether farmers, artisans, or women and children. Many of the Ethiopian slaves were sold in Arabia and India, leading to an exodus of Christians from Ethiopia. Thousands of other Christians converted to Islam in the wake of Imam Gurey's campaign. Most likely, Lebne Dengel's heavy-handed reign did little to endear Christians to their faith or their homeland, so when presented with the option of Islam or death, the choice was an easy one. Converting

57 Henze, *Layers of Time*, p.87.

58 Enrico Bossi, *Habesha and Ferengi* (Il Mio Libro, 2020), p.83.

59 Rita Pankhurst, 'Tayitu foremothers: Queen Eleni, Queen Sabla Wengel and Bati Del Wanbara', p.56.

60 Henze, *Layers of Time*, p.90.

from Christianity to Islam, and vice versa, was a common feature of the wars fought in the Horn of Africa. Muslim deserters and warrior captives could be absorbed into the Ethiopian regimental system described earlier, and "Christian deserters and prisoners of war could also be easily integrated into the Muslim military and social system. There was no limit to the burden that could be imposed on the peasant of either society."[61] Christian Ethiopians captured by Muslim forces could be found throughout Arabia, India, and even on the battlefields in Ethiopia, fighting against their fellow Christians as soldiers in Imam Gurey's army of *jihad*. Likewise, as previously noted, Arabs served in the Ethiopian Christian army, most notably at Amba Gesen in 1533, where they manned the Ethiopian cannon.

Italian adventurer Ludovico de Varthema described his stay in Yemen in the early sixteenth century, witnessing the army of one Muslim sultan who was preparing to attack a neighbouring province. He wrote:

> Two days afterwards, the Sultan took the field, and marched to the said city Sana with his army, in which there were three thousand horsemen, sons of Christians, as black as Moors. They were of those of Prester John, whom they purchased at the age of eight or nine years, and had them trained to arms. These constituted his own guard, because they were worth more than all the rest of the eighty thousand.[62]

According to this account, some of the best soldiers in the Arabian armies were Christian prisoners of war and slaves from Christian Ethiopia, belonging to "Prester John". Towards the end of the Ethiopian–Adal War, Christian converts to Islam formed the bulk of Imam Gurey's conquering army.

Seeking various types of expertise from other nations and people of other cultures and faiths was common in the fifteenth and sixteenth centuries, as it is today. Ethiopian king Lebna Dengel requested many different types of artisans, including weapons-makers, metallurgists, and other craftsmen. However, he was eager to acquire artisans whose skills were less vital and could make figurines for the royal court and decorate objects with gold leaf, such as goldsmiths. These requests were not motivated by any desire to gain a technological military edge or interest in foreign technology per se but by the wish to employ artisans in producing objects for courtly display. Ethiopia's court was lavishly decorated by many of these artisans, but the level of Ethiopian military technology seems not to have been advanced by their contacts with foreign merchants.[63] Perhaps the fact that Amda Seyon had created such a powerful military machine allowed his successors to focus on luxury items rather than enhancing the power of the military any further.

Ethiopians served in Imam Gurey's army in large numbers, but we should keep in mind that this practice was not unique to Ethiopians, and it should not be seen as a lack of dedication to their country or their faith. Even as

61 Aregay, 'Military Elites', pp.52–53.

62 De Varthema, *The Travels of Ludovico Di Varthema*, pp.63–64.

63 Marilyn E. Heldman, 'A Chalice from Venice for Emperor Dāwit of Ethiopia', *Bulletin of the School of Oriental and African Studies*, Vol. 53, No. 3 (1990), p.445.

Ottoman armies threatened the very heart of Christian Europe, "there were numerous French, Venetian, Genoese, Spanish, Sicilian, English, German, Hungarian, and Slavic experts working at the Ottoman cannon foundries", and "a considerable number of Christian smiths, stone carvers, masons, caulkers, and shipbuilders served in Ottoman Balkan fortresses".[64] Crusading zeal and hatred of Islam did not exist in the hearts of all Christian people. The employment of foreign military technicians and artisans does not necessarily indicate that the Ottomans were technologically inferior since this was a well-established practice worldwide. Most of the Ottomans' gunners and artillerists in their campaigns against the Christian Hungarians were of German and Italian origin. In the sixteenth century, like the Ethiopian kings and the Ottoman sultan, Spanish monarchs repeatedly employed Italian, German, and Flemish cannon founders, and "the lack of skilled workers was a significant problem for the Portuguese war industry as well, and even England lacked sufficient native gun founders".[65] Economic opportunity was the order of the day, as was the ability to make a profit. The idea that European technology was always superior to that of other cultures or that the Ottomans, the Indians, and the Arabs sought European weapons is largely unproven by the historical record. For example, in 1513:

> Albuquerque reported to the [Portuguese] king that the Muslim gunsmiths ... were capable of turning out iron cannon and matchlocks of a higher quality than anything produced in Germany, then considered the source of Europe's finest guns. From this point on, a tradition of German and Bohemian gun making that had been brought to India by the Portuguese seems to have merged with Turkish gun-making traditions already present in [India], producing what has been called an "Indo-Portuguese" tradition of matchlocks.[66]

While slaves made up a sizeable percentage of the soldiers fighting one another in Africa and India, many ships were also manned by sailors who were prisoners, captives, converts, or slaves. A record of the expenses incurred during the voyage of a Portuguese vessel by the name of *Santa Maria do Monte*, which sailed from Goa to Oman and Hormuz and back in the early 1520s, provides a picture of the amazing melting pot of peoples, ethnic groups, and religions in the early sixteenth century. Whilst it was a Portuguese vessel:

> its ledger clearly indicates that the European members were in a minority. Only 7% of the permanent crew were of European descent ... As the list makes plain, the crew was multi-ethnic and predominantly Muslim from a variety of

64 Gábor Ágoston, 'Behind the Turkish War Machine: Gunpowder, Technology, and War Industry in the Ottoman Empire, 1450–1700', in *The Heirs of Archimedes: Science and the Art of War through the Age of the Enlightenment*, Brett Steele and Tamara Dorland (eds) (Cambridge, MA: MIT Press, 2005), p.107.

65 Ágoston, 'Behind the Turkish War Machine', pp.106–107.

66 Richard M. Eaton, '"Kiss My Foot," Said the King: Firearms, Diplomacy, and the Battle for Raichur, 1520', *Modern Asian Studies*, Vol. 43, No. 1, *Expanding Frontiers in South Asian and World History: Essays in Honour of John F. Richards* (Jan 2009), p.298.

> locations throughout the western Indian Ocean, including the Arabian Peninsula, the Persian and Makran coastlines, and the west coast of India, as far south as Malabar, and East Africa. The crew also included a Florentine captain, Portuguese clerks, and the East African Christian wives of Portuguese agents.[67]

This diversity reflects the cosmopolitanism found in African, Arabian, and Indian Ocean ports such as Aden, Zeila, Massawa, Goa, Hormuz, and Cochin in the sixteenth century. It illustrates the many motives pursued not only by kings and sultans but also to which individuals aspired, often in opposition to the religious customs, values, and beliefs of their homelands and ethnic groups.

Coastal forts stretching from the Cape of Good Hope, up the eastern coast of Africa to Mombasa, and across the Indian Ocean to the *Estado da India* were the Portuguese Empire's backbone. Lacking the manpower to establish a presence in either Africa or India, the Portuguese were forced "to rely on a variety of local individuals and materials, particularly in Asia, in order to achieve their goals."[68] This reliance took the form of integrating non-Portuguese and non-Christians into the fleet and the army. Further illustrating the extent to which individuals laboured on behalf of what would commonly be perceived as the enemy, an examination of the ethnicity of the infamous Barbary Corsairs in the 1580s, albeit a generation after the end of the Ethiopian–Adal War, reveals that it was not only the Portuguese who benefitted from employing sailors from other kingdoms and cultures. Of the corsair captains and crews in Algiers in 1581, home to the pirates who were the scourge of Christendom:

> Out of 35, only 10 were Turks; 3 were sons of renegades and the remaining 22, renegades: one Hungarian, two Albanians, one French, three Greeks, six Genoese, two Spaniards … two Venetians, one Corsican, one Sicilian, and one Neapolitan. The Admiral himself, in this period, was a renegade from [Spain].[69]

The Ottoman Empire also deployed entire legions of Christian soldiers, known as the Janissary corps. The Janissary were modelled after the Byzantine Empire's legions, which were the mighty Roman legions' successors. Some scholars believe that Janissaries were probably recruited "not from the Christian tribute children, but from war prisoners".[70] However, others assert that:

---

67 Abdul Rahman al-Salimi and Eric Staples, 'Reflections of a Muslim-Portuguese maritime world in a sixteenth-century Portuguese source', *Proceedings of the Seminar for Arabian Studies*, Vol. 45, Papers from the forty-eighth meeting of the Seminar for Arabian Studies held at the British Museum, London, 25 to 27 July 2014 (2015), p.323.

68 al-Salimi and Staples, 'Reflections of a Muslim-Portuguese maritime world', p.325.

69 Henry and Renée Kahane, and Andreas Tietze, *The Lingua Franca in the Levant: Turkish Nautical Terms of Italian and Greek Origin* (Urbana, IL: University of Illinois Press, 1958), p.20.

70 William L. Langer and Robert P. Blake, 'The Rise of the Ottoman Turks and Its Historical Background', *The American Historical Review*, 37, No. 3 (Apr 1932), p.504.

> at some time between the years 1380 and 1390 a levy of Christian male children, from 8 to 15 years old, called the *dev irme*, was inaugurated. Approximately every three to five years after the initial conquest the Christian territories of the Balkans were visited to collect one boy from every 40 families. At its peak, under this system these children were brought to Constantinople, trained in the palace schools, and the majority of them relegated to the fighting troops that came to be known as the New Troops (*Yeni-Çeri*), the Janissaries.[71]

All the major powers in the sixteenth century employed soldiers and sailors impressed into service either from the pool of captured prisoners of war or from individuals who, for whatever reason, chose to fight under the banner of their former adversary. There was nothing uncommon about this practice, and the sympathies of modern patriotism and loyalty to country or faith should not prejudice our views of this phenomenon.

71 Virginia Aksan, 'Ottoman War and Warfare 1453–1812', 147–177. In Jeremy Black (ed.), *War in the Early Modern World* (London: Routledge, 1999), p.150.

Chapter 4

The Geopolitical Situation in 1540

Ethiopian resistance to the Sultanate of Adal had virtually collapsed over the 11 years since the Battle of Shembra Kure. As Imam Gurey ordered mosques to be built along Lake Tana's shores in the Ethiopian highlands, competition among the great powers for supremacy in the Mediterranean, the Red Sea (including what today would be termed the Middle East), and the Indian Ocean was at fever pitch. The year 1540 is a suitable time to pause and examine the overall geopolitical situation.

It is far too simplistic to assert that religious divides were the primary cause of the many wars in the sixteenth century. Although Christian kingdoms and states fought against Islamic powers, the sixteenth century was not merely a continuation of the Crusades of some three to five centuries earlier. The complexity of the political alignments is bewildering, and economic factors are at the heart of the alliance structures. Just as access to trade routes motivated the Ethiopian campaigns against the lowland Muslim sultanates from the fourteenth century, access to trade routes and the pursuit of economic supremacy motivated the European powers and the Ottoman Empire. One must keep in mind that Europe at the time was a panoply of primarily small kingdoms and principalities, with only a few states resembling what we could consider modern nations. The struggle to survive in this fragmented political environment led to an unprecedented level of technological experimentation and development. In fact:

> Europe's geographic balkanisation resulted in dozens or hundreds of independent, competing statelets and centers of innovation. If one state did not pursue some particular innovation, another did, forcing neighboring states to do likewise or else be conquered or left economically behind. Europe's barriers were sufficient to prevent political unification, but insufficient to halt the spread of technology and ideas.[1]

1 Jared Diamond. *Guns, Germs and Steel* (New York: W.W. Norton & C., 1999), p.416.

France and Spain were the premier powers in this balkanised Europe in the early sixteenth century, with Portugal, the Netherlands, and England on the rise. Some smaller states, such as Venice, wielded considerable economic and military power but would have offered little resistance to the rising Ottoman Empire without aligning with other smaller countries or with one or more of the major powers. Technological innovations in the realm of military armaments and navigational instruments helped propel Portugal to the forefront of European powers. Portuguese expansion and voyages of discovery would put them on a collision course with the Ottoman Empire.

The Ottoman Empire

While European nations established overseas colonies and empires, the Ottomans were similarly carving out their domains in south-east Europe, the Mediterranean, and the modern Middle East to include the Arabian Peninsula. So extensive were Ottoman trade routes that when the Portuguese explorer Vasco da Gama landed in Mozambique after rounding the Cape of Good Hope in 1498, the local ruler in Mozambique thought he was a Turk.[2] As one of the leading world powers of the Renaissance era, the Ottoman Empire was fully engaged in peripheral conflicts during the sixteenth century. Founded by the Turkoman king Osman I (r. 1299-1323), the Ottomans consolidated their control over the Anatolian peninsula (modern-day Turkey) in the late thirteenth century. With a disciplined army and determined leadership, the Ottomans expanded east towards Persia and west into Europe, conquering the Byzantine Empire in 1453 with the capture of the ancient city of Constantinople, the capital of the Eastern Roman Empire. Europe's Christian kings and princes watched with trepidation as Constantinople fell, and the Christian kingdoms and principalities in the Balkans knew that they would face an Ottoman onslaught. Conquest was the central driving force of the Ottoman Empire. *Jihad* and holy war were coming to Europe, as the remnants of the Christian empire of Trebizond, in what is today north-east Turkey, were swept away in 1461. The Ottomans went to war "for the sake of God and not the thrill of conquest".[3] The borders of the Ottoman Empire would continue to expand over the following decades. But the driving force behind this expansion was not much different from that which compelled the Christian states of Europe to expand and conquer – the trinity of faith, profit, and power.

While European maritime technology was, for the most part, superior to that of the Ottomans and most other civilisations at the turn of the sixteenth century, the Ottomans maintained a crucial advantage over their adversaries, including the Christian Europeans, in the area of firearms. The Ottomans did not enjoy a considerable technological or numerical advantage over their

2 Cemalettin Taşkıran, 'The Ottoman-Portuguese relationship in the 16th century', *Insight Turkey*, October 1998, No. 21, p.109.

3 Andrew C. Hess, 'The Evolution of the Ottoman Seaborne Empire in the Age of the Oceanic Discoveries, 1453–1525', *The American Historical Review*, 75, No. 7 (Dec 1970), pp.1902.

adversaries from a maritime perspective. In 1503, the Ottoman navy could muster some 300 ships.[4] However, both the Ottoman fleet and the Portuguese fleet would face innumerable problems keeping supplies of ammunition stocked to necessary levels to facilitate the use of cannons and firearms. For instance, in 1517, Sultan Selim I chastised his naval commanders for wasting valuable ammunition on training voyages while the Ottomans were planning the siege of Rhodes.[5] The ability to keep ships supplied was a major challenge, and logistics would play a key role in the wars fought during this time. Whichever nation mastered the art of producing and moving weapons, food, and troops across large distances to the exact spot where they were needed would likely be victorious. The ability to do this would require a centralised command structure, something which the Ottomans had developed by the early sixteenth century. The Ottoman military was a hierarchical organisation, with the elite infantry at the top of the pyramid, followed by the cavalry. Much like the Ethiopian army, the Ottomans used a crescent-shaped formation, but with cavalry on the wings, elite infantry in the centre, the opposite of the Ethiopian formation, which placed cavalry in the middle between two large infantry wings. Between 1389 and 1453, "most of the elements which made up the Ottoman military battle formation and strength were forged into a formidable balance of infantry, cavalry and artillery, supported by a well-regulated system of supply, a century before similar institutions were effectively in place in Europe."[6] Facing the Ottomans in battle was a risky proposition in the early sixteenth century.

From a maritime technology standpoint, once the Ottomans gained possession of significant portions of the Aegean and Black Sea coastal areas, which contained experienced seafaring populations, the Ottoman navy received a boost in its ability to build, man, and deploy maritime assets. Even in cases when the newly acquired territory was predominantly Christian, Ottoman policy was such that religious differences were tolerated as long as those who could contribute to the Empire's well-being were willing to do so.[7] Wars against the Mamluks of Egypt, the Habsburgs in south-east Europe, and the Safavid Persians occupied the Ottomans throughout the first decades of the sixteenth century. Sultan Selim I (r. 1512–1520) set out to defend *Sunni* Islam against the *Shi'a* branch, leading ultimately to the rise of the Ottoman Empire as the leader of the Muslim world, placing Selim in the position of Caliph. Ottoman weaponry had proven to be the crucial factor in their ability to expand their empire and subdue their adversaries. For Selim to carry out his ambitious schemes, he needed to control the Persian Gulf and the Red Sea, meaning he would be forced to conquer either Safavid Persia or Mamluk Egypt.[8] He chose to conquer both.

---

4 Palmira Brummett, 'Foreign Policy, Naval Strategy, and the Defence of the Ottoman Empire in the Early Sixteenth Century', *The International History Review*, 11 (Nov 1989), p.623.

5 Palmira Brummett. 'The Ottomans as a World Power: What We Don't Know About Ottoman Seapower', *Oriente Moderno, Nuova serie*, Anno 20 (2001), p.13.

6 Aksan, 'Ottoman War and Warfare', p.150.

7 Hess, 'Evolution of the Ottoman Seaborne Empire', pp.1901.

8 M. Longworth Dames, 'The Portuguese and Turks in the Indian Ocean in the Sixteenth Century', *The Journal of the Royal Asiatic Society of Great Britain and Ireland*, 1 (Jan 1921), p.3.

In the early sixteenth century, Safavid Persia was a powerful empire with a capable and efficient military. Persia was less of a threat to Europe, and so the Safavids do not appear in the historical memory with the same intensity as the Ottoman Turks.[9] In 1514 the Ottoman deployment of artillery against the Persians at the Battle of Chāldirān led the Ottomans to victory; however, fighting between the Ottomans and the Safavids continued. A decades-long contest between the Ottomans and the Persians ensued for control of eastern Anatolia and the province now known as Iraq. While still fighting against the Persians, Selim turned towards the Mamluk Sultans in Egypt. A driving factor behind the Ottoman decision to conquer Egypt was that the Portuguese had been at war with the Egyptians since 1505. Portuguese victory over the Mamluks, and the consequent Portuguese presence in Suez, would be a major setback to Ottoman plans for expansion in the region. The Ottoman–Mamluk War was a savage affair, ending with the complete overthrow of the Mamluks and Ottoman control over Egypt firmly established. Victory over the Egyptian Mamluks solidified the Ottoman position as leader of the *Sunni* Muslim world. The economic and financial benefits which the Ottomans achieved by conquering Egypt and expanding the Ottoman Empire south along the fertile shores of the Nile "resulted in direct financial benefits that served to fuel further military expeditions".[10] The Ottomans inherited the Egyptian navy after the Ottoman–Mamluk War ended in 1517, enhancing the dockyards in Suez and adding new ships to the fleet as fast as they could be built. Without any ports, coastal forts, or any land-based presence whatsoever in the Red Sea or the Indian Ocean, the Ottoman-controlled port of Suez gave Sultan Selim I the ability to project power into otherwise inaccessible parts of the globe.[11]

Immediately following the war against Egypt, Selim's death in 1520 brought Süleyman I "the Magnificent" to power. Egypt's defeat by the Ottomans turned the Red Sea into an "Ottoman lake, leading the coastal communities along the Red Sea to a position of prominence as they aligned themselves into the Ottoman trading block".[12] Also in 1520, Süleyman's first year in power, Portugal established the diplomatic mission in Ethiopia, which had been requested in 1507 by Queen Eleni. But helping Ethiopia was still not on the priority list of any European monarch. The threat of Ottoman expansion into the Balkans occupied the minds of many a Christian king, especially after Belgrade fell in 1521 to advancing Ottoman troops. Fearsome not only on the seas but also on land, the Ottoman army continued to overwhelm its adversaries. At the Battle of Mohács in Hungary on 29 August 1526, Ottoman troops defeated a Hungarian army, clearing the way for further advances into Christian Europe. But Christian nations continued to pursue their competition between themselves with the same, if not more, determination than they showed in joining together to meet the Ottoman threat. In fact, the

9 Jeremy Black, *War and the World: Military Power and the Fate of Continents, 1450–2000* (New Haven, CT: Yale University Press, 1998), p.21.

10 Hess, 'The Ottoman Conquest of Egypt', p.75.

11 Taşkıran 'Ottoman-Portuguese relationship', p.109.

12 Sargent, 'Following in Jesuit Footsteps', p.36.

Spanish court kept an eye on the expanding Portuguese since their maritime reach threatened Spanish global supremacy. Spanish merchants engaged in trading firearms to the Ottomans in the port of Zeila, the central port city of the Sultanate of Adal.[13] While Spain was more concerned with trade routes going from Europe to the Americas, ensuring that Portugal did not surpass Spain economically by exploiting their new maritime route to the *Estado da India* was also a Spanish policy objective. The King of Spain decided that helping the Ottomans keep the Portuguese tied down in the Red Sea and the Persian Gulf was a worthwhile objective.

The Portuguese advance into the Red Sea and the Indian Ocean actually enhanced the Ottoman position in the Euro-Asian sphere. Demonstrating their determination to keep the Red Sea free of Portuguese control, an Ottoman naval captain reported to his superiors in 1525 that "each [Ottoman] ship resembles a dragon with open mouth. It is impossible for anyone to appreciate the power of these arms and ships unless he actually sees them. Nor is it possible to describe them … when our ships are ready, and, God willing, move against [the Portuguese], their total destruction will be inevitable."[14] The Ottoman navy was ready to ensure that the Red Sea, the maritime gateway to the Holy Cities of Mecca and Medina, was cleared of infidels who might attempt to not only disrupt the pilgrimage but actually try to assault the cities. With large quantities of gunpowder weapons and an increasingly proficient navy, the Ottomans were the only power with the military resources to resist the Portuguese.[15] It was not lost on the Ottoman sultan that Portuguese plans included an attack against Mecca and Medina, as unlikely as it may have been that they would have been able to accomplish such an audacious objective.

The Ottomans had developed one of the most centralised and well-administered military forces in the world by the time their army had driven through the Balkans to lay siege to Vienna in 1529, the furthest west that their troops would advance into Europe. While Christian monarchs throughout Europe were only just beginning to form professional armies, the Ottomans wielded a highly trained and skilled military against their foes, including fellow Muslims such as the Persians and the Egyptians. Gunpowder technology had transformed warfare, and European states began to integrate firearms, including handguns and heavier artillery, into their militaries as early as the fourteenth century. After firearms were first developed and employed, it took decades for soldiers to use them regularly and in large enough quantities to be tactically significant. It would not be until the sixteenth century that these weapons altered battlefield tactics and influenced military strategy.[16]

The long history of gunpowder's impact on warfare is beyond the scope of his book. Still, the critical point to consider is not which nation was first

---

13 Trimingham, *Islam in Ethiopia*, p.86.

14 Salih Özbaran, 'A Turkish report on the Red Sea and the Portuguese in the Indian Ocean (1525)', *Arabian Studies*, IV (1978), pp.83–4.

15 Black, *War and the World*, p.23.

16 Ágoston, 'Behind the Turkish War Machine', p.103.

to employ firearms and artillery, but rather when were they "employed effectively enough to have a significant impact on the outcome of military conflicts".[17] The Ottomans had effectively deployed firearms against their Persian, Egyptian, and European enemies, expanding their empire's borders in the process. The firearm of the early fifteenth century was known as a matchlock, or an arquebus. Effectively employing the matchlock under combat conditions required great skill and intensive training. Wielding the firearm required the soldier to keep a short piece of burning rope close at hand, which would light the gunpowder in the pan. Gunpowder would also be put into the barrel of the gun, followed by the musket ball. The burning match cord would then be attached to the lock, which, when the trigger was pulled, would fall forward, allowing the burning cord to light the gunpowder in the pan, which ignited the gunpowder in the barrel, firing the ball. This slow firing process allowed a trained soldier to fire once per minute. Highly trained troops might be able to fire twice a minute, but this would be the exception. Many factors complicated the ability to put continuous fire against the enemy. Inclement weather, although not a factor in Ethiopia, could put a stop to sustained fire. Poor loading techniques, such as using too much gunpowder, could cause a small explosion, wounding or killing the matchlock man. Using too little gunpowder could cause merely a "flash in the pan" from which the contemporary term emerges.

Soldiers hit by a musket ball suffered horrible wounds. Unlike a modern bullet, which tends to make a cleaner wound, a round musket ball in the sixteenth century punched a gaping hole in the body, often pushing bone and tissue through the exit hole. A hit from a matchlock musket ball was frequently fatal.

Effective employment of firearms propelled Ottoman growth and expansion. In the early sixteenth century, the Ottoman Empire's major wars were against other Muslim powers, such as the Ottoman–Safavid War against the Persians and the Ottoman–Mamluk War against the Egyptians. Although religious elements permeated competition between the Ottomans and the Portuguese, the Portuguese–Ottoman rivalry was not front and centre in the struggle for supremacy between European rivals. In 1535 the Ottoman sultan Süleyman I chose to enter a quasi-alliance with the Catholic King of France, Francis I (r. 1494–1547), to facilitate Ottoman conquests in the Mediterranean against the Holy Roman Empire. The Holy Roman Emperor, Charles V (r. 1519–1556), was at war with France. Süleyman's reply to Francis was sent to the French court in Paris. The letter reveals Süleyman's worldview and his place in the hierarchy of nations. It read as follows:

> I who am the Sultan of Sultans, the sovereign of sovereigns, the dispenser of crowns to the monarchs on the face of the earth, the shadow of the God on Earth, the Sultan and sovereign lord of the Mediterranean Sea and of the Black Sea, of Rumelia and of Anatolia, of Karamania, of the land of Romans, of Dhulkadria, of Diyarbakir, of Kurdistan, of Azerbaijan, of Persia, of Damascus, of Aleppo, of

17 Gábor Ágoston, *Guns for the Sultan* (London: Cambridge University Press, 2009), p.21.

A matchlock musketeer in the sixteenth century. The small wooden flasks contain the powder which would have been used to keep the pan charged. The weapon weighed anywhere from 15 to 20 pounds. It discharged an enormous amount of smoke and could misfire if too much powder was placed in the pan, with potentially fatal consequences for the musketeer. Not enough powder would cause nothing but a flash in the pan. (Photo by the Chattanooga Times Free Press)

> Cairo, of Mecca, of Medina, of Jerusalem, of all Arabia, of Yemen and of many other lands which my noble fore-fathers and my glorious ancestors (may God light up their tombs!) conquered by the force of their arms and which my August Majesty has made subject to my flamboyant sword and my victorious blade, I, Sultan Suleiman Khan, son of Sultan Selim Khan, son of Sultan Bayezid Khan: To thee who art Francesco, king of the province of France ... You have informed me that the enemy has overrun your country and that you are at present in prison and a captive, and you have asked aid and succors for your deliverance. All this your saying having been set forth at the foot of my throne, which controls the world ... Our glorious predecessors and our illustrious ancestors (may God light up their tombs!) have never ceased to make war to repel the foe and conquer his lands. We ourselves have followed in their footsteps, and have at all times conquered provinces and citadels of great strength and difficult of approach ... May the God on High promote righteousness![18]

Such was Süleyman's greeting to Francis I, clearly indicating the perception of prestige and power that Süleyman had not only for himself but for the mighty Ottoman Empire.

European monarchs, whether Catholic or Protestant, received the news of this Christian–Muslim alliance in stunned disbelief. In joining this alliance with France, Süleyman also acted outside the accepted norms and violated the

18 Roger Bigelow Merriman, *Suleiman the Magnificent: 1520–1566* (Cambridge, MA: Harvard University Press, 1944), p.129.

Süleyman's grand signature reveals the glory and pride held by the Sultans of the Ottoman Empire. (Public domain)

idea that a permanent state of war existed between the *Dar al-Islam* (house of Islam) and the *Dar al-Harb* (house of non-believers). Aligning with the non-believers was as unprecedented for Süleyman as for Francis. Through this alliance, both leaders sought to transcend the bounds of religious principle in order to expand their power.

Francis I claimed that his alliance with the Ottomans was meant to offer Christians protection in Muslim lands, especially those ruled by the Ottomans. However, the real motive was to provide France with a powerful ally in their contest against the Holy Roman Empire. The stinging French defeat by the Empire's troops at the Battle of Pavia in 1525 compelled the French to find a powerful ally. While Süleyman ruled a unified empire, Charles V, supposedly the leader of the Christian war against Islam, had to contend with recalcitrant Christian kings and princes. Suleiman exploited these fissures, breaking the Spanish–Venetian alliance and forming an alliance of his own with the French. While Christian Europeans had been able to exploit divisions in the Muslim world, the Ottoman conquest of Egypt ensured that once solidified, the Ottoman Empire could now achieve its objectives by exploiting weakness and rivalry within the Christian world.[19] For both the French and the Ottomans, religious concerns were set aside, and the dictates of power politics were front and centre as Francis I and Süleyman the Great maintained their alliance throughout the rest of their reigns. France would remain allied in some form or another with the Ottomans until the nineteenth century.

19 Hess, 'The Ottoman Conquest of Egypt', p.72.

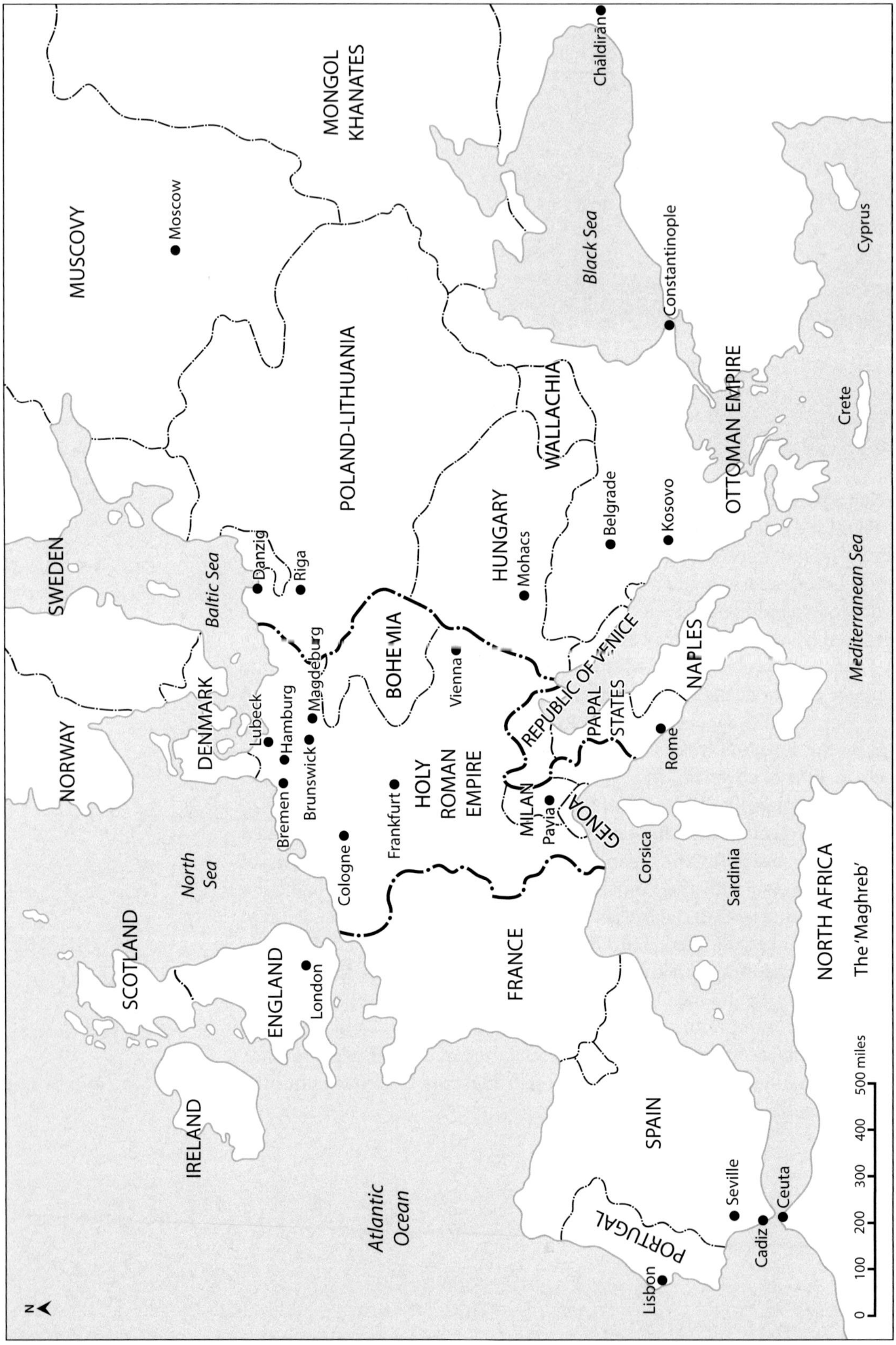

Europe and Africa in 1520.

The Portuguese–Ottoman War

The Portuguese went to war with the Ottoman Empire in 1538. Much like Süleyman's alliance with the French king exploited rivalries within the Christian world, "exploiting the animosity between Persia and the Ottoman empire in the sixteenth century was one of the main reasons why the Portuguese were able to preserve an edge in the Indian Ocean spice trade as long as they did".[20] The decision to go to war with the Ottomans placed logistical demands on the Portuguese government and military which were nearly beyond Portugal's capacity to handle. She did not have the luxury of simply embarking a large army and sending it by sea to Africa or India. Portugal had limited resources and only a small population from which to draw sailors, merchants, craftsmen, and soldiers. They would have to devise more clever ways (and in some cases, more devious ways) of accomplishing their objectives. By waging war against the mighty Ottoman Empire, "Portugal was embarking on a naval war of unprecedented length and difficulty against the greatest military power then existing."[21] One aspect of the conflict which worked to Portugal's advantage was that the Ottomans were still at war with Safavid Persia and were also still campaigning in the Balkans against the Hungarians and in the Mediterranean against the Habsburgs. Facing powerful adversaries, the Ottomans would not be able to put their full military weight against Portugal.

The Ottoman navy would face many challenges as well. The Portuguese were recognised as masters of the sea, and "the ease with which the Portuguese carracks and war squadrons established mastery over the major sea lanes" and their ability to bombard land settlements from a distance proved the usefulness of seaborne artillery – a lesson quickly learned and a practice soon to be emulated by Asian powers.[22] The Ottomans would be one of the first to challenge Portuguese power, and a Turkish manuscript in the British Museum summarises Ottoman strategy for the war against Portugal:

> Immediately on receipt of my orders will get ready your bag and baggage, and make preparations in Suez for a holy war, and having equipped and supplied a fleet and collected a sufficient army, you will set out for India and capture and hold those Indian ports; cutting off the road and blocking the way to Mecca and Medina you will avert the evil deeds of the Portuguese infidels and remove their flags from the sea.[23]

Departing from their newly acquired port in Suez, only recently taken from the Mamluk Egyptians, Süleyman I's sea captains wasted no time taking

20 Ivana Elbl, 'Cross-Cultural Trade and Diplomacy: Portuguese Relations with West Africa, 1441–1521', *Journal of World History*, 3, No. 2 (Fall, 1992), p.185.

21 Dames, 'Portuguese and Turks in the Indian Ocean', p.2.

22 Kirti N. Chaudhuri, 'The Portuguese Maritime Empire, Trade, and Society in the Indian Ocean During the Sixteenth Century', *Portuguese Studies* Vol. 8 (1992), Special Issue supported by the Comissão Nacional para as Comemorações dos Descobrimentos Portugueses, p.64.

23 E. Denison Ross, 'The Portuguese in India and Arabia, 1517–38', *The Journal of the Royal Asiatic Society of Great Britain and Ireland*, No. 1 (Jan 1922), p.14.

the offensive against the Portuguese. Having already severely degraded Portuguese trade in the Red Sea, the Ottoman plan was to engage the Portuguese fleet, which would be attacked and destroyed. The Portuguese *Estado da India* was to be conquered as well. This was a bold move for Süleyman. He would wage an offshore campaign against the Portuguese fleet, engaging in naval combat on the open seas, which would require greater skill and planning than the Ottoman navy had yet achieved. However, there was precedent for facing the Portuguese at sea. The Chinese had shown that the Portuguese fleet was not invincible, and at Tunmên in 1522, a Chinese fleet of lightly armed vessels defeated a Portuguese fleet. The Chinese were willing and able to take on the Portuguese in waters close to the Chinese mainland, where supply and logistic issues were minimised, and their ships did not have to venture far from port. The Chinese maintained a capable inshore naval capability, but they no longer deployed distant fleets.[24] They did not challenge Portuguese naval mastery in distant waters, as Süleyman would try to do by attacking the Portuguese in the Red Sea and the Indian Ocean. While seizing control of Portuguese maritime trade routes and conquering the *Estado da India* were top priorities, Süleyman had also kept a watchful eye on the Portuguese diplomatic mission that arrived in Ethiopia in 1520.

Suleiman sent a fleet to capture the Portuguese base at Diu, a major port along the Indian coast and an essential trade outlet for the *Estado da India.* The Ottomans deployed a force of "nearly 70 vessels and a crew of close to 10,000", which was the largest Ottoman naval effort yet seen in the Indian Ocean.[25] The Portuguese had not been idle, and Diu was well fortified and defended by walls and cannon. Ottoman forces were strengthened through the employment of troops from Gujarat. Using auxiliary troops was a common practice among the major powers, and the Ottomans employed Gujarati infantry in their assault on Diu in 1538. The Portuguese had made use of auxiliary forces many times. Employing auxiliaries from the African or Indian territory under their control helped compensate for Portugal's small military establishment. For example, in 1515, the Portuguese captain Albuquerque brought 1,500 Indian troops from Malabar to assault Hormuz, which was swiftly captured, and its Ottoman commander executed.[26] Both the Portuguese and the Ottomans employed auxiliary troops to make up for their lack of regular forces available in the Red Sea and Indian Ocean theatres. For the Portuguese, the logistical challenge of getting their troops to India was significant. For the Ottomans, more pressing concerns elsewhere in Europe, Persia, and North Africa required the best Ottoman forces to be deployed in these theatres. Also for the Ottomans, the province of Gujarat in north-west India had become a client state, and defending the Muslim Gujaratis from further Portuguese depredations factored into Ottoman imperial strategy.

24 Jeremy Black, *War in the Early Modern World* (New York: Routledge, 1998), p.7.

25 Jeremy Black, *War in the World: A Comparative History, 1450–1600* (New York: Palgrave, 2011), p.148.

26 Salih Özbaran and Dom Manuell de Lyma, 'The Ottoman Turks and the Portuguese in the Persian Gulf, 1534–1581', *Journal of Asian History*, 6, No. 1 (1972), p.46.

Despite a determined siege by the Ottoman fleet and the employment of Gujarat infantry, Diu did not fall, and it remained in Portuguese hands. Before returning to their base in Suez, the Ottoman fleet captured Aden on the Yemeni coast, hoping to at least salvage some military success from the enormous effort of equipping and sailing the fleet from Suez to Diu. Aden's capture by the Ottomans threatened Portuguese operations in the Red Sea but was not nearly as severe a threat to the *Estado da India* as the fall of Diu would have been. In December 1540 a Portuguese fleet would set sail to the Red Sea under the command of Estêvão da Gama, son of Portugal's greatest explorer, to attack the Ottoman port in Suez. This fleet would bring Portuguese forces into the Ethiopian–Adal War and will be part of the narrative in the next chapter.

Chapter 5

The Ethiopian–Adal War: Enter the Portuguese

In September of 1540, Ethiopian king Lebne Dengel died. Stunned by his defeat at Shembra Kure and unable to rally the Ethiopians to the cause of defending the homeland against Imam Gurey, he had been living as a hermit in a mountain fortress since 1530. It is believed that he had sent an emissary to Portugal to ask for military assistance against Imam Gurey. In a letter written in "late April or early May of 1540, the emperor bitterly laments his fate, saying, 'All of my nobility have rebelled against me in support of the Muslims'".[1] By 1540 most of the major monasteries were destroyed, and the Ethiopian army had been defeated in nearly every major engagement with the exception of their stand at Amba Gesen in November 1531 and again in 1533. Lebne Dengel's son Gelawdewos became the next king. As an infant, Gelawdewos was prophesied to "defeat his enemies and crush the unbelievers like a piece of earthenware".[2] While this may have been the prevailing vision at one time in his youth, in 1541 Gelawdewos was at the head of a very small force and was unlikely to crush Imam Gurey without some stroke of good fortune. *The Chronicle of King Gelawdewos* recounts the years following Imam Gurey's victories over the Ethiopian forces, describing conditions in Ethiopia in the 12 years between the Battle of Shembra Kure and Lebne Dengel's death in 1540:

> Victory was taken into the hands of the Muslims … and they had dominion over the Church of Ethiopia. They won all fighting in the direction of the east and west, and in the direction of the south and north even so far that they had destroyed shrines of prayer whose walls were built with gold, silver, and precious stones from India. They killed a large number of believers by the sword. They carried off the young men, the maidens, boys and girls even to the extent that they sold them for the task of miserable enslavement.[3]

1 Aregay, 'A Reappraisal', p.111, note 54.

2 Gebreyes, *Chronicle of King Galawdewos*, p.5.

3 Gebreyes, *Chronicle of King Galawdewos*, p.5.

Replica of a sixteenth-century sailing vessel, the *San Salvador*, which in 1542 explored the California coast, making its way from the Pacific coast of El Salvador to San Diego bay on 28 September. The Portuguese fleet which brought Cristóvão da Gama's troops to Ethiopia would have been composed of identical ships. The chronicler Gaspar Correa claims that 77 such ships were part of the fleet, which left India to attack Suez and to disembark troops in Ethiopia. (Photo by Robert Camp @ Maritime Museum of San Diego)

This idea of what might be called a "Christian *Jihad*" against Imam Gurey's invading forces is a recurring theme in *Chronicles of King Gelawdewos*.[4] As enticing as it might have been to Lebne Dengel to rally his people under the banner of Christianity, he was never able to inspire the same religious devotion in his people that Imam Gurey was able to do through the declaration of *jihad* against the non-believers of Christian Ethiopia. However, the Portuguese would bring a crusading zeal to Ethiopia's conflict, helping turn the tide against Imam Gurey's forces.

In 1540, having learned that the Ottomans were assembling another fleet at Suez to attack Diu for a second time, and with news coming from Ethiopia that the war against the Sultanate of Adal was not going well, the newly appointed viceroy of the *Estado da India*, Estêvão da Gama – son of the great Vasco da Gama – decided to send a powerful armada to the Red Sea. According to Gaspar Correa, another of the Portuguese chroniclers of the Ethiopian–Adal War, the armada comprised 77 minor ships, three galiots, and 12 major ships, laden with artillery and more than 2,000 rowers. Estêvão da Gama's younger brother Cristóvão, and João Bermudez sailed aboard one of the flagships. The expedition's main objective was to destroy the Ottoman fleet at Suez. The secondary objective was to land forces on the African mainland to rescue their Ethiopian "ally".[5] Deciding it was time to act decisively, Estêvão da Gama led the Portuguese fleet from India on 10

4 Demoz, 'Moslems and Islam', p.6.

5 Andreu Martínez d'Alòs-Moner, 'Early Portuguese Emigration to the Ethiopian Highlands: Geopolitics, Mission and Métissage', in *Reinterpreting Indian Ocean Worlds: Essays in Honour of Kirti N. Chaudhuri*, ed. Stefan Halikowski Smith, 2–32. Newcastle Upon Tyne: co, 2011, p.7.

The crew and passengers, to include Cristóvão da Gama's troops, would have dined in the cramped spaces of the ships which transported them from India to the Red Sea and ultimately to Ethiopia. (Photo by Julia Lee)

Medical instruments laid out on one of the beds in the *San Salvador*. Cristóvão da Gama would almost certainly have brought a surgeon with his force of 400 soldiers to Ethiopia. In many cases, a quick death would have been preferable to the surgeon's knife and saw. (Photo by Julia Lee)

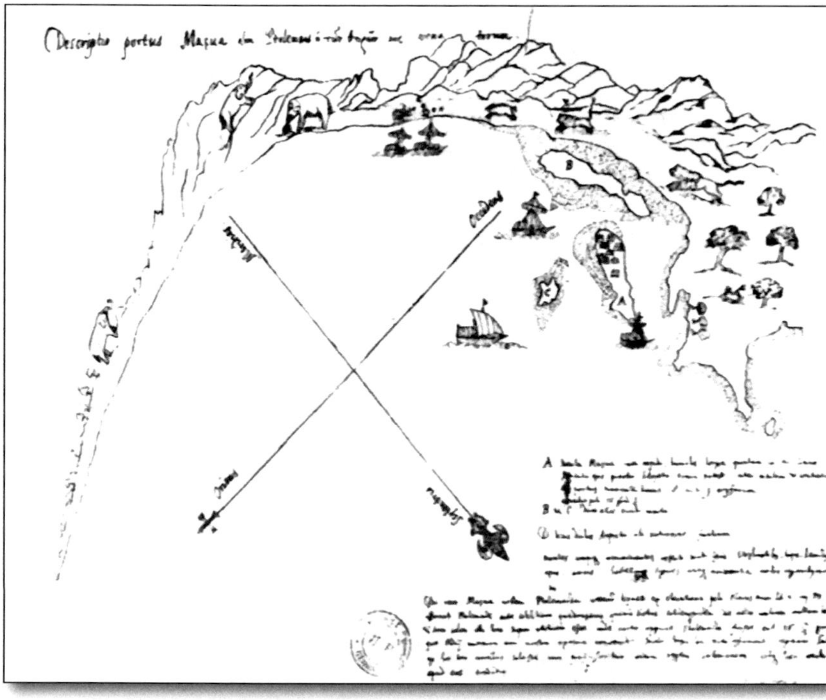

This drawing of the port of Massawa was done by either João de Castro himself or one of his cartographers. It depicts the Ethiopian coastline and is one of a series of drawings that chronicled the Portuguese maritime expedition from Goa to attack the Ottomans at Suez in 1541. (Public Domain)

February 1541 and sailed into the Ottoman-controlled Red Sea. One of the captains in this fleet was João de Castro, who recorded his observations of the land along the coast of the Red Sea and also provided his observations of the Ethiopian people, indicating that he must have accompanied the landing party ashore in Ethiopia at some point, but then returned with the fleet to India. De Castro maintained a great interest in other cultures, and he co-authored a book on Indian art in his later years. His home in Portugal was decorated with gems and stones from India.

On the way to attack the Ottoman naval base at Suez, the fleet made a brief stop in Massawa on the Ethiopian coast of the Red Sea, where the heaviest ships were left in the harbour to await the return of the strike fleet, which continued on to Suez. Another of the Gama brothers, Manuel, remained with the heaviest Portuguese ships in port at Massawa and a few hundred sailors, with orders not to go ashore or leave the ships until the main fleet returned from Suez.

After suffering in the ship's sweltering quarters, about 60 of the sailors disregarded their orders and went ashore. Searching for food and fresh water, they made their way inland for miles, meeting patrols sent out by the Adal army. Promising the sailors food and drink if they would give up their weapons, an Adal captain lured the sailors into a trap. On the verge of starvation and suffering from thirst, the Portuguese complied, and upon disarming themselves they were slain. Two escapees made their way back to the ships, where Manuel da Gama arranged for a force to venture inland and capture those responsible for the deaths of so many Portuguese. The Adal captain who tricked the Portuguese sailors was found and killed, his severed head delivered to Queen Sabla Wengel, the mother of King

Gelawdewos.[6] The Queen rejoiced that finally some of the invading soldiers were vanquished, and the prospect of further help from the Portuguese was an encouragement to the Ethiopians who had suffered for so long under Imam Gurey's rule.

Unable to overcome the powerful Ottoman fleet and Suez's defences, Estêvão da Gama sailed his fleet back to Massawa on Ethiopia's Red Sea coast to execute the secondary plan of sending troops inland to help save Ethiopia from complete collapse at the hands of Imam Gurey's *jihad*. In Massawa he met with Ethiopian emissaries who confirmed that Muslim armies had nearly overrun the Christian kingdom over the last 12 years. It may have been at this juncture that Portuguese captain João de Castro recorded his observations of the Ethiopians.[7] He wrote that:

> The [Ethiopians] are naturally ceremonious men, and full of points of honour. Their only weapons are darts, in which they figure to themselves the lance with which our Saviour was wounded, and the cross on which he died, though some wear short swords. They are very expert horsemen, but badly apparelled … In their own country they are dastardly cowards, but in other countries valiant; insomuch that in India they say that a good Lascarin, or what we call a soldier, must be an [Ethiopian]; and they are so much esteemed in Ballagayat, Cambaya, Bengal, and other places, that they are always made captains and principal officers in the army. Their clothing is vile and poor. They wear linen shirts, and the great personages have a kind of upper garment called Beden. The vulgar people are almost quite naked. They eat bollemus and raw flesh; or if held to the fire, it is so little done that the blood runs from it. In the whole land there are no cities or towns, so that they live in the field under tents and pavilions like the Arabs.[8]

While in port in Massawa, Estêvão da Gama considered his options and learned that 60 Portuguese sailors had disobeyed orders, gone ashore, and met their demise at the hands of the invaders. Gama considered departing Ethiopia for India, replenishing his supplies at Goa, and making another attempt at defeating the Ottoman fleet in Suez. Or he could press ahead with the secondary plan to join forces with Prester John's army and help turn the tide against Imam Gurey. There seemed little choice but to return to India after failing to take Suez; if the Ottoman navy gained undisputed control of the Red Sea, resupplying troops in Ethiopia would be exceptionally difficult. However, the Portuguese soldiers thought otherwise and declared their

6 D. João Bermudez, 'A Short Account of the Embassy to Ethiopia', in R.S. Whiteway, *The Portuguese Expedition to Abyssinia in 1541–1543* (Alpha Editions, 2019), pp.139–143. Bermudez provides the only account of the loss of the 60 Portuguese sailors prior to the Portuguese fleet's return to Ethiopia from Suez.

7 As with many historical accounts of the Ethiopian–Adal War, Robert Kerr's English translation of Castro's account of Ethiopia states that "This account of the first interference of the Portuguese in the affairs of Abyssinia … is rather meagre and unsatisfactory, and the names of places are often so disguised by faulty orthography as to be scarcely intelligible." However, a few of Castro's general observations are of interest to the overall narrative of the war.

8 Robert Kerr, *General History and Collection of Voyages and Travels* (Edinburgh: William Blackwood), 1824, p.281.

unwavering support for remaining in Ethiopia, avenging their comrade's death, and joining Prester John's forces to defeat Imam Gurey's Muslim armies in accordance with the proselytising mission that had been the driving force behind so much of Portugal's overseas adventurism.

Emissaries from the Ethiopian court were in Massawa with the Queen, including Yeshak, the *bahrnagash* (ruler of the sea), the Ethiopian chief of the northern coastal provinces, which today make up the nation of Eritrea. Yeshak proclaimed that the Ethiopian Church would switch allegiance from the Coptic Church to the Roman Church if the Portuguese would provide military assistance. Yeshak also had a force of about 500 Ethiopian soldiers who were prepared to join with the Portuguese and attempt to make their way inland to join forces with King Gelawdewos's larger Ethiopian army. Estêvão da Gama acquiesced to the *bahrnagash*'s request and finally decided to leave 400 of his soldiers in Ethiopia along with about 130 Indian slaves who would serve as auxiliary troops and could be used to carry weapons and supplies and even join in the fighting if necessary.

While Yeshak the *bahrnagash* and Queen Sabla Wengel were hosting the newly arrived Portuguese along the Red Sea coast, King Gelawdewos was busy fighting the Muslim army in Showa. If Imam Gurey could destroy the remnants of the main Ethiopian army, he could turn his attention to the tiny Portuguese contingent approaching from the north-east and crush it with ease. Even if the Portuguese linked up with King Gelawdewos and his army in Showa, Imam Gurey would still outnumber the combined force by well over two to one. At the Battle of Sahart on 24 April 1541, Gelawdewos was defeated by a detachment led by one of Imam Gurey's captains. The precise location of Sahart is unknown, and "most of the Ethiopian sources are vague about the king's [Gelawdewos'] refuge at this time".[9] However, the Ethiopian army was still resisting Imam Gurey, and Gelawdewos refused to give in while there was still a chance to liberate his country. He was, after all, the fabled Prester John (although he would not have been aware of this), and his Portuguese hosts were on the way to his rescue.

Estêvão's brother Cristóvão da Gama, Vasco's fourth son, would lead the Portuguese expedition into Ethiopia in search of Prester John. Aged 25, Cristóvão had experience fighting in the East Indies, and although he was young he had the respect of his troops.[10] Five captains accompanied Gama, and would serve as sub-commanders during the expedition into the Ethiopian highlands. They were Manuel da Cunha, João da Fonseca, Inofre de Abreu, Francisco de Abreu, and Francisco Velho.[11] On 9 July 1541, Estêvão da Gama set sail from Massawa back to India, leaving the small contingent of 400 Portuguese soldiers and his brother Cristóvão, one of Portugal's leading sons, to their fate. The soldiers marched inland, regarding themselves "as

---

9 C.F. Beckingham, 'A Note on the Topography of Ahmad Gran's Campaign in 1542', *Journal of Semitic Studies*, Vol. IV (October 1959), p.370.

10 Laband, *Bringers of War*, p.94.

11 Miguel de Castanhoso, *A Discourse on the Deeds of the very Valorous Captain Dom Christavao da Gama in the Kingdoms of the Preste John with the four hundred Portuguese, his Companions*, in R.S. Whiteway, *The Portuguese Expedition to Abyssinia in 1541–1543* (Alpha Editions, 2019), p.12.

crusaders, even Christian martyrs, setting forth under the banner of the Order of Christ on a chivalric quest from which there was scant hope of ever returning alive to Portugal".[12] Not one of them questioned their mission; all willingly accepted the task ahead.

Miguel de Castanhoso was one of the Portuguese soldiers in the expedition. He recorded the journey from Massawa to the Ethiopian highlands, providing details on the terrain, weather, food, and the reception given to the Portuguese by the local populace and by the Queen, Lebne Dengel's widow Sabla Wengel. The Queen had assumed the diplomatic role representing her son, King Gelawdewos, who was with the remnants of the Ethiopian army some hundreds of miles to the south-west in the province of Showa.[13] Cristóvão da Gama spoke to the Queen in the fall of 1541 (the exact date is not provided), and he proclaimed to her:

> Most Christian Queen, the Governor of India [Estêvão da Gama] was with his fleet in the Red Sea, defeating the infidels of our holy faith in the service of our most Christian King of Portugal, my lord; after he had wasted many towns and places, he was in the port of Massawa, on his return to India, when there arrived this captain [Yeshak, the *bahrnagash*], who holds your highnesses bridle, on an Embassy from the Preste your son [King Gelawdewos], and bringing letters from you, begging the Governor, in the name of God and the King of Portugal, to take pity on this Christian kingdom, so wasted and tyrannized over by the enemy; begging him to send some aid, as it was his custom to assist the helpless, because for fourteen years the enemy had occupied his country, doing much harm and injury. When the Governor [Estêvão da Gama] learned what need this kingdom had of help, and what service he would do to God and the King in helping it at this time, he sent him (me) and these soldiers for the moment; in the coming year he will send more men so that with the help of our Lord God, that kingdom will soon again be prosperous; and that trust can be placed in his (my) words, for all the Portuguese who were there had come ready to die for the faith of Christ and the salvation of that kingdom.[14]

Breaking down Gama's speech to the Queen, he had clearly stated that the arrival of the 400 Portuguese soldiers was a result of requests from Ethiopia, from "the Preste your son", meaning King Gelawdewos (whom the Portuguese considered to be Prester John), the son of the late King Lebne Dengel and Queen Sabla Wengel, although the request probably came from Lebne Dengel while he was in seclusion in the years following the disaster at Shembra Kure. Following the speech, the Portuguese soldiers performed military drills for the Queen. In the Ethiopian army, only the emperor's elite *Çäwa* troops performed any kind of regular training, and this would have

12 Laband, *Bringers of War*, p.95.

13 Margaux Herman, *Sabla Wangêl, the queen of the Kingdom of Heaven*. Addis Ababa University Institute of Ethiopian Studies XVII International Conference of Ethiopian Studies, Nov 2009, Addis Ababa, France, p.15.

14 Castanhoso, *Portuguese Expedition*, pp.19–20.

taken place in the katama camp in full view of the emperor.[15] None of the Ethiopian military training involved the use of firearms.

Castanhoso refers to the Portuguese drill performed for Queen Sabla Wengel using the word *soica*, a word of Swiss origin, which implies that the Portuguese were using Swiss marching drill.[16] They performed the *caracol*, a marching manoeuvre designed to allow the front rank to fire and then the second rank to take their place in an orderly manner, which Castanhoso describes impressed the Queen greatly, especially as the Ethiopian soldiers had not been able to employ this method successfully, which must have been known to the Queen. According to Castanhoso's account, while watching the drill, the Queen was "very pleased ... especially [with] the closing and opening of the *caracol*, in which her people fail."[17] It is unlikely that the Portuguese actually fired their matchlocks while performing this drill since they must have realised that resupply would be unlikely. Whether they did or not, they impressed the Queen and received a warm welcome from their Ethiopian hosts.

The Portuguese contingent traversed the Ethiopian highlands throughout the remainder of 1541, seeking to join forces with Prester John's main Ethiopian army, which was about 400 miles south-west in the province of Showa. The gruelling journey required physical exertion that tested the Portuguese troops' endurance. Not only was the terrain a challenge, but the small force could not risk falling into a trap. If Imam Gurey's main army encountered the Portuguese force before they had a chance to rendezvous with the Ethiopian army, the result would have been certain defeat for Gama's 400 soldiers and their servants, and the 500 Ethiopians led by the *bahrnagash*. Cristóvão da Gama led his force of about 1,000 troops cautiously, keeping a dedicated reconnaissance force in the lead. Castanhoso wrote that there were:

> four horses, on which four men always accompanied [Da Gama] in visiting the line, from the van to the rear; the two captains who were in front with the carts, half a league in advance, were changed every day, for the work was hard, as in places they found the roads such that the cattle could not drag the carts, and our men had to carry them over their shoulders.[18]

The Portuguese horses were likely provided by their Ethiopian hosts, which allowed the mounted scouting party to march ahead of the main body of troops. Local Ethiopian guides kept an eye out for Imam Gurey's sentries. Progress across the mountainous, rocky terrain was painfully slow and treacherous.

15 Richard Pankhurst and Andreu Martínez d'Alòs-Moner, 'Military Units and Organization', in Merid Aregay et al. (eds), *Encyclopedia Aethiopica*, Vol. 5 (Wiesbaden: Harrassowitz Verlag, 2003), p.433.

16 Castanhoso, *Portuguese Expedition*, note 4, p.20.

17 Castanhoso, *Portuguese Expedition*, p.20.

18 Correa, vol. iv, p.353.

Baboons in the Ethiopian highlands as Miguel de Castanhoso and the Portuguese soldiers would have seen them as they marched inland to join with Prester John's Ethiopian army. Castanhoso wrote that there were "elephants, lions, leopards, and other wild beasts which we do not know here" (Castanhoso, p.236). Marco Polo also recorded having seen baboons on his return to Venice 250 years earlier. (Author's photo)

Christmas was celebrated with a day-long mass, replete with musical instruments. In the evening, Castanhoso remembered that "we all confessed". At the same time, Queen Sabla Wengel looked out upon the Christmas festivities and solemnities with astonishment at the differences between the Ethiopian and Portuguese customs. After celebrating Christmas, the Portuguese force "reached a very high hill", so high in fact that all their carts had to be disassembled and carried by pieces over the precipice. This travel method took a toll not only on the soldiers and porters themselves but on the carts and the artillery carriages, which degraded each time they were taken apart and put back together. The year 1541 ended without any major engagements between the Muslim army and the Ethiopians or their Portuguese allies.

Continuing their westward march to join Prester John, the Portuguese contingent spent over a week during the Epiphany encamped on a plain near the town of Agamé, according to Castanhoso. The time spent in camp seems excessive for a force moving in the vicinity of a much larger enemy army, but the reasons for moving slowly are possibly twofold. First, reassuring the local population that the Portuguese were here to restore the Christian kingdom required that their presence be seen, which would help establish a sense of security. Second, it is likely that Cristóvão da Gama had it in the back of his mind that if he waited long enough, reinforcements that his brother Estêvão promised he would send might reach him.

The Battle of Amba Senait

Imam Gurey's forces had taken up a position on a small hill close to Agamé, a perfect location to observe Portuguese movements and dispositions. Lacking firearms, these Muslim troops relied on their strong defensive position and numbers to deter a Portuguese attack. With their usual elan and crusading zeal, the Portuguese attacked the hill on 4 February 1542. Queen Sabla Wengel objected to the move, fearing that Imam Gurey's main force would retaliate, jeopardising the progress that Gama's force had made in moving towards the main Ethiopian army, still hundreds of miles away to the south. Gama's Portuguese captured the small garrison of Muslim troops and took no prisoners. However they did capture many women, both Christian women who had been taken as wives by the Muslim soldiers as well as many Muslim women. These women were all turned over to Queen Sabla Wengel. The Christian women were freed, but in accordance with the pitiless nature of the religious conflict which had characterised warfare in the Horn of Africa since the days of Amda Seyon some 200 years earlier, all the Muslim women were put to death.[19] Gama set up camp atop the newly captured hill, hoping that it might accrue more defensive advantage to his small force than it had to the Muslims whom he had just defeated and slain.

Within days, news reached him that a Portuguese vessel had docked in Massawa. Estêvão da Gama, while still the Viceroy of the *Estado da India*, had sent a ship from Goa to Massawa to gain any news about his brother Cristóvão's Ethiopian expedition. Cristóvão, therefore, sent a 40-man patrol back to Massawa to meet the vessel to collect any supplies that it might have brought from India. His force now reduced in size, he could not simply sit idly until the patrol returned from Massawa. He could not retreat, as this would alarm the Ethiopians and possibly anger Queen Sabla Wengel. He had to move, and in the martial tradition imbued into every Portuguese warrior, he moved towards Imam Gurey's vastly stronger Muslim army. The day before Palm Sunday, 1 April 1542, the Portuguese prepared to attack the Imam's army. Having established an observation post on another hill overlooking the Portuguese camp, Imam Gurey sent a messenger to Gama, asking for the Portuguese troops to realise their chances of defeating his powerful Muslim army were slim. Vastly outnumbered and still far from the main Ethiopian force under King Gelawdewos, Gama decided to at least receive the messenger from Imam Gurey under a flag of truce. Gurey offered Gama the opportunity to depart Ethiopia unmolested, or if this was not to his liking, he could join forces with Imam Gurey and help rule the new Islamic Kingdom of Ethiopia. Gama sent his reply to Imam Gurey via a young boy to the Muslim camp, expressing no desire to do anything except obey the King of Portugal's orders, which were to save Ethiopian Christianity and defeat Imam Gurey. In a gesture meant to offend Gurey, Gama sent a mirror and a pair of tweezers, clearly implying that the Imam was a woman and could use the two items for his grooming. This act of levity on the part of

19 Castanhoso, *Portuguese Expedition*, note 2, p.36.

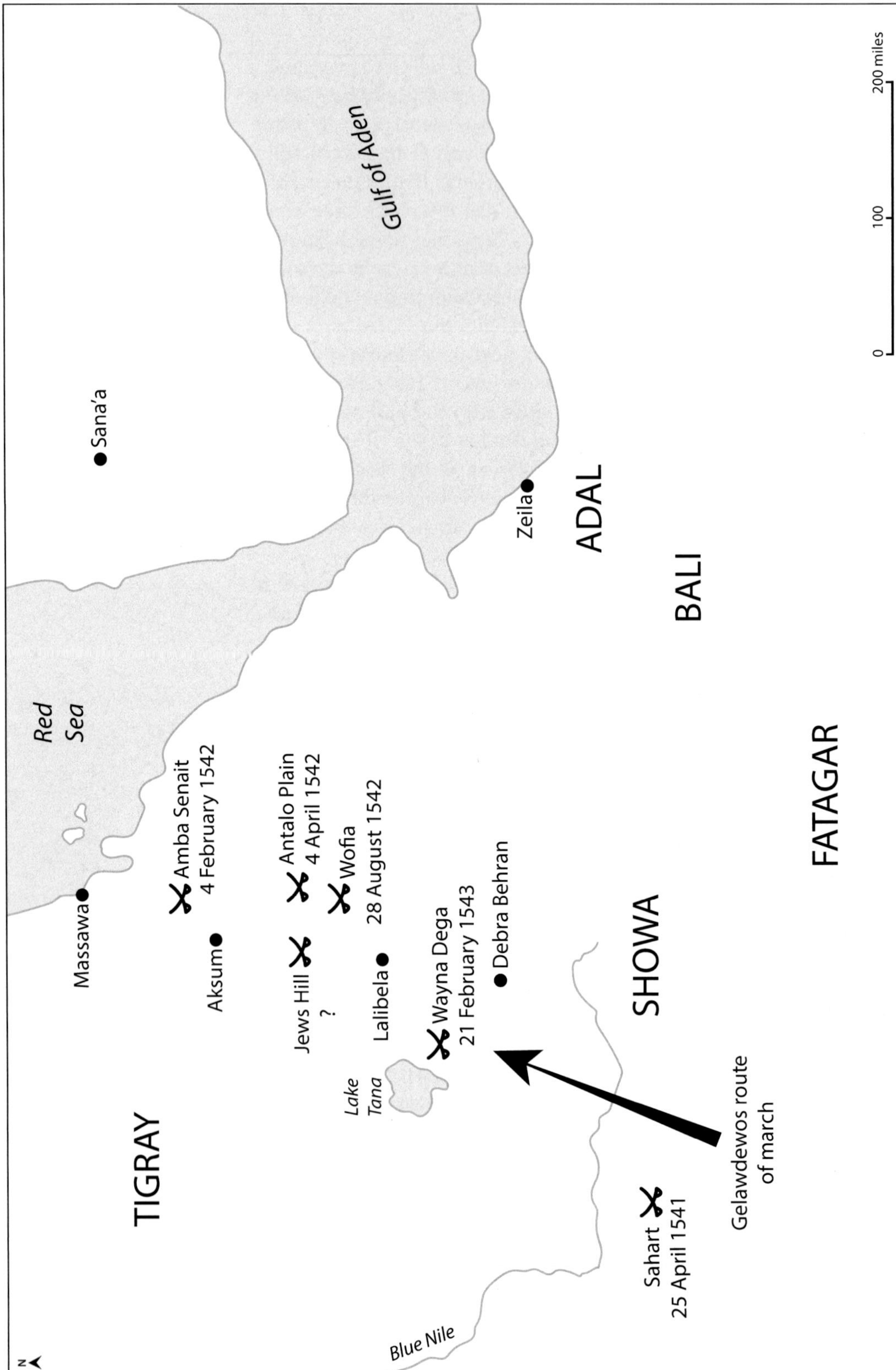

The major battles between the Portuguese and Imam Gurey from 1541–1543. The location of Jews Hill is an estimate. Sahart is also shown only to illustrate that King Gelawdewos continued to resist Imam Gurey's main army while the Portuguese were marching inland from Massawa. No evidence for Sahart's location exists in any of the literature.

the Portuguese leadership would come back to haunt da Gama in the coming weeks. Imam Gurey did not take kindly to Gama's offering.

The Battle of Antalo Plain

The Portuguese prepared for battle. Still not having joined forces with King Gelawdewos, the Portuguese would stand alone against Imam Gurey's mighty army at the Battle of Antalo Plain.

Imam Gurey formed his army for battle, preparing to take his place at the front of the line. While his troops formed ranks, Castanhoso remembered that:

> the king of Zeila [Imam Gurey] ascended a hill with several horse and some foot to examine us: he halted on the top with three hundred horse and three large banners, two white with red moons, and one red with a white moon, which always accompanied him, and [by] which he was recognized.[20]

Gama surveyed his 360 Portuguese troops (40 soldiers had left the force to go back to Massawa to meet the hoped-for ship from India), encouraging them and motivating them to stand firm against their foe. Arrayed against him were, according to Portuguese estimates, some 15,000 of Gurey's infantry, "all archers and bucklermen [swordsmen]; fifteen hundred horse, and 200 Turkish arquebusiers, of whom [the Imam] thought a great deal, and with whom they had conquered all that country".[21] Gama must have known what he was up against, and in a sense, the Battle of Antalo Plain represents a microcosm of the entire Portuguese overseas enterprise in the sixteenth century. A small nation of fewer than one million inhabitants, a sliver of land on the far western end of the European continent, Portugal relied upon unquestioned valour, steadfast courage, and a crusading zeal which continued to burn nearly three centuries after the Muslims were thrown out of Portugal in 1249. Portuguese conquistadors and explorers for the past few decades had willingly accepted battle against enemies far superior in number, and Cristóvão da Gama was not about to waiver in the face of his enemy. On 4 April 1542, facing odds of over 60 to 1, with cross in one hand and sword in the other, the Portuguese attacked.

Seething with anger over the gift of tweezers and mirror, Imam Gurey ordered his troops to crush the Portuguese. Skirmishing between the Portuguese and Ottoman gunners foreshadowed the fighting to come. Both armies' elite troops took the field as they tried to dislodge one another from the rocky terrain around the Portuguese camp. As Castanhoso recalled:

> Mahomet began the attack with only ten horsemen, against whom as many Portuguese were detached, who fired with so much exactness, that nine of the Moors fell, and the tenth with great difficulty made his escape. This omen of good

20 Castanhoso, *Portuguese Expedition*, p.41

21 Castanhoso, *Portuguese Expedition*, p.44.

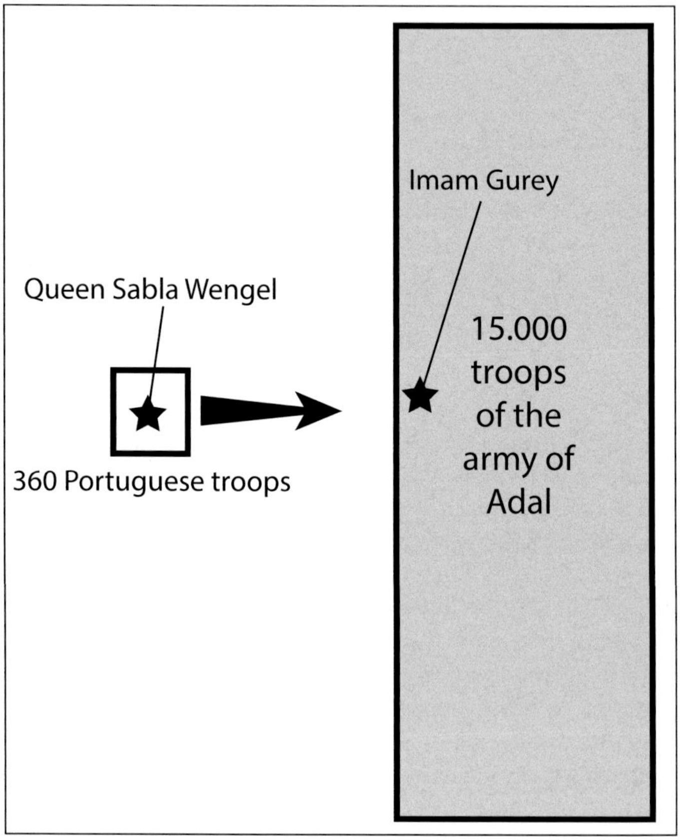

The Battle of Antalo Plain. Demonstrating that they were ready to pay with their lives to save Ethiopia from submission to Islam, the Portuguese attacked against great odds. Protecting Queen Sabla Wengel was also one of their primary objectives.

> fortune gave the soldiers great encouragement; the action grew hot, and they came at length to a general battle; but the Moors, dismayed by the advantages our men had obtained at first, were half defeated before the fight. The great fire of our muskets and artillery broke them immediately.[22]

The small canons that Gama's troops had worked so hard to transport over the rough terrain began to fire, as did the matchlocks, covering the area with smoke and giving Imam Gurey a firm indication that the Portuguese expected to give him no ground, and likely no quarter should any of his soldiers fall into Portuguese captivity. Castanhoso remembered that:

> when the Moors saw us advancing towards them, they raised such a noise of shouting, trumpets, and kettledrums, that it seemed as if the world were dissolving; they showed great joy, thinking they had us already in their net. At this we began to do our duty with matchlocks and artillery, so that we cleared the plain as we advanced.[23]

Imam Gurey again advanced his Ottoman gunners, giving him the best chance at dislodging the Portuguese artillery. The Portuguese force formed a

22 Lobo, *A Voyage to Abyssinia*, n.p.
23 Castanhoso, *Portuguese Expedition*, p.45.

square, albeit a small one, with Queen Sabla Wengel and a few hundred non-combatants inside. Like a tiny turtle, the square advanced slowly into the murderous hail of fire from the Ottoman gunners. Firing cannon from the corners and matchlocks across the square's front three faces, the Portuguese braved the Ottoman fire. Gama was wounded by a musket ball, as were about 50 other Portuguese, 11 of whom were killed. If the Ottomans and Imam Gurey expected that Gama's wound would somehow weaken Portuguese resolve, they were wrong. As Castanhoso recalled, once Gama received his second leg wound, it was "for him an honour, for, wounded as he was, he behaved himself and acted as we find no example of any notable Captain in ancient or modern histories".[24] What greater fortune could have befallen a Portuguese conquistador in battle than to be bleeding from both legs and one arm while still driving your troops forward against a far more numerous foe? To his soldiers, and especially to the Ethiopian infantry under Yeshak the *bahrnagash*'s command, Gama's continued determination to see the battle through to victory despite his serious wounds must have been nothing short of miraculous.

As the Ottomans continued to pour fire into the Portuguese square, a Portuguese soldier aimed his musket at the three banners which always accompanied Imam Gurey, hitting the Imam in the leg. The musket ball penetrated his flesh and killed his horse. Now both leaders were injured, and the value of having troops trained to employ firearms in combat was evident to both sides. While Cristóvão da Gama's wounds gave him the aura of invincibility, once Imam Gurey was wounded his army stopped its advance, lifted up the Imam and retreated, leaving the Portuguese in shocked disbelief as the Muslims withdrew from the battlefield. Once the smoke cleared it became apparent that nearly 30 Ottoman musketeers lay dead, along with many more Arab soldiers and a few of Imam Gurey's leading captains. Castanhoso recalled that the Portuguese were too tired to pursue, but the chances are good that most of them were also on one knee thanking God for his favour on this fateful day.

Although wounded, Imam Gurey did not waste time over the following days. With both the Portuguese army and Imam Gurey's army still encamped on the Antalo Plain, Gurey called for reinforcements. He was able to make up his losses, and in full view of the Portuguese the appearance of additional soldiers joining the Imam's forces must have been foreboding, even if they were almost all regular foot soldiers equipped with swords, spears, and shield. There were no reinforcements available anywhere for the Portuguese/Ethiopian army, and so on 16 April Gama decided to take the offensive again. Forming into another small square, the Portuguese advanced, meeting the Muslim army, which was still led by Imam Gurey in the front rank. He was not fully recovered from his wound and had to be carried in a litter. Gama was nowhere near recovered either, but he walked with his troops, prepared to meet his fate.

24 Castanhoso, *Portuguese Expedition*, p.46.

Imam Gurey's *Malassy* cavalry, the elite arm of his force, nearly succeeded in penetrating the Portuguese square, but very soon after the battle began a barrel of gunpowder exploded, panicking the horses and forcing them back in complete disarray. Gurey's army followed, fleeing from the field for the second time in two weeks. First at Amba Senait, and now on the Antalo Plain, the tiny Portuguese force had bested Imam Gurey's battle-tested veterans. For the first time since the successful defence of Amba Gesen in 1531 and 1533, Muslim forces had been decisively defeated on an Ethiopian battlefield. But the war was far from over. While the Portuguese were a formidable force, their small size must have led Imam Gurey to think that it would only be a matter of time before they were destroyed on the battlefield. Ethiopia was his, and under no circumstances would a small force of foreign interlopers deprive him of his conquest. Taking no precautions, Gurey selected a defensible position for his camp, tended to his wounds, gathered food and provisions, and most importantly appealed to the Ottoman governor in Arabia for more soldiers to subdue the elite Portuguese gunners.

Firearms had made their first real impact on the military history of Ethiopia at the Battle of Antalo Plain. Deploying his 10 artillery pieces and 360 musketeers, Cristóvão da Gama twice repulsed attacks against overwhelming numbers of Muslim cavalry and infantry. The 200 Ottoman gunners who were with Imam Gurey were overwhelmed by Portuguese artillery fire. According to Merid Aregay, "the various artillery that [Gurey] had collected earlier do not figure in any of his campaigns against the Portuguese or Lebne Dengel's successor, Gelawdewos".[25] Earlier battles featuring one or two cannons and maybe a few muskets were decided by better leadership and morale rather than by gunpowder. At Antalo Plain, gunpowder and cannonballs were the decisive factor. The Portuguese had changed the nature of warfare in the Horn of Africa.

King Gelawdewos, almost certainly having heard about the bravery and martial valour demonstrated by the small Portuguese force, began to move north from Showa to join forces with Cristóvão da Gama and Yeshak the *bahrnagash*. The *Chronicle of King Gelawdewos* describes the king as humble, pious, and loved by his people. The *Chronicle* recounts that "he led in his way, by keeping the word of God glorious and the most high rather than maintaining a large number of horses and soldiers".[26] Gelawdewos would not rule in the same manner as past kings, such as Amda Seyon and even his father Lebne Dengel, who chose to lord over their subjects with brute force. Gelawdewos would not have the option to rule in this manner, especially since the instrument of brute force, the Ethiopian army, had been degraded, defeated, and largely destroyed by Imam Gurey over the last 13 years. Whatever his inclinations might have been before assuming the crown, he had no choice but to adopt the mantle of humility and Christian piety as king. His army was whittled away, and chances were good that soon he would be captured and killed, and the Ethiopian Christian kingdom relegated to the dustbin of history.

25 Aregay, 'A Reappraisal', p.112.

26 Gebreyes, *Chronicle of King Galawdewos*, p.9.

Assessing Portuguese and Ottoman Strategy

How well did the Portuguese employ a military strategy to accomplish their policy objectives in the middle of the sixteenth century? Specifically, did their attempt to enter an alliance with Prester John in Ethiopia help or hinder the attainment of their objectives? Portuguese and Ottoman involvement in Ethiopia was fundamentally different from any of their other conflicts. For Portugal, supporting the 400 soldiers dispatched to Ethiopia was a logistical challenge that was never resolved. For the Ottomans, the extent to which their involvement in Ethiopia was part of an overall strategic policy is unclear. However, military theorists such as Julian Corbett and Carl von Clausewitz can help us evaluate the choices the Portuguese and the Ottomans made, which led to their involvement in the Ethiopian–Adal War. British historian Julian Corbett (1854-1922) wrote *Some Principles of Maritime Strategy* in 1918. Corbett's writing focuses on sea power, and although he was a naval historian, "it is probably more accurate to consider him as a student of war specialising in the naval aspects".[27] Although Corbett discussed neither the sixteenth-century Portuguese nor the Ottomans in his writing, both powers conducted themselves in accordance with some of Corbett's primary principles of war.

Writing in the early twentieth century, the nature of the nation state had changed substantially from the age of exploration in the sixteenth century. Neither Portugal nor the Ottoman Empire resembled a modern state. Corbett described how maritime strategy could support national policy objectives as determined by a centralised government, with a deliberate military strategy designed to support the government's goals. The Portuguese *Estado da India* did not necessarily look to Lisbon to establish and pursue what would today be considered national military objectives. Individuals such as Alfonso de Albuquerque and even Estêvão do Gama determined their policies and often acted outside the Portuguese crown's purview, even though ostensibly the objective of expanding Portuguese power and influence was an objective shared by the king in Lisbon and the viceroys, whether in India or Brazil. For example, during the first decade of Portuguese expansion in the Indian Ocean, King Manuel I ordered an attack on the Indian coastal port city of Goa in 1509. Albuquerque received this order, but he determined that his fleet "was not in a position to execute the order immediately", and thus he "decided to sail to the Red Sea to seek the Egyptian fleet and attack it".[28] Preferring to rely on the strategy which had so far led Portuguese forces to victory, Albuquerque took the offensive only when he had overwhelming strength. He understood the King's intent but carried out the order as the regional dynamics dictated. Even during the Portuguese–Ottoman War:

27 John B. Hattendorf, *Sir Julian Corbett on the Significance of Naval History* (Salem, MA: Peabody Museum of Salem, 1971), p.280.

28 B.S. Shastri, 'Some Aspects of the First Conquest of Goa by the Portuguese', *Proceedings of the Indian History Congress*, 39, Volume I (1978), p.388.

> the nature of the *Estado da India* as it had emerged – its distance from the metropolis, its internal divisions, and dissensions, the lack of accountability of many of the central actors – the course of events would always be the result of the interaction of local and regional dynamics, and the broader ideological and architectural considerations of makers of imperial policy.[29]

However, one must keep in mind that the Portuguese *Estado da India* was given a threefold mission by the King and the government in Lisbon: "to face and destroy, if feasible, the naval forces of the Mamluks in the Red Sea, attacking the port of Jeddah; to establish friendly relations with the Amir of Aden; to explore the Abyssinian coast and try and establish a Portuguese base there, using the opportunity to disembark an ambassador sent by King Manuel I to Prester John."[30] While the objectives were clear, the means to accomplish those objectives were determined by the representatives of the *Estado da India* in Goa.

To many Portuguese government officials both in Lisbon and dispersed throughout the global empire, the concentration of power in the governors generals' and viceroys' hands was perceived by many as a threat to the king's powers. However, when examining Portuguese strategy and operations in the Ethiopian–Adal War, we can still rely on Julian Corbett's analysis to determine the efficacy of their actions and decisions, even if these decisions were not explicitly laid out by the King and his court in Lisbon. After the Ottoman admiral Hadim Suleiman Pasha, sent by order of the Sultan, was able to secure Ottoman hegemony in the Red Sea and surrounding areas, contemporary Portuguese sources, produced within the *Estado da India*, often mention a "perigo turco", or Ottoman menace. Thus, "the idea, born in India among Portuguese authorities, came about of organising a powerful military expedition to the Red Sea. Empowered as governor in 1540, Dom Estêvão da Gama immediately started preparing for such an expedition."[31] This expedition brought the Portuguese contingent of 400 soldiers to Ethiopia to fight alongside "Prester John" against Imam Gurey.

Corbett proposed the concept of a "disposal force", "designed not for permanent conquest, but as a method of disturbing our enemy's plans and strengthening the hands of [one's] allies and our own position".[32] Explaining how maritime powers can best accomplish their policy objectives, the disposal force, composed of those troops which are not absolutely necessary for defensive purposes, can be employed to frustrate the plans and strategies of one's adversary. Describing the employment of a portion of one's forces, Corbett explained, "it would seem, therefore, that these operations were distinguished not so much by the nature of the object as by the fact that we devoted to them, not the whole of our military strength, but only a certain

29 Sanjay Subrahmanyam, *The Portuguese Empire in Asia, 1500–1700: A Political and Economic History* (West Sussex: Wiley Blackwell, 2012), p.85.

30 Loureiro, 'Portas do Estreito', p.132.

31 Loureiro, 'Portas do Estreito', p.133.

32 Julian Corbett, *Some Principles of Maritime Strategy* (Annapolis: Naval Institute Press, 1988), p.61.

part of it which was known as our 'disposal force.'"[33] He further explained that:

> where its object is to wrest or secure from the enemy a definite piece of territory that to a greater or less extent can be isolated by naval action. Its operative power, in fact, appears to bear some direct relation to the intimacy with which naval and military action can be combined to give the contingent a weight and mobility that are beyond its intrinsic power.[34]

Although Corbett never referenced the Portuguese adventure in Ethiopia in the sixteenth century, few better examples of a disposal force can be found in the annals of military history than Cristóvão da Gama's excursion into Ethiopia in 1541. The Portuguese attempt to challenge Ottoman power in the Red Sea and the Persian Gulf and associated support for Christian Ethiopia did not require a strategy of extensive territorial conquest. Instead, the Portuguese relied on their fleet, the series of coastal forts which they had established along the African and Indian coast over the last 40 years, and the dispatch of a disposal force to assist the king of Ethiopia, whom they thought was Prester John, against the Sultanate of Adal.

Once in Ethiopia, did the Portuguese follow a tactically sound plan? Undoubtedly a brave soldier and a stalwart example of Portugal's finest conquistadors, Cristóvão da Gama made decisions which could have had catastrophic consequences for Ethiopia. He manoeuvred his force inland from Massawa in an effort to join forces with the main Ethiopian army in Showa under the command of King Gelawdewos, but in doing so, he chose on three occasions to engage in open battle with the vastly larger Muslim army led by Imam Gurey. Even the combined Portuguese–Ethiopian army would have been less than half the size of Imam Gurey's force. Risking open battle with Imam Gurey may not have been wise, but as previously noted, Portugal staked everything on aggression and audacity. Not attacking an enemy in striking distance might have been seen as cowardice by his own troops and by the very people he had come to rescue. Queen Sabla Wengel recognised the dangers inherent in attacking Imam Gurey before joining forces with her son's army, but as Cristóvão da Gama assured her, there was nothing to fear, since they were Portuguese. He may have been right, but as C.F. Beckingham has noted, "it was not in the interests of the Portuguese to seek battle with [Gurey], but for reasons of prestige they could hardly avoid it if he confronted them".[35] From Portugal's first military involvement in Africa in Morocco in 1415 to their many battles in India, and finally in 1541 in Ethiopia, "Portuguese soldiers, particularly the noblemen and their subordinates, chose an individual action instead of a collective one, as well as sudden attacks instead of planned operations."[36] Consistent with this ideal,

---

33 Corbett, *Some Principles*, p.61.

34 Corbett, *Some Principles*, pp.62–63.

35 C.F. Beckingham, 'A Note on the Topography of Ahmad Gran's Campaign in 1542', p.372.

36 Vitor Luís Gaspar Rodrigues, 'The Portuguese Art of War in Northern Morocco during the 15th Century', *Athens Journal of History*, Vol. 3, Issue 4, p.334.

Cristóvão da Gama relied on audacity, but when combined with the more conservative vision offered by Queen Sabla Wengel, Ethiopia's fate rested in capable hands.

The Ottoman expedition to support the Sultanate of Adal against Ethiopia represents a much smaller proportional military effort than the Portuguese excursion in support of the Ethiopians. Following their victory over the Mamluk Egyptians in 1517, the Ottomans were placed in direct competition with the Portuguese over access to the spice trade in the Indian Ocean and the gold and slave trade in Africa. While Ottoman military effort could have been deployed to threaten Portugal directly, the sultan's imperial policy focused on territorial expansion into the agriculturally more fertile and populous Balkan territories. The sultan's strategic interests maintained a religious element, just as Portugal's and most of the Christian states did in the early sixteenth century. Concern for the well-being of Muslims, whether in India, the Arabian Peninsula, or even the Crimea "prompted clashes with the Portuguese in Arabia, Yemen, and the [Indian] coast early in the sixteenth century; they also led to conflict with [Russia] on the Ukrainian steppes and with the Portuguese in Morocco."[37] Protecting Muslim communities and kingdoms was a key part of Ottoman policy throughout the sixteenth century.

Had the Ottomans focused on adding the North African coast to its empire, with its numerous excellent ports, perhaps the Ottoman fleet could have attempted to deny the sea route around Africa to the Portuguese. The Ottomans would challenge Portuguese naval ascendancy, but in the Red Sea and the Indian Ocean rather than in the Mediterranean and the Atlantic. In practice, the Ottomans practiced two types of warfare, and a military thrust across the North African coast to the Atlantic shores to deny Portugal the sea route to the east does not quite fit into either type. On the one hand, the Ottomans fought wars of conquest, which both protected Muslim communities and added new converts into the community of believers, the *Ummah.* These familiar wars of conquest and conversion are known as *jihad*, the likes of which Imam Gurey had so successfully conducted against Ethiopia from 1529-1540. The second type of war "was a matter of incessant raids, skirmishes, and prolonged blockades" known as *ghazi* warfare.[38] Neither *jihad* nor *ghazi* would have been an appropriate intellectual template for justifying an Ottoman strike through North Africa, as it was already part of the Islamic *Dar al-Harb*, and the Ottomans did control some territory along the Mediterranean coast of the Maghreb. Portugal's sea lanes around the North African coast were not directly challenged by Ottoman naval power, compelling the Ottomans to engage the Portuguese in *ghazi* warfare in the Red Sea and Ethiopia.

As previously noted, Portuguese strategy in the sixteenth century was primarily driven by the demands and requirements of the viceroys and

37 John F. Guilmartin, Jr., 'Ideology and Conflict: The Wars of the Ottoman Empire, 1453–1606', *The Journal of Interdisciplinary History*, 18, No. 4, The Origin and Prevention of Major Wars (Spring, 1988), p.737.

38 Guilmartin, 'Ideology and Conflict', p.726.

governor generals dispersed throughout the Portuguese Empire. The fact that the Ottomans did not more aggressively pursue their conflict with Portugal was similarly a result of the requirements of a ruling class based primarily on agriculture. Thus, military ventures into the Balkans were more important in serving the interests of an important element of the Ottoman nobility. By contrast, Portugal was focused much less on securing fertile land and almost exclusively on bringing commercially valuable territories under direct conquest and political control for specifically economic purposes.[39] For both the Portuguese and the Ottomans, strategies designed to influence the Ethiopian–Adal War's outcome were not necessarily designed or even supported by the royal courts and the sovereigns in Lisbon and Constantinople. Local and regional subalterns and governors called the shots and acted on their own initiative within the broader context of imperial ambition.

The Ottoman military machine was the primary instrument Süleyman I used to achieve Ottoman policy objectives. His large, efficient and feared army incorporated land into the empire through direct conquest and subjugation of enemy forces and governments. Being such a small nation, the Portuguese lacked a large army comparable to the Ottomans or comparable to most other European nations. Portugal was able to achieve its objectives by dividing its opponents and setting them against one another. Their strategy was always to extend their empire, add coastal forts to the route around the Cape of Good Hope and up the east African coastline, and, when necessary, as a last resort, exercise direct military force. This was their preferred modus operandi in the Red Sea, the Maldives, Malabar and India, and further east in China.[40] Operating in this fashion was the key to building its commercial empire. In this manner:

> the imperial adventure of the Portuguese skipped along the coast of West Africa, touching the shore here and there at strategic outposts, which were defended later on by many of the techniques the Venetians practiced: the division of political opponents, the employment of economic resources for political ends, and the use of superior military technology when other measures failed.[41]

As a result, extensive territorial conquest was not required to achieve Portuguese goals. Instead, they relied on their maritime strength, coastal bases and forts manned by only a small number of troops, most of whom were local auxiliaries only marginally loyal to the Portuguese, and in 1541 the dispatch of a small force sent to assist Prester John's Ethiopian army against the Islamic Sultanate of Adal.[42] Seen from this perspective, Cristóvão da Gama's 400 Portuguese soldiers were a key element in Portugal's overall strategy against the Ottomans.

---

39 Alexander Anievas and Kerem Nişancioğlu, *How the West Came to Rule* (London: Pluto, 2015), p.105.

40 Bhattacharyay, 'Portuguese Maritime Strategies', p.274.

41 Hess, 'Evolution of the Ottoman Seaborne Empire', p.1900.

42 Black, *War in the Early Modern World*, p.12.

The Ottomans and the Portuguese used their fleets for transport, to protect merchantmen, and to supply their land forces. Ships were tied to trade and transport. Seizing control of maritime trade routes was best achieved by capturing the port cities from which trade goods moved. The scale of the Ottoman naval building programme and the fearsome reputation that Ottoman sea captains had carved out for themselves helped deter other states through intimidation. But naval operations in the Mediterranean and elsewhere were directed primarily at providing for the security of trade.[43] Engaging an adversary fleet in ship-to-ship combat was not the preferred method of warfare for either the Portuguese or the Ottomans in the Red Sea and the Indian Ocean in the mid sixteenth century.

The Prussian military philosopher and theorist Carl von Clausewitz explained the advantages of opening or contesting a secondary theatre in his classic treatise *On War*. He wrote that "the principle of aiming everything at the enemy's centre of gravity admits of only one exception – that is when secondary operations look exceptionally rewarding. But we must repeat that only decisive superiority can justify diverting strength without risking too much in the principal theater."[44] Was it wise from a strategic standpoint for the Portuguese to open a new theatre in Ethiopia if their overall strategic objective was to ensure dominance in the spice trade? Suppose one accepts that one of Portugal's primary political objectives was to fight Islam wherever it was found. In that case, their foray into Ethiopia might be considered a principal theatre of war and not a secondary one. However, Portugal's limited ability to put troops on the ground anywhere in the world necessitates viewing anything other than a naval excursion, such as the *Armadas da India*, as a secondary theatre, according to Clausewitz. Ultimately, Portugal benefitted from Ethiopia's survival as a Christian nation on the East African coast, which was able to keep the Ottomans occupied well into the latter half of the sixteenth century. Thus, from a Clausewitzian perspective, Portugal's decision to open a new theatre in Ethiopia was justified. Had they not done so, Ethiopia might have been absorbed into the *Dar al-Islam* and eventually into the Ottoman Empire, an outcome that would not have been in Portugal's interest or the interest of any European state.

In the sixteenth century the Ottomans fought on land in Europe and North Africa and at sea in the Mediterranean, Red Sea, Persian Gulf, and the Indian Ocean. They attacked Persia and overran Egypt, both well-developed, powerful Islamic states deploying large cavalry armies. The Ottomans also fought less powerful polities ranging from Bedouin Arabs to opponents in the Caucasus.[45] At what point the Ottomans intervened in Ethiopia on Imam Gurey's behalf is a matter of some conjecture. While "Ottoman" musketeers are noted as having served in the early battles such as Antukyah in 1531, these may not have been regular Ottoman troops sent by Sultan Suleiman I. They might have been mercenaries or some other Arab infantry armed with

43 Brummett, 'Foreign Policy', p. 627.

44 Carl von Clausewitz, *On War*, edited and translated by Michael Howard and Peter Paret (Princeton: Princeton University Press, 1989), p.618.

45 Black, *War in the Early Modern World*, p.10.

firearms. The Jesuit historian Manuel Tellez, writing in 1660, knew nothing of Turks fighting at Shembra Kure in 1529.[46] While the Yemeni sultan and local Ottoman rulers certainly knew about Imam Gurey's *jihad* sweeping through Ethiopia, their participation in the *jihad* was conducted primarily through the slave and firearm trade between ports such as Zeila on the African shore of the Red Sea and Aden on the Arabian side. Likely Adal did not, before 1539, receive a substantial number of matchlocks or artillery pieces directly from the Ottomans. In fact, the Ottoman Sultan Suleiman I transferred most of his cannons and ammunition from Suez to the Mediterranean in 1532, just a few years after Shembra Kure, since the Ottoman military effort against the Habsburgs "was of greater concern to him".[47] Any firearms acquired by the Sultanate of Adal were obtained through trade over the 15 years before the *jihad* against Ethiopia began, and any "Turkish" troops fighting with Imam Gurey's army were not likely to have been part of a coordinated Ottoman strategy, at least not during the first decade of the Ethiopian–Adal War. As French scholar Amélie Chekroun has noted:

> According to the Portuguese and Ethiopian Christian sources, the so-called "Turks" are presented as the soldiers sent by the Ottomans to strengthen [Imam Gurey's] weakened army, a couple of years before his death. However, as the origin of these "Turks" within the wide Ottoman Empire, the involvement of the central Turkish authorities in the military campaigns launched by the [Adal] Sultanate remains quite blurry.[48]

It is thus difficult to evaluate the Ottoman effort through a Corbettian lens. Still, there is little dispute that by 1540, the Sultan had decided to intervene in Ethiopia to challenge the Portuguese effort. How much of this effort he personally directed and how much he delegated to regional commanders is unclear. One factor that may have compelled some Ottoman intervention in Ethiopia was that famine ravaged much of Arabia in 1539 and 1540. This forced many Ottoman troops garrisoned at Zebid and Aden on the Arabian Peninsula to cross the Red Sea to Ethiopia in search of food, although having arrived in Ethiopia, they would have learned much to their chagrin that there was a famine there as well. Castanhoso and Correa do not agree as to whether all the 200 Ottoman soldiers that Imam Gurey had with him in 1542 when he faced the Portuguese expedition were such freelancers, or if they included some men sent explicitly to Ethiopia by the Ottoman sultan.[49]

While Portugal and the Ottoman Empire battled for economic supremacy globally, by 1542 their respective forces contributed to a crucial regional struggle in Ethiopia. Their participation in the Ethiopian–Adal War would have repercussions long outlasting many of the strategic outcomes achieved by either Portugal or the Ottomans in many other parts of the globe.

46 Aregay, 'A Reappraisal', p.103.
47 Black, *War in the World*, p.149.
48 Amélie Chekroun, 'Ottomans, Yemenis and the "Conquest of Abyssinia" (1531–1543)', Université Paris Panthéon Sorbonne – Centre d'études des mondes africains (CEMAf), p.177.
49 Aregay, 'A Reappraisal', p.112.

Chapter 6

The Ethiopian–Adal War: Into the Valley of Death

In late April, after the battles of Amba Senait and Antalo Plain, the 40 soldiers that Cristóvão da Gama had sent to Massawa to rendezvous with the Portuguese ship returned to camp. They brought the sad news that they could not contact the ship; the Ottoman navy had chased it out of port. Whatever supplies and reinforcements it might have had on board were either captured by the Ottoman fleet or driven out of the Red Sea and back to India. Gama could only hope that another ship, or maybe a small armada, would force its way into Massawa. His force needed supplies, and additional troops would certainly be welcome. Unknown to Gama, control of the Red Sea had slipped away from the Portuguese and the Ottoman navy now sailed unopposed into and out of their main port in Suez. The *Estado do India*'s viceroys and captains were no longer following Albuquerque's grand strategy, and no further attempts would be made to send reinforcements or supplies to Ethiopia.

Furthermore, the Portuguese command authorities in the *Estado do India* did not share the crusading zeal that had led to the deployment of the 400 soldiers to Ethiopia. In fact, Portuguese gunsmiths in Goa worked side by side with their Muslim Indian counterparts as they tried to refine and improve upon firearm technology. Goa was the largest arsenal in the world at the time, manned by Christian Portuguese and Muslim Indian workers and overlords, each seeking to expand their economic domain at the expense of their adversaries.[1] More pressing concerns had arisen elsewhere, leaving Cristóvão da Gama's expedition stranded at the bottom of a long list of more important priorities. The small expedition was on its own, left to its fate.

Despite the bad news that he would not be receiving supplies or reinforcements, at least Gama had his 40 soldiers back. He would need them as Gurey advanced north from his camp to meet the Portuguese in what he hoped would be a final, decisive encounter. Cristóvão da Gama's enthusiasm

1 Rainer Daehnhardt, *The Bewitched Gun: The Introduction of the Firearm in the Far East by the Portuguese; Espingarda Feiticeira: A Introducao Da Arma De Fogo Pelos Portugueses No Extremo-Oriente* (Texto Editoria, 1994), p.42.

for another fight may have waned by this time, having survived three encounters with the Imam's vastly larger army. Could his luck hold out? How much confidence he had left by the late summer of 1542 is hard to say. The rainy season in Ethiopia runs from June to September, a time when travel is a challenge, and keeping the cord of a matchlock lit in battle would be difficult, if not impossible. With no reinforcements on the way, little prospect of joining forces with the main Ethiopian army (Prester John's force), and still nursing a wound, Gama's judgement in selecting his camp after the battle of Antalo Plain may have been slightly off. He chose a spot near a hill that blocked his view of Imam Gurey's army, a tactical error uncharacteristic of a veteran field commander, even one as young as 25. Gama was unable to ascertain any of Gurey's intentions. He also did not observe the nearly 900 Ottoman reinforcements that arrived to bolster Gurey's already vastly more powerful army. During this time, Imam Gurey:

> was not idle; he solicited the assistance of the Mahometan princes, pressed them with all the motives of religion, and obtained a reinforcement of two thousand musketeers from the Arabs and a train of artillery from the Turks. Animated with these succors, he marched out of his trenches to enter those of the Portuguese, who received him with the utmost bravery, destroyed prodigious numbers of his men, and made many sallies with great vigour, but losing every day some of their small troops, and most of their officers being killed, it was easy to surround and force them.[2]

The Ottoman Pasha of Zebid sent these 900 troops, along with 10 cannons, in return for expected tribute from Imam Gurey. Other Arab volunteers likely accompanied the Ottomans, as well as Persian archers and 20 Ottoman cavalry.[3]

Cristóvão da Gama may not have known that the additional reinforcements and the 10 cannons were on their way to Imam Gurey's camp, which was about 20 miles away from the Portuguese camp. He did, however, send an emissary to bring news to King Gelawdewos that the Portuguese, along with Ethiopian forces led by Yeshak the *bahrnagash*, had met and defeated Imam Gurey's army in battle. It would take months for the emissary to deliver the message and return to the Portuguese camp with any word about King Gelawdewos's intentions, and Gama was thus forced to decide what to do next. Retreating to Massawa was out of the question. With Imam Gurey reinforcing his army, the prospect of European Christianity aligning with the powerful Prester John seemed more remote than ever. Gama had to know that he would not be joining forces with the Ethiopians before his next battle with Imam Gurey.

---

2 Lobo, *A Voyage to Abyssinia*, n.p.

3 Laband, *Bringers of War*, pp.101–102.

The Battle of Jews Hill

Good fortune intervened when a Jewish Ethiopian village chief approached the Portuguese camp. This man had been the chief of a small community that lived atop an amba that had been captured by Imam Gurey's forces some years earlier. The chief informed Cristóvão da Gama that King Gelawdewos' army had traversed the hill on their way south to Showa, from where Gama was awaiting his return. However, the chief explained that Gelawdewos's army was too small to recapture the hill, causing Gama much consternation, since in his mind Gelawdewos (Prester John) was at the head of a formidable force.[4] Gama decided to take the hill with his own troops since it was said that there were plenty of horses on the hilltop, which would be useful for further operations against Imam Gurey. Disappointed and quite concerned over the news that his small army might be larger than the main Ethiopian army under King Gelawdewos, Gama ordered preparations for an attack on "Jews Hill". On the mountain itself, Imam Gurey:

> had a garrison of 400 men. Having inquired into the truth of this information, and found that it was to be depended upon, Don Christopher marched thither with two companies of Portuguese and some Abyssinians, and came to the foot of the mountain which is twelve leagues in compass. Some Moors who guarded the passes were slain in the ascent, and on the top the Moorish commander met him with all his men, but Don Christopher running at him with his lance thrust him through the body. The shot of the Portuguese soon constrained the Moors to make a precipitate flight, after losing a great number of men, and the mountain was completely reduced. Great numbers of horses and mules were found in this place, which was inhabited by about 800 Jews in six or seven villages, who were reduced to obedience.[5]

In addition to the horses captured on the hill, Gama had acted wisely. Rather than continue to attack Imam Gurey's much larger army, Gama's tired troops could rest atop Jews Hill and await the rendezvous with King Gelawdewos' army which was marching north from Showa.

The Battle of Wofla

In August, having received word from the Portuguese emissary that Imam Gurey had been defeated on the battlefield, King Gelawdewos was very slowly marching north from Showa to rendezvous with the Portuguese and with the *bahrnagash* Yeshak's Ethiopian force. Too weak to take on Imam Gurey himself, King Gelawdewos likely did not want to risk a battle and face the possibility of losing the last Ethiopian army, as well as his own life, so he proceeded slowly and cautiously on his northward advance in order not to fall into a trap. On 28 August, while King Gelawdewos was continuing

---

4 R.S. Whiteway, *Introduction*, p.lviii.

5 Robert Kerr, *General History*, p.297.

his northward march from Showa, Imam Gurey marched out to meet the Portuguese again, offering them the opportunity to achieve another victory or face certain demise. The 500 Ethiopian spear-armed soldiers under the command of the *bahrnagash* fled once they spotted Imam Gurey's army approaching, knowing that much of the Muslim force was composed of captured Christians who would be unlikely to take any prisoners This left Gama with only about 350 remaining Portuguese, their Indian slaves, and the Queen. Instead of forming a square as he had on the battlefields in April, in which he was victorious, Gama sent his matchlock-armed men to separate positions in the hills to try to put the advancing Muslims in a crossfire. This deployment was somewhat successful, but the sheer weight of numbers wore down the Portuguese. After an hour-long engagement, Gama was wounded by a musket ball in both legs and his arm; four of his five captains were dead, and as were nearly half of his soldiers. The fate of Christian Ethiopia was in the balance, and as night fell the Imam's army held the field. Gama's force tried to escape, admitting defeat for the first time, but they saved the Queen, who accompanied the remaining soldiers up a wooded hill in the hope of finding shelter for the night. Not able to keep up with the main force, Gama and some soldiers helping him walk were captured as they tried to hide in a thicket of brush. They were taken to Imam Gurey, who had not forgotten the insulting gift of tweezers and mirror which Gama had given him four months earlier. Suffering through hours of torture, Gama maintained his pride and honour through to the end. He was beheaded, dismembered, and his body parts distributed to Gurey's leading captains as proof of the final Portuguese defeat.

Only a few hundred Portuguese soldiers remained alive. Under Manuel da Cunha's command, about 50 made the long journey back to Massawa where they hoped a ship would meet them to bring them to India and from there eventually home to Portugal. The narrator of so much of the Portuguese effort in Ethiopia, Miguel de Castanhoso, was among this group. Another 120 soldiers retreated to Jews Hill with Queen Sabla Wengel. At this point, in early September 1542, King Gelawdewos finally joined the few remaining Portuguese near Jews Hill, a rendezvous of two tired and ragged forces that together would attempt to save Christian Ethiopia from extinction.

With Cristóvão da Gama dead, Imam Gurey almost certainly assumed that the war was finally over. Had he captured and killed King Gelawdewos, the entire Ethiopian army would have surrendered. The Ottoman troops who fought at Wofla likely felt their job was done, and they petitioned Imam Gurey for gold as recompense for their services. In fact, Imam Gurey "sent the Turks home, though he treated them well, giving them 2000 *tikyas* of gold. There is no indication … that any Turks stayed behind with [Gurey]."[6]

Portuguese and Ethiopian sources differ on the events following the Battle of Wofla in August 1542 and the first months of 1543. Clearly, Imam Gurey

6 C.F. Beckingham, 'A Note on the Topography of Ahmad Gran's Campaign in 1542', p.373. Beckingham cites an unpublished source translated from Arabic (the *Tirib al-Sibri)* by R.B. Serjeant which describes the relationship between Imam Gurey and his Ottoman (Turkish) musketeers after the Battle of Wofla.

must have thought the war was finally over, and the Islamic Kingdom of Ethiopia would be bothered no more by the infidel intruders from Portugal. He could now turn his attention to locating and destroying the remaining Ethiopian army under the command of the young king Gelawdewos, who was himself preparing to face Imam Gurey in battle. According to a second-hand account written by João de Castro, the Ethiopian army marching north from Showa encountered Muslim reinforcements moving to join Imam Gurey after the Battle of Wofla. Castro wrote that:

> The emperor [Gelawdewos] marched soon afterwards against the king of Zeyla [Imam Gurey], accompanied by 90 of the Portuguese who had joined him after the former defeat, to whom he gave the vanguard of his army, in consideration of the high opinion he had of their valour. At the foot of the mountain of Oenadias in the province of Ambea, they met a body of 700 horse and 2000 foot going to join the king of Zeyla. Fifty Portuguese horse went immediately to attack them, and Antonio Cardoso who was foremost killed the commander of the enemy at the first thrust of his lance. The rest of the Portuguese followed this brave example, and slew many of the enemy, and being seconded by the Abyssinians, first under the *Baharnagash* and afterwards by the king in person [Gelawdewos], eight hundred of the enemy were slain and the rest put to flight.[7]

By this account, Yeshak the *bahrnagash* and a number of Portuguese who still had possession of their horses were able to rally after the disaster at Wofla and continue the fight against Imam Gurey. The bravery and valour of the Ethiopian forces led by Yeshak as well as by King Gelawdewos is evident, and the determination by their Portuguese allies to continue the fight to save Christian Ethiopia from complete subjugation at the hands of Imam Gurey's army was apparent to both sides. The location of this encounter recounted by Castro is not known, but it indicates that between the Battle of Wofla in August 1542 and the final battle in February 1543 there was contact between the two armies.

By February 1543, nearly six months after Gama's death, Manuel da Cunha's 50 Portuguese soldiers had rearmed themselves with matchlocks, made gunpowder from locally sourced saltpetre, and joined with their compatriots and with King Gelawdewos' (Prester John's) Ethiopian army, ready to avenge the death of their leader. The army of Prester John numbered 8,000 infantry and about 500 cavalry, a far cry from the mighty hordes that the Portuguese had hoped would materialise.[8] However, both the Ethiopian army and Imam Gurey's army prepared for another battle and spent the intervening weeks assembling as many reinforcements as possible, procuring supplies, and tending to their wounded.

7 Kerr, *General History*, p.299.

8 Tellez, *Travels of the Jesuits in Ethiopia*, p.127.

The Battle of Wayna Dega

Every soldier in both armies must have sensed that the next major battle would be the final contest in the struggle to control Ethiopia. For the first time in many years, an Ethiopian army took the field against Imam Gurey's force with the determination to fight to the last man. According to Castanhoso, "the Christians and Muhamedans remained for some days in sight of each other; there were skirmishes, but, knowing the importance of the engagement, neither side cared to risk a decisive battle."[9] For Imam Gurey and King Gelawdewos, as well as for Manuel da Cunha and the few remaining Portuguese soldiers, there could have been no doubt that this day's victor would rule Ethiopia, either under the crescent or the cross.

On 21 February 1543 both sides advanced towards each other. The battle developed slowly, beginning as a series of small skirmishes. Imam Gurey planned to break through the Ethiopian lines with his elite *Malassy* cavalry – the core of his force since the early days of the war – and then roll up both flanks of his enemy, crushing Gelawdewos and ending the conflict.[10] The Ethiopian author of the *Chronicle of King Gelawdewos* described the Muslim advance:

> They were ready for combat being as strong as the lion and as swift as the eagles. Among them some were cavalry and clothed with steel armour. Some were infantry who were confident with the armed shields and carried swords and spears. There were some who bent the bow and fired as the sons of Ephraim (Efrem). There were those who fought with firearms like the warriors of Yo'an. (King John) and they appeared poor to those who saw them, like the pot in the direction of the north. There were those who were hurling stones with slingshots. None of these warriors had the habit of fear of combat and at the time of the battle, they rushed with their ardour like a hunting dog that sees wild animals for the first time.[11]

One Portuguese secondhand account described the battle this way:

> At Break of Day the Army drew out, the Portuguese leading the Van, with 250 Ethiopian Horse, and 350 Foot. The Emperor brought up the Rear with 250 Horse more, and 4,500 Foot. In this Posture they advanced towards the Enemy, who moved in two Lines also, [Gurey] leading the first, with 200 Turkish Musquetiers, 600 Moorish Horse, and 7,000 Foot, the second was commanded by another General, and consisted of 600 Horse, and 7,000 Foot. Both Armies charged with great Fury.[12]

---

9 Whiteway, *Portuguese Expedition to Abyssinia*, p.lxxi.

10 Manfred Kropp, 'King Claudius's Short Energetic Campaign', manuscript in preparation.

11 Gebreyes, *Chronicle of King Galawdewos*, p.17. According to the translator, the meaning of the term "like the pot in the direction of the north" is unclear.

12 Tellez, *Travels of the Jesuits in Ethiopia*, p.128.

Father Tellez wrote that Pedro Paez recited this account of the battle and that he was told these stories by creditable sources, including eyewitnesses to the battle.[13] We can surmise that both the Ethiopian/Portuguese army commanded by King Gelawdewos and Imam Gurey's forces were each drawn up in two lines. In the centre of the front line for each side were the elite troops. The Portuguese gunners were in the centre of the Ethiopian front line, facing the *Malassy* cavalry and the Ottoman gunners in Gurey's front line. Gurey advanced his army, intent on enveloping the smaller Ethiopian force and destroying it. Ethiopia's conquest would be complete.

The situation facing King Gelawdewos at Wayna Dega differed in a number of important respects from that faced by his father, Lebne Dengel, at the Battle of Shembra Kure 14 years earlier. Lebne Dengel was held in low esteem by his army and by the people of Ethiopia for his pride and avarice. Gelawdewos was regarded as a noble and benevolent leader if for no other reason than the fate of Christian Ethiopia rested in his hands. Lebne Dengel brought a large army into the field at Shembra Kure, an army led by a host of sub-commanders from many of Ethiopia's provinces. Jealousy and distrust plagued his army in 1529. By Ethiopian standards, the army that King Gelawdewos fielded at Wayna Dega was tiny, not worthy of comparison to the armies which had regularly crushed Ethiopia's enemies during the reigns of the great warrior kings such as Amda Seyon and Zara Yaqob. Gelawdewos' small army had only a few sub-commanders who had no choice but to give their full loyalty and devotion to the final cause of victory over Imam Gurey. There was no room for pettiness in this army; it was fight or die. Finally, the Ethiopians faced a much different army at Wayna Dega than they had at Shembra Kure. Imam Gurey's army was, by 1543, composed nearly entirely of Ethiopian Christian slaves. The fire of *jihad* did not burn in the hearts of these Ethiopians, but they could not be sure what kind of treatment they would receive if they were captured, so their determination to fight should not be underestimated.

For all that was riding on this epic battle, it did not last long. Ethiopia's fate hung in the balance, as did both Imam Gurey's and Gelawdewos' life. The few surviving Portuguese soldiers had nothing left to lose, and avenging Cristóvão da Gama's death remained their only objective. Mounted on horses provided for them by the Ethiopians, the Portuguese troops rode into battle with loaded weapons, intent on finding Imam Gurey early and delivering a fatal shot. One of the Portuguese soldiers, John the Galician, saw the Imam surrounded by his banners and his few remaining Ottoman gunners, aimed his matchlock, and fired. Hit in the chest, Imam Gurey fell from his horse, and according to legend he swung his sword at a tree in anger, leaving a slash mark that is still said to be visible to this day. Although the *Chronicle of King Gelawdewos* attributes Gurey's death to an Ethiopian soldier, Ethiopian soldiers "were not familiar with the use of the gun and it was possible only in the hand of the Portuguese".[14] Both Ethiopian and Portuguese courage was

13 Tellez, *Travels of the Jesuits in Ethiopia*, p.128.

14 Solomon Gebreyes Beyene, *The Chronicle of King Gälawdewos* (1540–1559): A Critical Edition with Annotated Translation. A Dissertation submitted to the Faculty of Humanities at

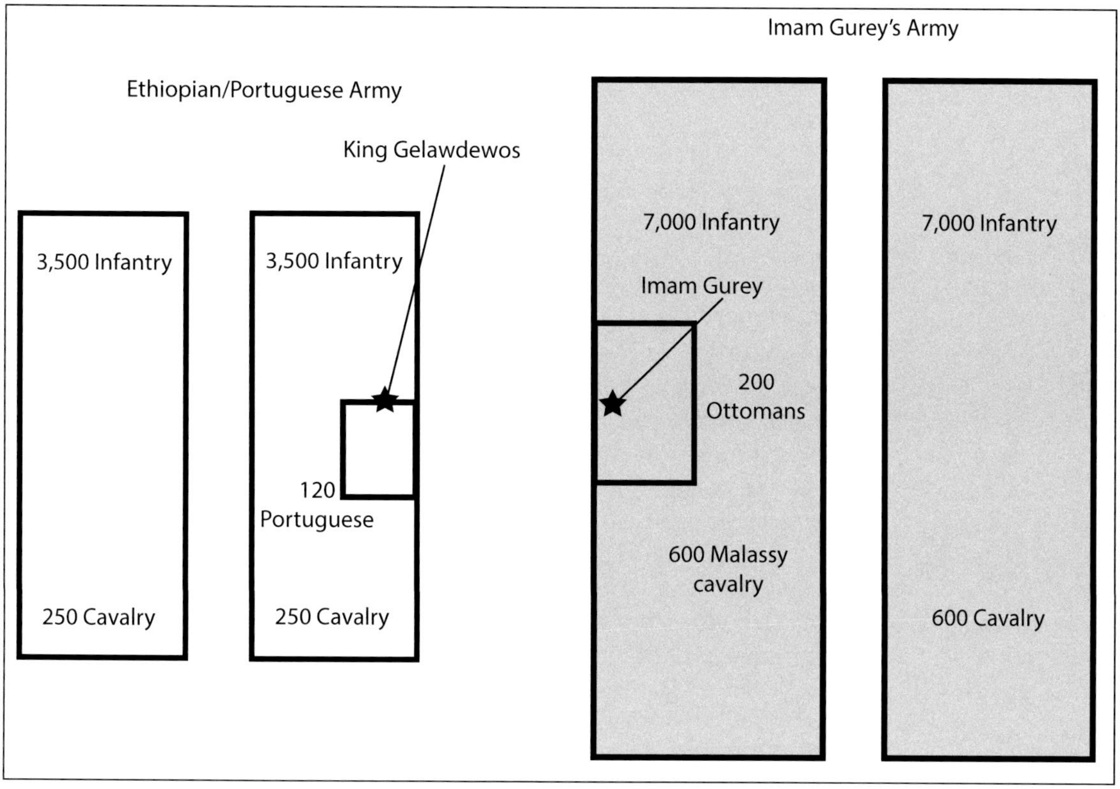

The Battle of Wayna Dega. King Gelawdewos is in the front rank with his troops, unlike his father who remained behind the main army at Shembra Kure.

evident at Wayna Dega, for without King Gelawdewos' army, the remaining Portuguese soldiers would have been hunted down and killed. The Ethiopian author of the *Chronicle of King Gelawdewos* gives only cursory mention to the Portuguese military effort. He wrote, "children of Tubal, son of Japheth, strong and brave men, who were thirsty for combat like wolves and hungry for killing like a lion, came up from the sea".[15] These "strong and brave men" were the Portuguese soldiers led by Gama. While the Portuguese are mentioned, the chronicler ultimately gives credit to King Gelawdewos and his Ethiopian army for the final victory over Imam Gurey. This is deserved, since if the Portuguese were on their own in 1543, they would likely not have returned from Massawa to face Imam Gurey again. Also, just as most Europeans had little if any knowledge of the Ethiopians, the Ethiopians, including the author of the *Chronicle of King Gelawdewos*, also knew nothing about these people who came from afar in small numbers.

The *Chronicle of King Gelawdewos* describes Wayna Dega as a violent clash. The chronicler wrote that:

> a fierce battle took place between him [King Gelawdewos] and Imam Gurey, and God, whose name be blessed, decorated as the winner King Gelawdewos, peace be

---

the University of Hamburg, in partial fulfillment of the requirements, for the degree of Doctor of Philosophy in Athiopistik (2016), p.56.

15 Gebreyes, *Chronicle of King Galawdewos*, p.12. Tubal and Japheth are characters from Genesis 10:2.

> upon him. And Imam Gurey died by the hands of one of his servants. They killed also a large number of soldiers from the Turks … Among those who survived, half of them fled in the direction of the sea with the wife of Imam Gurey. Half of the soldiers, taking Mehmad, the son of Imam Gurey, surrendered themselves into the hands of the glorious King Gelawdewos and they became subjects under his feet. But he was merciful and clement; he did not hurt a man who had behaved badly towards him, but he behaved to him as a benefactor.[16]

Amazingly, and in contrast to the savagery of religious conflict that had torn the Horn of Africa asunder for centuries, King Gelawdewos did not execute Imam Gurey's son Mehmad. But the Muslim prisoners, of which there were hundreds, if not thousands, were instantly put to the sword. Some 40 of the surviving Ottoman soldiers carried Gurey's wife, Beti Del Wanbara, back to safety, eventually arriving home in Adal. On that fateful day in February 1543 the mighty Muslim army which had conquered so much of Ethiopia over the past 14 years was gone.

Christians who had converted to Islam and fought with Imam Gurey were among the many thousands of Ethiopians repatriated, receiving absolution and clemency from King Gelawdewos. Two of these Christians who fought for Imam Gurey claimed to have personally participated in torturing Cristóvão da Gama. However, they too received clemency from the king, but when the Portuguese found out about this, "two Portuguese went into that Ethiopians Tent, and stabbed him in many Places with their Daggers".[17] Gelawdewos may have had clemency in mind, but clearly the few surviving Portuguese soldiers did not.

This Ethiopian stamp depicts King Lebne Dengel leading Ethiopian troops to battle. Issued in 1962, it is surprising that the stamp does not commemorate King Gelawdewos instead. It is not known what battle the stamp commemorates.

16 Gebreyes, *Chronicle of King Galawdewos*, p.17.
17 Tellez, *Travels of the Jesuits in Ethiopia*, p.130.

Aftermath

Imam Gurey's severed head was impaled on a stake and paraded throughout the highlands, proof that the scourge of Ethiopia had been slain, his armies driven from the land. A large blue velvet robe with enormous sleeves, claimed to have been the Imam's, is kept in the monastery of Mertule Maryam in Gojjam, and to this day is shown to visitors, tourists, and Christian pilgrims who travel to the site. Through the spring and summer of 1543 King Gelawdewos liberated Ethiopia, driving the remnants of Gurey's defeated forces out of the Christian kingdom. His brother Minas was brought home and exchanged for Imam Gurey's son, Mehmad. Adal soldiers launched a half-hearted attempt to challenge the Ethiopians in 1548, but the Ethiopian army, still led by King Gelawdewos, brushed this effort aside. Churches and monasteries, many lying in heaps of stone and rubble, were rebuilt, and Christianity was restored throughout the kingdom. The people returned to their homes, many having been refugees in the mountain amba fortresses for the last decade or more.

King Gelawdewos sent a letter to Portuguese King John II in 1550, expressing his thanks and his satisfaction with the performance of Portuguese arms in turning the tide against Imam Gurey. He wrote:

> May God make you a great lord in the land, and place in your hand the sea, the islands, and the continent. May He make you a greater lord in the heavens for all eternity, as He does to His friends and holy men. Through your prayers God worked us great good; with the help of your men we conquered the Moors and have always been victorious over them. The Captain, D. Cristóvão, landed from the sea, and entered my country with four hundred Franks, and many bombards and matchlocks and other arms ... I heard that [Imam Gurey] had killed D. Cristóvão and many Franks ... At this news I was so sorrowful that I wept with sadness and passion.[18]

Gelawdewos knew that Ethiopia owed the Portuguese their devotion. But when Ethiopia was attacked again by Ottoman forces in 1557, the Portuguese did not come to their aid for a second time. The Ottomans captured the port city of Massawa and advanced inland. King Gelawdewos resisted, but the fighting was not nearly as intense or threatening to Ethiopia as Imam Gurey's invasion in 1529.

The Portuguese soldiers who fought in Ethiopia suffered grievous casualties; about half of the expedition died during the two years of fighting against Imam Gurey's army. Because of their gallantry and devotion, they gained the affection of their Ethiopian hosts. Many of them remained in Ethiopia to reap the rewards promised to them by King Gelawdewos, which included the possibility of marriage to local wives. Of the almost 170 survivors who were still alive after the Battle of Wayna Dega, about 120 remained in Ethiopia.[19] The legacy of those Portuguese who came to her aid lives on in the form of the *Birtukan*, the Ethiopian term for the descendants of the 400 Portuguese soldiers who came to Prester John's rescue in 1541.

---

18 Castanhoso, *Portuguese Expedition*, p.116.

19 D'Alòs-Moner, 'Early Portuguese Emigration', p.8.

The Portuguese fort of St John in Muscat. The Portuguese and Ottomans continued their maritime contest for control of the Red Sea after the Ethiopian–Adal War ended. The Ottoman admiral Piri Reis commanded 24 galleys in a successful 18-day siege of Muscat in 1552, but the Portuguese retook the town in 1554. After the Ottomans sacked Muscat for the second time in 1582, the Portuguese built Fort St John (Forte de Sao João), which dominated the harbour, to protect the valuable trading port from the invading Ottoman forces. As Portuguese power in the Indian Ocean began to decline with the competition from Dutch and English traders during the seventeenth century, Omani forces captured the fort in 1650, renaming it Fort al-Jalali. (Photo by Grant Rhode)

The Portuguese Bridge, near the Debra Libanos monastery. Most likely built in the late 1570s by Portuguese soldiers who settled in Ethiopia after the war, it is unlikely that they would have had time to build this bridge while fighting Imam Gurey's forces between 1541–1543. (Author's photo)

Chapter 7

Epilogue

Portugal and the Ottoman Empire suffered little in this war, but both Ethiopia and the Sultanate of Adal were severely weakened. While Ethiopian territory had been restored after 1543, trade routes into the Mediterranean had not been reopened. Since the earliest days of Aksum, these maritime trade routes were Ethiopia's lifeline, yet they were still not firmly under King Gelawdewos' control. The Ottomans also had not secured control of the Red Sea, and within 20 years after the Ethiopian–Adal War the Portuguese once again were supreme in the Red Sea and in the Indian Ocean.[1] The Ethiopian–Adal War was an example of a conflict that was influenced by religion but was not fought primarily to achieve religious objectives. The two sides were drawn along religious lines, and religious passions helped both prolong the war and add to the ferocity of the fighting. Still, economic and geopolitical considerations were the primary motives for the war's expansion from a localised conflict between Ethiopia and the Sultanate of Adal to a more widespread conflict involving the Portuguese and Ottoman empires. The war also served to degrade relations between Muslims and Christians within Ethiopia. For many Christian Ethiopians, their view was "not only related to the perception of Islam as an external threat but also denoted the concern whether Ethiopian Muslims would be loyal to the Ethiopian state or would side with external forces".[2] This issue continues to challenge Ethiopia in the twenty-first century.

Portugal and the Ottoman Empire

The Ethiopian–Adal War occurred at a time of significant change in Europe. The Ottoman threat to the Balkans and the siege of Vienna was of great concern to kings and princes throughout Europe, focusing their attention on south-eastern Europe while diverting attention from their own religious troubles brewing in their kingdoms. The Protestant Reformation was nearly

1 Dames, 'Portuguese and Turks in the Indian Ocean', p.20.

2 Patrick Desplat and Terje Ostebo, *Muslim Ethiopia: The Christian Legacy, Identity Politics, and Muslim Reformism* (New York: Palgrave Macmillan, 2013), p.6.

a decade old when the Ottomans laid siege to Vienna in 1529. Perhaps without the Ottoman threat, Catholic kings would have been able to quell the Reformation. It has been said that the Sultan [Süleyman I] was "Luther's best ally".[3] Most Christian kings were preoccupied with domestic challenges and could not spare any forces to search for Prester John. Only a small contingent of Portuguese troops from India was sent to Prester John's kingdom (Ethiopia) in 1540. The pace of spectacular events shaking the foundations of the Christian world was unprecedented, and the Ethiopian–Adal War fell squarely into the centre of this non-stop conflagration. As Professor Douglas Howard explained:

> In October of the same year in which Selim's armies took Cairo [1517], Martin Luther published his Ninety-five Theses in Wittenberg. The main sponsor of anti-Protestant activity in Central Europe, the Habsburg dynasty, now ruled not only homelands in Austria and (because of Mohács) an empire with large Slavic territories on the Ottoman frontier in Europe, but also Spain and an empire in the Americas and the Pacific. Suleiman's alliance with Francis I, the King of France, who was surrounded by the Habsburgs, became the occasion for the first direct contact between the Ottomans and a sovereign of Northwestern Europe. All of these radical changes took place in full view of a single generation, the same generation that witnessed the discovery of the New World.[4]

The Ethiopian–Adal War may not have shared the spotlight with many of these events, but the significance of this seminal conflict should not be overlooked. The events taking place in Europe and Asia were directly intertwined with the fighting in Ethiopia from 1529 to 1543.

Wrestling with how to deal with the many crises facing the world, a Spanish priest named Ignatius Loyola founded the Society of Jesus in 1539.[5] Pope Paul III approved the Society, which would come to be known as the Jesuits, in 1540, the same year in which Imam Gurey camped comfortably on the shores of Lake Tana in conquered Ethiopia, and one year before the arrival of the Portuguese who rescued their Christian brethren from certain defeat. The Jesuits carried cross and sword throughout the world, sending missionaries to Asia, Africa, and the Americas. A Portuguese Jesuit, Father Jerome Lobo, served as a missionary in Ethiopia from 1624-1631. Among his many observations of the land and the people, he recorded his journey to discover Cristóvão da Gama's gravesite:

> We took with us an old Moor, so enfeebled with age that they were forced to carry him: he had seen, as I have said, the sufferings and death of Don Christopher de Gama; and a Christian, who had often heard all those passages related to his father, and knew the place where the uncle and nephew of Mahomet were

3 Norman Davies, *Europe: A History* (Oxford: Oxford University Press, 1996), p.560.

4 Douglas Howard, *History of the Ottoman Empire* (Cambridge: Cambridge University Press, 2017), p.93.

5 See Cristina Osswald, 'The Jesuits', in Jeffrey M. Shaw (ed.), *War and Religion: An Encyclopedia of Faith and Conflict* (Santa Barbara, CA: ABC-CLIO, 2017), pp.420–423.

> buried, and where they interred one quarter of the Portuguese martyr. We often examined these two men, and always apart; they agreed in every circumstance of their relations and confirmed us in our belief of them by leading us to the place where we took up the uncle and nephew of Mahomet, as they had described. With no small labour we removed the heap of stones which the Moors, according to their custom, had thrown upon the body, and discovered the treasure we came in search of. Not many paces off was the fountain where they had thrown his head, with a dead dog, to raise a greater aversion in the Moors. I gathered the teeth and the lower jaw. No words can express the ecstasies I was transported with at seeing the relics of so great a man, and reflecting that it had pleased God to make me the instrument of their preservation, so that one day, if our holy father the Pope shall be so pleased, they may receive the veneration of the faithful. All burst into tears at the sight.[6]

Lobo recorded many other such observations, which were as fresh in the minds of the people he encountered as if the war had just ended, although it had been nearly 80 years since Imam Gurey's defeat. Unwisely, Portuguese Jesuits like Lobo would attempt to compel the Ethiopian Church to follow Roman Catholicism over the ensuing years. Ethiopia's Orthodox Christian church leaders were "just as adamant in preserving their ancient Monophysite Christianity as in repelling their Muslim opponents" from their homeland.[7] Having helped save Ethiopia from subjugation by Imam Gurey's Muslim army, the Portuguese overplayed their hand. The Jesuits wielded the cross as if it were a sword, and they were banished from Ethiopia in 1633.

Indicative of Portugal's global reach, within a few months of the Portuguese/Ethiopian victory over Imam Gurey's army at Wayna Dega in 1543, a ship carrying Portuguese traders was blown ashore in a storm at Tanegashima, a small Japanese island. Some of these Portuguese were armed with muskets, the same type of firearm that Gama's 400 troops used to fight Imam Gurey's forces in Ethiopia. The arrival of this musket in Japan changed the balance of power not only within Japan but in North East Asia. The "Tanegashima" musket helped facilitate Japanese unification under the Shogun Toyotomi Hideyoshi. The musket would also arm many of the 150,000 samurai that Hideyoshi sent to Korea in 1592, leading to the brutal and devastating six-year conflict known as the Imjin War.

Süleyman the Magnificent continued his campaigns against Christian Europe. He passed away among his troops in Hungary in September 1566, continuing his *jihad* against Christian Europe until his last day. His successors never proved equal to the task of maintaining the empire. Islam did not put down deep roots in European soil. The Ottoman Empire began its slow decline, and it would linger on as the "sick man of Europe" for another 350 years.

6 Lobo, *A Voyage to Abyssinia*, n.p.
7 Davis, 'The Sixteenth Century *Jihad*', p.568.

Adal and Ethiopia

The walls surrounding the city of Harar were built after the Ethiopian–Adal War. King Gelawdewos' liberation of Ethiopia after Imam Gurey's defeat brought the Ethiopian army to the city after subjugating the Sultanate of Adal in its entirety. The walls around Harar were a defensive measure, and the walls remain to this day. (Photo by Marco Vigano)

During and immediately after the Ethiopian–Adal War, the Oromo people moved into the Ethiopian Christian highlands. Over time, some of the Oromo adopted Christianity, and some adopted Islam, while others maintained their pastoral religious traditions. These migrations were followed by a period of feudal anarchy known as the Age of the Princes, where figurehead Solomonian monarchs were put on the throne by Oromo generals while the country was, in reality, ruled by independent feudal lords.[8] The Ethiopian military hierarchy put in place during the reigns of Zara Yaqob and Amda Seyon had atrophied to the point where the king no longer maintained firm control over the military, leaving the door wide open for mass migrations into the Ethiopian heartland. The Oromo are the largest ethnic group in Ethiopia in the twenty-first century, having displaced the Tigray and Amhara, who make up the second and third largest ethnic groups.

In the years after the Ethiopian–Adal War, the Sultanate of Adal disappeared entirely from the map. Contemporary Somali historians have claimed that Imam Gurey may have been a patrilineal ancestor of Siyad Barre, president of the Somali Republic in 1977. Barre harnessed the twin passions of ethnic conflict and Somali irredentism, which led to The Ogaden War of 1977-1978 between Ethiopia and Somalia. This war was fought over much the same ground as the Ethiopian–Adal War. However, linking Siyad Barre to Imam Gurey is a tenuous argument, especially as it would be impossible "to trace the genealogy of Barre in the twentieth century to the Imam who lived in the sixteenth century through oral sources".[9] While the Ethiopian–Adal

8 Paulos Milkias and Getachew Metaferia, *The Battle of Adwa* (New York: Algora, 2005), p.16.
9 Hinika, 'Genealogy and Ethnic Identity', p.25.

War in the sixteenth century wrought unparalleled havoc in Ethiopia, the Ogaden War did much the same, although this war was confined mostly to the lowlands around Dire Dawa and Jijiga.[10] The origins of the Ogaden War between Somalia and Ethiopia are often traced to the Ethiopian–Adal War.

Access to trade routes and managing ethnic discord has driven much of Ethiopia's foreign policy since the days of the Kingdom of Aksum. The same holds true in the twentieth and twenty-first centuries. Ethiopia fought a brutal civil war with Eritrea, a nation established in 1958 that now controls the port city of Massawa, once Ethiopia's link to the outside world. With Eritrea's independence, Ethiopia became a landlocked nation. This long war was finally brought to an end by Ethiopian President Ahmed Abiy in 2018, for which he received the Noble Peace Prize. However, Ethiopia is in the grip of a brutal civil war as this book is heading to print. Internal discord between two of Ethiopia's most numerous peoples, the Tigrayan and the Oromo, has boiled over into open conflict. As Ethiopians navigate the vexing issues of ethnic tension and access to Red Sea ports, problems which have challenged Ethiopia since Aksumite times, the memory and legacy of the war against the Sultanate of Adal over 450 years ago continues to live on in their collective memory.

10 See Jeffrey M. Shaw, 'The Ogaden War – A Case Study of Cold War Politics', in Frank Jacob (ed.), *Peripheries of the Cold War* (Würzburg: Königshausen & Neuman GmbH, 2015), pp.103–117.

Appendix I

Ethiopian Kings: Solomonic Restoration to the end of the Ethiopian–Adal War

Yekunno Amlak	1270–1285
Yag'be Seyon	1285–1294
Sanfa Ared IV	1294–1295
Hezba Asgad	1295–1296
Qedma Asgad	1296–1297
Jan Asgad	1297–1298
Saba Asgad	1298–1299
Wedem Arad	1299–1314
Amda Seyon I	1314–1344
Newaya Krestos	1344–1372
Newaya Maryam	1372–1382
Dawit I	1382–1413
Tewodros I	1413–1414
Yeshaq I	1414–1429
Andreyas	1429–1430
Takla Meryam	1430–1433
Sarwe Iyasus	1433
Amda Iyasus	1433–1434
Zara Yaqob	1434–1468
Baeda Meryam I	1468–1478
Eskender	1478–1494
Amda Seyon II	1494
Na'od	1494–1508
Lebne Dengel	1508–1540
Gelawdewos	1540–1559

Ottoman Sultans to the end of the Ethiopian–Adal War

Osman I	*c.* 1300-24
Orhan	1324-60
Murad I	1360–89
Bayezid I	1389–1402
Mehmed I	1413–21
Murad II	1421–44
Mehmed II	1444–46
Murad II (second reign)	1446–51
Mehmed II (second reign)	1451–81
Bayezid II	1481–1512
Selim I	1512–20
Süleyman I	1520–66

Appendix II

Paean to Imam Gurey before the Battle of Shembra Kure by Arab Faqih

He it is who arranges matters;
who is the regulator of the wars.
audacious in attacking during battle;
He is [like] the blows of a sword.
For the sake of the *jihad*, he is the destroyer
of disunity that stubbornly resists, by subterfuge, the
one who knows the divine secrets.
He is the spearman who bests his strong opponent
with his thrust;
And with his iron sword,
he is a wielder of blows.
The infidels he has left wallowing in the dust:
the tear ducts of any who survive, overflow.
He had launched attacks against them with
a tumultuous din:
He struck them indefatigably
With humiliation and torment
O you who ask me about Ahmad
He is a lover of the just
And hater of a man who lies
He is the respecter of the law of the religion of
His Prophet:
Humble towards his Lord, and also fearful of Him.
He is unceasing in his observance
Of the prescriptions [of the Law];
Preserving in his observance
Of legally binding acts of devotion.
O Lord, guard him by your grace for all to see;
O merciful one, make him last as a strong wind lasts.[1]

1 Šihab ad-Din, *Futuh Al-Habaša*, pp.74–75.

Appendix III

Ethiopian Soldier's Song

Zān, succeeder in victory,
His ancestor was Adal Mabraq.
As a hyena eats poison,
When he surprised Adal,
Their spirit declined-
Vulture of David, vulture.
Follow behind me,
I'll feed you meat in pieces,
I'll give you pure blood to drink,
Follow behind me.
Having pierced with knife,
Having thrust with spear, We swear to you,
May we be given to spear, to be thrown like one.
Should we use (your) wing for shade,
May we be given a strung bow.
Come what may, we will not eat our oath.
If our body looked (red) like a red garment of Fatagar,
If our mouth looked red like the red hand of a woman,
If our finger looked like a fly whisk covered in blood,
Our name is 'Jackals of Zān':
We will not eat our oath.[1]

This song, likely chanted by Ethiopian soldiers in the early battles of the Ethiopian–Adal War, likely was composed during either Amda Seyon's or Zara Yaqob's reign. Both "Adal Mabraq" and "Jackals of Zān" are Ethiopian military regiments, probably of the elite *Çäwa* units that guarded the *katama* camp. "Adal Mabraq" is Amharic for "lightning on Adal", a fitting name for an elite Ethiopian regiment. The red hand of a woman is a reference to the common practice of *henna*, which involved a red dye used as a type of make-up.

1 Huntingford, *Glorious Victories*, pp.131–32.

Further Reading

There are no English language books specifically on the Ethiopian–Adal War, nor are there any books published in any language that cover the entire war from 1529–1543. This edition from Helion is likely the only one available to cover the war and situate the entire conflict in the broader history of the sixteenth century. In order to gain a greater understanding of the many other historical events taking place at the same time that this war-ravaged Ethiopia, the following books are highly recommended.

The Ottoman Empire is a subject of growing interest to military historians. De Giancarlo Casale's *The Ottoman Age of Exploration* (Oxford: Oxford University Press, 2010) provides a sweeping overview of the Ottomans and the consolidation of their empire. Douglas Howard's *History of the Ottoman Empire* (Cambridge: Cambridge University Press, 2017) is another outstanding historical account of the Ottoman rise to power. The most comprehensive account of Ottoman–Portuguese rivalry is Salih Özbaran, *Ottoman Expansion towards the Indian Ocean in the 16th Century* (Istanbul: Bilgi University Press, 2009). Özbaran integrates Turkish and Portuguese sources into the definitive study on this topic.

There are many accounts of the Portuguese in Africa, most of which explain the Portuguese intervention in Ethiopia in general terms. Of note in this field is John Laband's *Bringers of War: The Portuguese in Africa during the Age of Gunpowder and Sail from the Fifteenth to the Eighteenth Century* (London: Frontline, 2013). This gripping account of the Portuguese voyages of exploration and conquest sheds light on the age of exploration and the brutal nature of the Portuguese voyages to Africa and Asia. Other books that examine Portugal's rise to world power status and the creation of their empire include Roger Crowley's bestselling *Conquerors: How Portugal Forged the First Global Empire* (New York: Penguin, 2015) and Sanjay Subrahmanyam's excellent *The Portuguese Empire in Asia, 1500-1700: A Political and Economic History* (West Sussex: Wiley Blackwell, 2012).

Dr Jeremy Black's numerous books on military history and warfare include many volumes that provide an overview of warfare's changing nature in the sixteenth century. Specifically, readers will benefit enormously from *War and the World: Military Power and the Fate of Continents, 1450-2000* (New Haven, CT: Yale University Press, 1998), *War in European History, 1494-1660* (Washington, Potomac Books, 2006), *War in the World: A*

Comparative History, 1450-1600 (New York: Palgrave, 2011), *European Warfare 1494-1660* (Psychology Press, 2002), and *A Brief History Of Portugal* (Robinson, 2020).

Also available in English are first-hand accounts of the conflict written by Miguel de Castanhoso and Bermudez and Correa, as discussed earlier in this book. The recently published compendium of the three Portuguese first-hand accounts, *The Portuguese Expedition to Abyssinia in 1541-1543* (Alpha Editions, 2019), contains the introduction by R.S. Whiteway and is an invaluable source for the Portuguese contribution to the war. The English language edition of the *Futuh Al-Habaša*, translated by Paul Lester Stenhouse (Hollywood, CA: Tsehai Publishers and Distributors, 2003), is also available and highly recommended.

Bibliography

Primary Source Material

Bermudez, D. João, 'A Short Account of the Embassy to Ethiopia', in R.S. Whiteway, *The Portuguese Expedition to Abyssinia in 1541–1543* (Alpha Editions, 2019)

Castanhoso, Miguel de, *A Discourse on the Deeds of the very Valorous Captain Dom Christavao da Gama in the Kingdoms of the Preste John with the four hundred Portuguese, his Companions,* in R.S. Whiteway. *The Portuguese Expedition to Abyssinia in 1541-1543* (Alpha Editions, 2019)

Gebreyes, Solomon, trans., *Chronicle of King Gâlawdéwos (1540-1559)* (Lovanii: Peters, 2019)

Huntingford, G.W.B., trans., *The Glorious Victories of Amda Seyon, King of Ethiopia* (Oxford: Clarendon, 1965)

Polo, Marco and Rustichello of Pisa, *The Travels of Marco Polo, Volume 2* <http://www.gutenberg.org/cache/epub/12410/pg12410.html>

Schloss, Wilfred, trans. *The Peryplus of the Erythraean Sea: Travel in the Indian Ocean by a Merchant of the First Century* (New York: Longmans, Green & Co., 1912)

Šihab ad-Din, Ahmad bin Abd al-Qader bin Salem bin Utman, *Futuh Al-Habaša: The Conquest of Abyssinia [16th Century].* Translated by Paul Lester Stenhouse (Hollywood, CA: Tsehai Publishers and Distributors, 2003)

Whiteway, R.S., *The Portuguese Expedition to Abyssinia in 1541-1543* (Alpha Editions, 2019)

Secondary Sources

Adejumobi, Saheed A., *The History of Ethiopia* (Westport, CT: Greenwood, 2007)

Ágoston, Gábor, 'Behind the Turkish War Machine: Gunpowder, Technology, and War Industry in the Ottoman Empire, 1450-1700', in Brett Steele and Tamara Dorland (eds), *The Heirs of Archimedes: Science and the Art of War through the Age of the Enlightenment* (Cambridge, MA: MIT Press, 2005), pp.101-133

Ágoston, Gábor, *Guns for the Sultan* (London: Cambridge University Press, 2009)

Abdussamad H. Ahmad, 'Ethiopian Slave Exports at Matamma, Massawa and Tajura, c. 1830–1885', in *The Economics of the Indian Ocean Slave Trade in the Nineteenth Century*, ed. William Gervase Clarence-Smith (New York: Routledge, 2013), pp.93–102

Aksan, Virginia, 'Ottoman War and Warfare 1453–1812', in Jeremy Black (ed.), *War in the Early Modern World* (London: Routledge, 1999), pp.147-177

Bausi, Alessandro (ed.), *Languages and Cultures of Eastern Christianity: Ethiopia* (London: Ashgate, 2012)

The Holy Bible: King James Version (Dallas, TX: Brown Books Publishing, 2004)

Black, Jeremy, *War and the World: Military Power and the Fate of Continents, 1450-2000* (New Haven, CT: Yale University Press, 1998)

Black, Jeremy, *Why Wars Happen* (London: Reaktion, 1998)

Black, Jeremy, *War in the Early Modern World* (New York: Routledge, 1998)

Black, Jeremy, *European Warfare, 1494-1660* (London: Routledge, 2002)

Black, Jeremy, *War in the World: A Comparative History, 1450-1600* (New York: Palgrave, 2011)

Boxer, C.R., *The Portuguese Seaborne Empire in Asia, 1415-1825* (London: Hutchinson, 1969)

Amélie Chekroun, Bertrand Hirsch. *The Muslim-Christian Wars and the Oromo Expansion: Transformations at the End of the Middle Ages* (*c.*1500–*c.*1560). S. Kelly (ed.). *Companion to Medieval Ethiopia and Eritrea*, 2020

Anievas, Alexander, and Kerem Nişancioğlu, *How the West Came to Rule* (London: Pluto, 2015)

Clausewitz, Carl von, *On War*, edited and translated by Michael Howard and Peter Paret (Princeton: Princeton University Press, 1989)

Corbett, Julian, *Some Principles of Maritime Strategy* (Annapolis: Naval Institute Press, 1988)

Crowley, Roger, *Conquerors: How Portugal Forged The First Global Empire* (New York: Random House, 2015)

D'Alòs-Moner, Andreu Martínez, 'Early Portuguese Emigration to the Ethiopian Highlands: Geopolitics, Mission and Métissage', in Stefan Halikowski Smith (ed.), *Reinterpreting Indian Ocean Worlds: Essays in Honour of Kirti N. Chaudhuri* (Newcastle Upon Tyne: co, 2011), pp.2-32

Daehnhardt, Rainer, *The Bewitched Gun: The Introduction of the Firearm in the Far East by the Portuguese; Espingarda Feiticeira: A Introducao Da Arma De Fogo Pelos Portugueses No Extremo-Oriente* (Texto Editoria, 1994)

Davies, Norman, *Europe: A History* (Oxford: Oxford University Press, 1996)

Desplat, Patrick and Terje Ostebo, *Muslim Ethiopia: The Christian Legacy, Identity Politics, and Muslim Reformism* (New York: Palgrave Macmillan, 2013)

Diamond, Jared, *Guns, Germs, and Steel* (New York: W.W. Norton & C., 1999)

Doresse, J., *L'Empire du Pretre-Jean*, Vol. II (Paris: Plon, 1957)

Dunn, Ross E., *The Adventures of Ibn Battuta: A Muslim Traveler of the Fourteenth Century* (Berkeley, CA: University of California Press, 1986)

Gann, Lewis H. and Peter Duignan, *Africa and the World* (New York: University Press of America, 2000)

Gibbon, Edward, *The Decline and Fall of the Roman Empire*, vol. 56 (New York: Peter Fenelon Collier, 1899)

Hattendorf, John B., *Sir Julian Corbett on the Significance of Naval History* (Salem, MA: Peabody Museum of Salem, 1971)

Henze, Paul B., *Layers of Time: A History of Ethiopia* (New York: Palgrave, 2000)

Herodotus, *The Histories*, translated by Henry Cary (New York: D. Appleton & Co., 1904)

Howard, Douglas, *History of the Ottoman Empire* (Cambridge: Cambridge University Press, 2017)

Huntingford, G.W.B., *The Historical Geography of Ethiopia, From the First Century A.D. to 1704* (New York: Oxford University Press, 1989)

Kahane, Henry and Renée, and Andreas Tietze, *The Lingua Franca in the Levant: Turkish Nautical Terms of Italian and Greek Origin* (Urbana, IL: University of Illinois Press, 1958)

Kerr, Robert, *General History and Collection of Voyages and Travels* (Edinburgh: William Blackwood), 1824, p.299. Available online: <http://www.columbia.edu/itc/mealac/pritchett/00generallinks/kerr/>

Krebs, Verena, 'Crusading Threats? Ethiopian-Egyptian Relations in the 1440s', in Benjamin Weber (ed.), *Croisades en Afrique: Les expéditions occidentales à destination du continent africain, Xllle–XVIe siècles* (Toulouse: Presses Universitaires du Midi Meridiennes, 2019), pp.245-274

Laband, John, *Bringers of War: The Portuguese in Africa during the Age of Gunpowder and Sail from the Fifteenth to the Eighteenth Century* (London: Frontline, 2013)

Levine, Donald N., *Wax and Gold* (Chicago: University of Chicago Press, 1972)

Lipsky, George A., *Ethiopia* (New Haven, CT: H.R.A.F. Press, 1962)

Marcus, Harold G., *A History of Ethiopia* (Berkeley, CA: University of California Press, 1994)

Merriman, Roger Bigelow, *Suleiman the Magnificent: 1520-1566* (Cambridge, MA: Harvard University Press, 1944)

Milkias, Paulos & Getachew Metaferia, *The Battle of Adwa* (New York: Algora, 2005)

Munro-Hay, Stuart, *Aksum: An African Civilization of Late Antiquity* (Edinburgh: Edinburgh University Press, 1991)

Ofcansky, Thomas P. and David H. Shinn, *Historical Dictionary of Ethiopia* (Lanham, MD: Scarecrow Press, 2004)

Osswald, Cristina, 'The Jesuits', in Jeffrey M. Shaw (ed.), *War and Religion: An Encyclopedia of Faith and Conflict* (Santa Barbara, CA: ABC-CLIO, 2017) pp.420-423

Pankhurst, Richard, *An Introduction to the Economic History of Ethiopia* (London: Sidgwick & Jackson, 1961)

Pankhurst, Richard, *The Ethiopian Borderlands: Essays in Regional History from Ancient Times to the End of the Eighteenth Century* (Lawrenceville, NJ: The Red Sea Press, 1997)

Pankhurst, Richard and Andreu Martínez d'Alòs-Moner, 'Military Units and Organization', in Merid Aregay et al., (eds), *Encyclopedia Aethiopica* Vol. 5 (Wiesbaden: Harrassowitz Verlag, 2003)

Payne, Robert, *The History of Islam* (New York: Dorsett Press, 1959)

Reid, Richard, *Warfare in African History* (New York: Cambridge University Press, 2012)

Salvadore, Matteo, *The African Prester John and the Birth of Ethiopian–European Relations, 1402–1555* (London: Routledge, 2016)

Sargent, Jesse, 'Following in Jesuit Footsteps: British Expeditions to Ethiopia in the Early Victorian Era', in Robert Aleksander Maryks and Mkenda Festo (eds), *Encounters between Jesuits and Protestants in Africa* (Leiden: Brill, 2018), pp.33–58

Serjeant, R.B., *The Portuguese off the South Arabian Coast* (Beirut: Libraire du Liban, 1974)

Shaw, Jeffrey M., 'The Ogaden War – A Case Study of Cold War Politics', in Frank Jacobs (ed.), *Peripheries of the Cold War* (Würzburg: Königshausen & Neuman GmbH, 2015), pp.103–117

Shaw, Jeffrey M., and Tim Demy (eds), *War and Religion: An Encyclopedia of Faith and Conflict* (Santa Barbara, CA: ABC-CLIO, 2017)

Snowden, Jr., Frank M., *Blacks in Antiquity: Ethiopians in the Greco-Roman Experience* (Cambridge, MA: Belknap Press, 1971)

Subrahmanyam, Sanjay, *The Portuguese Empire in Asia, 1500–1700: A Political and Economic History* (West Sussex: Wiley Blackwell, 2012)

Trimingham, J. Spencer, *Islam in Ethiopia* (London: Oxford University Press, 1952)

Journal Articles

Ahmed, Hussein, 'The Historiography of Islam in Ethiopia', *Journal of Islamic Studies*, Vol. 3, No. 1 (January 1992), pp.15–46. <http://www.jstor.org/stable/26196528>

al-Salimi Abdul Rahman and Eric Staples, 'Reflections of a Muslim-Portuguese Maritime World in a Sixteenth-Century Portuguese Source', *Proceedings of the Seminar for Arabian Studies*, 2015, Vol. 45, Papers from the forty-eighth meeting of the Seminar for Arabian Studies held at the British Museum, London, 25 to 27 July 2014 (2015), pp.321–327. <http://www.jstor.org/stable/43783641>

Aregay, Merid, 'Military Elites in Medieval Ethiopia', *Journal of Ethiopian Studies*, Vol. 30 (June 1997), pp.31–73. <http://www.jstor.org/stable/41966063>

Aregay, Merid, 'A Reappraisal of the Impact of Firearms on the History of Warfare in Ethiopia (c. 1500–1800)', *Journal of Ethiopian Studies,* 14 (January 1980), pp.98–121. <http://www.jstor.org/stable/41965889>

Ayenachew, Deresse, 'Evolution and Organisation of the *Č̣äwa* Military Regiments in Medieval Ethiopia', *Annales d'Éthiopie* 29 (2014), pp.83–95

Ayenachew, Deresse, 'A historical overview of the Wärǧəḥ Muslim community in the Christian highland of Šäwa', Afriques [Online], Varia, Online since 3 November 2016, connection on 31 January 2017. URL <http://afriques.revues.org/1944>

Beckingham, C.F., 'A Note on the Topography of Ahmad Gran's Campaign in 1542', *Journal of Semitic Studies*, Vol. IV (October 1959), pp.361–373

Bhattacharyay, Ujjayan, 'The Portuguese Maritime Strategies and Options in the Eastern Indian Ocean Region (1515–1526)', *Proceedings of the Indian History Congress*, Vol. 57 (1996), pp.262–276

Bonaci, Giulia, 'Revisiting Slavery and the Slave Trade in Ethiopia', *Northeast African Studies* Vol. 17, No. 2 (2017), pp.5–30

Braukämper, Ulrich, 'Islamic Principalities in Southeast Ethiopia Between the Thirteenth and Sixteenth Centuries (Part 1)', *Ethiopianist Notes*, Vol. 1, No. 1 (Spring 1977), pp.17–25, 27–45, 47–56

Brummett, Palmira, 'The Ottomans as a World Power: What We Don't Know About Ottoman Seapower', *Oriente Moderno, Nuova serie*, Anno 20 (2001), pp.1–21

Brummett, Palmira, 'Foreign Policy, Naval Strategy, and the Defence of the Ottoman Empire in the Early Sixteenth Century', *The International History Review*, 11 (Nov 1989), pp.613–627

Chaudhuri, Kirti N., 'The Portuguese Maritime Empire, Trade, and Society in the Indian Ocean During the Sixteenth Century', *Portuguese Studies*, 1992, Vol. 8, Special Issue supported by the Comissão Nacional para as Comemorações dos Descobrimentos Portugueses, pp.57–70

Chaudhuri, Kirti N., 'The World-System East of Longitude 20°: The European Role in Asia 1500-1750', *Review (Fernand Braudel Center)*, Vol. 5, No. 2 (Fall, 1981), pp.219-245

Chekroun, Amélie, 'Conquête(s) et conversions religieuses en Éthiopie du XVIe siècle', Archives de Sciences Sociales des Religions, Vol. 182 (2018), p.149–166

Chekroun, Amélie, 'Ottomans, Yemenis and the "Conquest of Abyssinia" (1531-1543)', Université Paris 1 Panthéon Sorbonne – Centre d'études des mondes africains (CEMAf), pp.173-184, <https://halshs.archives-ouvertes.fr/halshs-02505465/>, accessed 13 Oct 2020

Chekroun, Amélie, 'The Mäṣḥafä Seddät and the Futūḥ al-Ḥabaša: a case of contact between Islamic and Christian manuscripts from Ethiopia in the 16th century?', *Open Edition Journals*. DOI <https://doi.org/10.4000/afriques.2025>

d'Alòs-Moner, Andreu Martínez, 'Conquistadores, Mercenaries, and Missionaries: The Failed Portuguese Dominion of the Red Sea', *Northeast African Studies* 12 (2012), pp.1-28. <http://www.jstor.org/stable/41960556>

Dames, M. Longworth, 'The Portuguese and Turks in the Indian Ocean in the Sixteenth Century', *The Journal of the Royal Asiatic Society of Great Britain and Ireland* 1 (Jan 1921), pp.1-28. DOI <https://doi.org/10.1017/S0035869X00062870>

Davis. Asa J., 'The Sixteenth Century *Jihad* in Ethiopia and the Impact on its Culture (Part One)', *Journal of the Historical Society of Nigeria*, Vol. 2 (December 1963), pp.567-592. <http://www.jstor.org/stable/41856679>

Davis. Asa J., 'The Sixteenth Century *Jihad* in Ethiopia and the Impact on its Culture (Part Two): Implicit Factors Behind the Movement', *Journal of the Historical Society of Nigeria*, Vol. 3 (December 1964), pp.113–128. <https://www.jstor.org/stable/41856692>

Demoz, Abraham, 'Moslems and Islam in Ethiopic Literature', *Journal of Ethiopian Studies* 10 (January 1972) p.1-11. <http://www.jstor.org/stable/41965840>

Eaton, Richard M., '"Kiss My Foot," Said the King: Firearms, Diplomacy, and the Battle for Raichur, 1520', *Modern Asian Studies*, Vol. 43, No. 1, *Expanding Frontiers in South Asian and World History: Essays in Honour of John F. Richards* (Jan 2009), pp.289–313. <https://www.jstor.org/stable/20488080>

Elbl, Ivana, 'Cross-Cultural Trade and Diplomacy: Portuguese Relations with West Africa, 1441–1521', *Journal of World History*, 3, No. 2 (Fall, 1992), pp.165–204

Ghazanfar, S.M., 'Vasco da Gama's Voyages to India: Messianism, Mercantilism, and Sacred Exploits', *Journal of Global Initiatives: Policy, Pedagogy, Perspective* (13) 2018, pp.15-40. <https://digitalcommons.kennesaw.edu/jgi/vol13/iss1/3/>, accessed 20 Jul 2020

Godsal, John R., 'Richard Burton's Somali Expedition, 1854-55: Its Wider Historical Context and Planning', *Journal of the Royal Asiatic Society*, 2001, Vol. 11, No. 2, pp.135-173. <http://www.jstor.org/stable/25188129>

Guilmartin, John F. Jr., 'Ideology and Conflict: The Wars of the Ottoman Empire, 1453-1606', *The Journal of Interdisciplinary History* 18, No. 4, *The Origin and Prevention of Major Wars* (Spring, 1988), pp.721-747. DOI <https://doi.org/10.2307/204822>

Hassen, Mohammed, 'Reviewed Work(s): Ethiopia and the Red Sea: The Rise and Decline of the Solomonic Dynasty and Muslim-European Rivalry in the Region by M. Abir', *Northeast African Studies*, Vol. 6, No. 3 (1984), pp.60-65. <http://www.jstor.org/stable/43660165>

Heldman, Marilyn E., 'A Chalice from Venice for Emperor Dāwit of Ethiopia', *Bulletin of the School of Oriental and African Studies*, Vol. 53, No. 3 (1990), pp.442-445. <http://www.jstor.org/stable/618118>

Herman, Margaux, *Sabla Wangêl, the Queen of the Kingdom of Heaven*. Addis Ababa University Institute of Ethiopian Studies XVII International Conference of Ethiopian Studies, Nov 2009, Addis Ababa, France. Available online at <https://www.academia.edu/>

Hess, Andrew C., 'The Evolution of the Ottoman Seaborne Empire in the Age of the Oceanic Discoveries, 1453-1525', *The American Historical Review*, 75, No. 7 (Dec 1970), pp.1892-1919. DOI <https://doi.org/10.2307/1848022>

Hess, Andrew C., 'The Ottoman Conquest of Egypt (1517) and the Beginning of the Sixteenth-Century World War', *International Journal of Middle East Studies*, Vol. 4, No. 1 (Jan 1973), pp.55-76. DOI <https://doi.org/10.1017/S0020743800027276>

Hinika, Mohammed Hassen, 'The Genealogy and Ethnic Identity of Ahmed Ibn Ibrahim Al-Gazi (Gragn) of Ethiopia: A Historiographical Reappraisal', *East African Journal of Social Sciences and Humanities* (2017) Vol. 2, pp.21–40 <https://www.semanticscholar.org/paper/The-Genealogy-and-Ethnic-Identity-of-Ahmed-Ibn-of-A-Hinika/1cb1d0e1b1bd35243357afb8138d8e7336620516?p2df>, accessed 5 Aug 2020

Horvath, Ronald J., 'The Wandering Capitals of Ethiopia', *The Journal of African History*, Vol. 10, No. 2 (1969), pp.205-219. <http://www.jstor.org/stable/179511>

Kennedy Cooke, B. and B. Kennedy-Cooke, 'The Red Sea Coasts in 1540', *Sudan Notes and Records*, 16, No. 2 (1933), pp.151–159. <https://www.jstor.org/stable/41716059>

Kurt, Andrew, 'The search for Prester John, a projected crusade and the eroding prestige of Ethiopian kings, c.1200–c.1540', *Journal of Medieval History*, 2013, pp.291-320. DOI <http://dx.doi.org/10.1080/03044181.2013.789978>

Langer, William L. and Robert P. Blake, 'The Rise of the Ottoman Turks and Its Historical Background', *The American Historical Review*, 37, No. 3 (Apr 1932), pp.468-505. DOI <https://doi.org/10.2307/1837961>

Levine, Donald, 'The Masculinity Ethic and the Spirit of Warriorhood in Ethiopian and Japanese Cultures', *International Journal of Ethiopian Studies*, Vol. 2 (Summer/Fall 2005-2006), pp.161-177. <http://www.jstor.org/stable/27828860>

Levine, Donald N., 'A Revised Analytical Approach to the Evolution of Ethiopian Civilization', *International Journal of Ethiopian Studies*, 2012, Vol. 6 (2012), pp.29-70. <http://www.jstor.org/stable/41756934>

Lewis, Herbert S., 'The Origins of the Galla and Somali', *The Journal of African History*, Vol. 7 (1966), pp.27-46. <http://www.jstor.org/stable/179457>

Lewis, I.M., 'The Somali Conquest of the Horn of Africa'. *The Journal of African History* 1 (1960), pp.213-230. <http://www.jstor.org/stable/180241>

Loureiro, Rui Manuel, 'Portas do Estreito: The ports of the Red Sea and the Gulf of Aden according to 16th century Portuguese iconographic sources', *Orientierungen Themenheft* 2013, pp.126–142

Mariam, Mesfin Wolde, 'The Background of the Ethio-Somali Border Dispute', *The Journal of Modern African Studies* 2 (July 1964), pp.189-219. <http://www.jstor.org/stable/158818>

Markham, Clements R., 'On the Early Portuguese Expeditions to Abyssinia', *Proceedings of the Royal Geographic Society of London* 12 (1867-68), pp.11-19. DOI <https://doi.org/10.2307/1799506>

Martin, E.G., 'Mahdism and Holy Wars in Ethiopia Before 1600', *Proceedings of the Seminar for Arabian Studies* (1974), pp.106-117. <http://www.jstor.org/stable/41223140>

Miftah, Mukerrem, 'Key Dimensions in Abyssinia-Ottoman Relations in the Sixteenth and Seventeenth Centuries: A Critical Review of Literatures', *Africology: The Journal of Pan African Studies*, 10, no.1, (March 2017), pp.265-279. <http://www.jpanafrican.org/docs/vol10no1/10.1-16-Miftah.pdf>, accessed 11 Jun 2020

Molvaer, Reidulf K, 'The Tragedy of Emperor Libne-Dingil of Ethiopia (1508-1540)', *Northeast African Studies* New Series, 5, No. 2 (1998), pp.23-46. <http://www.jstor.org/stable/41931161>

Moore, Dale H., 'Christianity in Ethiopia'. *Church History* 5 (September 1936), pp.271-284. <http://www.jstor.org/stable/3160789>

Özbaran, Salih and Dom Manuel de Lyma, 'The Ottoman Turks and the Portuguese in the Persian Gulf, 1534–1581', *Journal of Asian History* 6, No. 1 (1972), pp.45-87. <http://www.jstor.org/stable/41929749>

Pankhurst, Richard, 'Guns in Ethiopia', *Transition* 20 (1965), pp.26-33. <https://www.jstor.org/stable/2934388>

Pankhurst, Richard and Hartwig Breternitz, 'Barara, the Royal City of 15th and Early 16th Century (Ethiopia). Medieval and Other Early Settlements Between Wechecha Range and Mt Yerer: Results from a Recent Survey', *Annales d'Ethiopie* 24, (2009), pp.209–249. <https://www.persee.fr/doc/ethio_0066-2127_2009_num_24_1_1394 >

Pankhurst, Rita, 'Tayitu foremothers: Queen Eleni, Queen Sabla Wengel and Bati Del Wanbara', Proceedings of the 16th International Conference of Ethiopian Studies 1 (2009), pp.51–65. Available online: <https://zethio.files.wordpress.com/2014/04/ethiopian-studies-volume-1.pdf>

Phillips, Jacke, 'Punt and Aksum: Egypt and the Horn of Africa', *The Journal of African History*, 38, No. 3 (1997), pp.423-457. <http://www.jstor.org/stable/182543>

Phillipson David W., 'Aksum in Africa', *Journal of Ethiopian Studies*, 23 (November 1990), pp.55–65. <http://www.jstor.org/stable/44324722>

Rodrigues, Vitor Luís Gaspar, 'The Portuguese Art of War in Northern Morocco during the 15th Century', *Athens Journal of History*, Vol. 3, Issue 4, pp.321–336. <https://www.athensjournals.gr/history/2017-3-4-4-Rodrigues.pdf> accessed 12 March 2021

Ross, E. Denison, 'The Portuguese in India and Arabia, 1517-38', *The Journal of the Royal Asiatic Society of Great Britain and Ireland,* No. 1 (Jan 1922), pp.1-18. <http://www.jstor.org/stable/25209837>

Shastri, B.S., 'Some Aspects of the First Conquest of Goa by the Portuguese', *Proceedings of the Indian History Congress 39*, Volume I (1978), pp.385-392. <http://www.jstor.org/stable/44139374>

Tamrat, Taddesse, 'A Short Note on the Traditions of Pagan Resistance to the Ethiopian Church (14th and 15th Centuries)', *Journal of Ethiopian Studies*, 10 (January 1972), pp.137-150. <http://www.jstor.org/stable/41965851>

Taşkıran, Cemalettin, 'The Ottoman–Portuguese relationship in the 16th century', *Insight Turkey*, no. 21, 1998, pp.109-119. <https://www.jstor.org/stable/26726823>

Ullendorff, Edward, 'The Glorious Victories of Amda Seyon, King of Ethiopia', *Bulletin of the School of Oriental and African Studies, University of London* Vol. 29 (1966), pp.600-611. DOI <https://doi.org/10.1017/S0041977X00073432>

Yasin, Mohammed Yasin, 'Political History of the Afar in Ethiopia and Eritrea', *Africa Spectrum* 43, No. 1, Horn of Africa (2008), pp.39-65. <http://www.jstor.org/stable/40175221>

Online Books

Alvarez, Fr. F., *Narrative of the Portuguese Embassy During the Years 1520-27*, ed. & trans. Lord Stanley of Alderley (London, 1881). <https://babel.hathitrust.org/cgi/pt?id=ien.35556025358086>, accessed 4 May 2020

Bassett, Rene, *Études Sur L'histoire D'éthiopie* (Paris: Imprimerie Nationale, 1882). <http://archive.org/details/tudessurlhistoi00bassgoog/>, accessed 13 Apr 2020

Bossi, Enrico, *Habesha and Ferengi* (Il Mio Libro, 2020), p.83. <https://ilmiolibro.kataweb.it/libro/storia-e-filosofia/531043/habesha-and-ferengi-9/>, accessed 1 Feb 2021

Bruce, James, *Travels to Discover the Source of the Nile: In the Years 1768, 1769, 1770, 1771, 1772, and 1773* (London: Ruthven, 1790). <https://www.biodiversitylibrary.org/item/130732#page/13/mode/1up>, accessed 1 Feb 2020

Budge, Sir Ernest Alfred Wallis, *A History of Ethiopia, Nubia & Abyssinia: (according to the Hieroglyphic Inscriptions of Egypt and Nubia, and the Ethiopian Chronicles)* (London: Methuen & Company Limited, 1928). <https://archive.org/details/in.ernet.dli.2015.499166>, accessed 11 May 2020

de Varthema, Ludovico, *The Travels of Ludovico Di Varthema in Egypt, Syria, Arabia Deserta and Arabia Felix, in Persia, India, and Ethiopia, 1503 to 1508*. Translated by John Winter Jones (London: Hakluyt Society, 1863). <https://publicdomainreview.org/collection/the-travels-of-ludovico-di-varthema-1863>, accessed 11 May 2020

Edwards, Frederick A., 'The Conquest of Abyssinia', *The Asiatic Quarterly Review & Quarterly and Colonial Record,* 3rd Series, XIX, 37 & 38, Jan–Apr 1905, pp.320-361. <https://babel.hathitrust.org/cgi/pt?id=nyp.33433081828182&view=1up&seq=8>, accessed 23 Mar 2020

Lobo, Fr. Jerome, *A Voyage to Abyssinia*. Translated from French by Samuel Johnson (London: Cassell & Co, Ltd, 1887). <https://www.gutenberg.org/files/1436/1436-h/1436-h.htm>, accessed 17 Aug 2020

Ludolphus, Job, *A New History of Ethiopia*. Translated by J.P. Gent (London, 1684). <https://babel.hathitrust.org/cgi/pt?id=osu.32435017829573&view=1up&seq=5&skin=2021>, accessed 11 Apr 2020

Ofcansky, Thomas P. (ed), *Ethiopia: A Country Study* (Washington DC: Library of Congress, 1993). <https://www.loc.gov/item/92000507/>, accessed 12 Jul 2020

Pankhurst, Richard, *The Chronicle of the Emperor Zara Yaqob (1434–1468)*, <https://tezetaethiopia.wordpress.com/2005/06/01/the-chronicle-of-the-emperor-zara-yaqob-1434-1468/>, accessed 1 Jun 2021

Tellez, Fr. Balthazar, S.J., *The Travels of the Jesuits in Ethiopia* (London: Knapton, 1710). <http://www.fondazioneintorcetta.info/pdf/biblioteca-virtuale/documento848/Ethiopia.pdf>, accessed 11 Oct 2020

Dissertations

Atçil, Muhammet Zahit, State and Government in the Mid-Sixteenth Century Ottoman Empire: *The Grand Vizierates of Rüstem Pasha (1544–1561)*. A Dissertation submitted to the Faculty of the Division of the Humanities in Candidacy for the Degree of Doctor of Philosophy in the Department of Near Eastern Languages and Civilizations University of Chicago (2015)

Beyene, Solomon Gebreyes, *The Chronicle of King Gälawdewos (1540–1559): A Critical Edition with Annotated Translation*. A Dissertation submitted to the Faculty of Humanities at the University of Hamburg, in partial fulfillment of the requirements, for the degree of Doctor of Philosophy in Athiopistik (2016)

Chekroun, Amélie. '*Le "Futuh Al-Habaša": écriture de l'histoire, guerre et société dans le Bar Sa'ad ad-din (Ethiopie, XVIe siècle)*'. Thèse de doctorat d'histoire Histoire. Université Panthéon-Sorbonne – Paris I, (2013)

Hassen, Mohammed, *The Oromo of Ethiopia, 1500–1850: With Special Emphasis on the Gibe Region*. PhD Diss., University of London, School of Oriental and African Studies (1983)

Owens, Travis J. *Beleaguered Muslim Fortresses and Ethiopian Imperial Expansion from the 13th to the 16th Century*. Master's Thesis, Naval Postgraduate School (June 2008)

Tamrat, Taddesse, *Church and State in Ethiopia: 1270–1527*. PhD Diss., University of London (February 1968)

Online News Article

Pankhurst, Richard, 'Did the Imam Reach Lalibela'? *Addis Tribune* (2003). Available online: <https://web.archive.org/web/20070927213855/http://www.addistribune.com/Archives/2003/11/21-11-03/Story.htm>

Unpublished Work

Kropp, Manfred, 'King Claudius's Short Energetic Campaign', manuscript in preparation